NICOLAJ VAN DER MEULEN, JÖRG WIESE

Culinary Turn

Aesthetic Practice of Cookery

in collaboration with ANNELI KÄSMAYR
and in editorial cooperation with RAPHAELA REINMANN

[transcript]

Bibliographic information published by the Deutsche Nationalbibliothek
The Deutsche Nationalbibliothek lists this publication in the Deutsche Nationalbibliografie; detailed bibliographic data are available in the Internet at http://dnb.d-nb.de

© 2017 transcript Verlag, Bielefeld

Cover layout: Kordula Röckenhaus, Bielefeld,
    based on a Design by Philipp Möckli, Basel
Cover: Stefan Wiesner is inventing and cooking the »Brother Klaus-Soup«,
    photography by Nicolaj van der Meulen, November 2014
Typeset by Michael Rauscher, Bielefeld
Printed in Germany
Print-ISBN 978-3-8376-3031-2
PDF-ISBN 978-3-8394-3031-6

Content

Discourse

Perception

Culinary Criteria Creation in an Open Society
Jürgen Dollase | 285

Foreword

The present book is the first of a series that will be brought out in coming years by transcript Verlag and which we have entitled "Aesthetic Practice". The intention is not only to explore the epistemic potential of aesthetic practices in art, design and related fields, but also to dovetail aesthetic practices and the associated discourses that are otherwise carefully distinguished from one another as systemic units in society and often co-exist more or less in isolation. If in this regard we construe objects and processes as the embodiment of knowledge, and knowledge itself as an object and process, then in the volumes in this series we will address the question of how a concept of knowledge can be better consolidated and advanced beyond purely language-based concepts. We believe that it would be promising to return to and make productive use of the concept of critique as an act of differentiating, assessing and suspending final judgments, among others taking our cue from Michel Foucault and Judith Butler. We wish hereby to develop the concept of critique dialogically as a critique of art, culture and taste. We proceed from the assumption that the discourse itself, be it in the form of lectures, dialogues, seminars, or performances constitutes aesthetic practice. Aesthetic practice can be fostered performatively along the interfaces and nodes of social systems, be it in the form of hybrid authorship or as an admixture of individuals, media and discourses. If only because it is suitable for bridging the hiatus of theory and practice.

For the current volume on the "Culinary Turn. Aesthetic Practice of Cookery" we have selected different genres of texts and images that cast a bright light on the social fields of cookery, food and nutrition – as discourses, treatises, recipes, confessions, assertions, conversations, and definitions of positions. If we have assembled the texts and images under the heading of a "culinary turn", then it is not to claim that we seek to prove this or that theory or hypothesis. However, our intention is to bring together in a volume those text and image genres that would not normally be encountered in one and the same book because they originate in different discourses and practices. If one considers the topic of cookery as broadly as possible, then the discourses and practices relating to it seem so complex as to prevent them being boiled down to a single common denominator. The resulting heterogeneity is thus intentional or at least conceded.

The term "culinary turn" is chosen to express a broad social turn towards questions of food, of cooking and nutrition, one driven by a new proximity of cooking and eating to cultural techniques in art and design. A key indicator of the "culinary turn" is not only how cookery and food are spilling over into other walks of life, but also the related emergence of paradoxes. Thus, the "culinary turn" is formulated as genuineness and authenticity that functions as a counter program to a digitalized, connected and globalized world, although both qualities have first to be constructed and staged.[1] And where it lays claim to independence and a "more genuine genuineness", its content still derives from the relationship to a community from which it distinguishes itself but which it needs to be able to develop authentically in the first place. The slightly overweight TV chef-lecturers have given way to athletic tattooed doers in their best years. However, the seedbed for the "culinary turn" are less the artists or cooks, and above all those who move across the system boundaries: the amateurs, hipsters, cultural scholars that publish their own cookbooks, creative hobby cooks, curators, and authors of culinary and rural magazines, not to mention their subscribers. Their flag is the curly kale.

The idea for the present volume arose in the context of the preparations for the research project, now supported by the Swiss National Fund, on "Cooking and Eating as Aesthetic Practice". One of the triggers for the research project was the encounter with Swiss chef Stefan Wiesner. He had converted a barn in the rear courtyard of his inn, the *Rössli* in Escholzmatt/ Entlebuch, into an experimental lab. Alongside a kitchen, the lab is choc-a-bloc with books, old and new tools, apocryphal spices, plant essences, aromas and countless woods, some of them several thousand years old. From here, Stefan Wiesner heads off into the countryside close at hand to discover ingredients for his thematic gourmet menus. The latest of these, called "Nature speaks", is made up of 14 units: water, earth, fire, air, sun, brook, wood, flame, wind, Big Bang, metal, soil, stone, ash. The tenth course, the "Big Bang", is composed as follows: "Salt crucible sounded at 108 Hz, covered with a Chioggia beet in pink pepper water, carrot mousse with rose-water, carrot greens jelly, black Palatinate beet chips, violet Palatinate beet straw, black salsify in caramel nutmeg milk, yellow beet with sweet-sour pimento, parsley root from the smoker with juniper, parsnip candied with walnut, celeriac with a crust of salted thyme, kohlrabi with coriander in wine vinegar, sunflower root with clementine leaves, oat root in laurel-cheese water, yam root parboiled, root of chervil in alcohol and Szechuan pepper 50 Hz". Wiesner explains the history behind each course with great precision and explains the thinking behind them.

Well before the triumphant march of Nordic cuisine, in fact for over 25 years, Stefan Wiesner has been exploring the various substances in the world, in part as a counter to so-called molecular cuisine, in order to transform them in culinary terms. When we first spoke with him, at the end of 2013, Wiesner commented: "If a chef learned under me then he

---

1 | See Menke: 1996, pp. 198–201 on authenticity.

must be able to analyze an Art Deco clock such that he can derive a recipe from it." The typography of the clock face, the materiality of the casing and clockwork, the stylistic and social conditions of the epoch when the clock was made all lead to certain recipe ideas as regards the choice of components and cooking technique that Wiesner then develops through sketches. Put differently: The clock gets cooked, in part directly using components such as gold or leather. Stefan Wiesner is therefore not bragging when he says: "I can actually serve a dish on any topic. You simply have to state the topic." What we can see here is a specific interpretation of cooking as a symbiosis of art, craftsmanship and experience in which the focus is not only on cooking tasty dishes, but on using cooking as a way to analyze the world and transform it into a gustatory experience. In this way, and in part for the very first time, things get grasped in culinary terms. Understood in this light, cooking constitutes an aesthetic practice that seeks a dialogue with other artistic practices, with nature and with our stocks of knowledge of the world. While the path taken by artistic Modernism can obviously be read as a path from figuration to abstraction, the path of a history of cooking probably runs the other way: It starts with pure material, as it were with the abstraction of essences, and from there increasingly moves towards the figurative and to representational concepts. This explains why an entire carrot or meat on a bone has become more important than mash, tartar, pie dough and free aromas: On a plate prepared by Stefan Wiesner landscapes, objects and abstract entities are raised to the level of culinary representation. Those who sit down to a Stefan Wiesner gourmet menu may well be profoundly touched by tastes that they have never experienced before or that reach back into the depths of childhood and in a strange way interlink the past and future in the present. At this level cooking can clearly be understood as a speculative practice which, unlike its most recent equivalent, the "speculative turn", is able to reach practical conclusions from the precedence of the world over human thought.

The present volume is subdivided into five chapters or episodes: *kitchen, production, concept, discourse* and *perception*. The *kitchen* chapter (Krausse/ Leinfelder/von Mende, Regan, Rützler/Reiter, Surmann, Wiesner) brings together historical, political and social perspectives on the culinary theme. The conversation with Stefan Wiesner has been placed at the beginning, as it is key to the concept and thrust of this book. The *production* chapter (Bartha, de La Falaise, Flammer, Home/Oehen, Stromberg) contains fundamental angles on the agricultural, botanical and socio-economic preconditions of the current aspects of cuisine that focus on diversity and regionality. They also show how the latter two aspects have become cultural and social paradigms. The chapter *concept* gets its teeth into the conceptual richness of cooking and into the biographical-narrative dimensions of ingredients and aromas. Anneli Käsmayr picked constituents that make sense in terms of cooking practice (meats, vegetables, fats, acids, herbs and salt), to which Samuel Herzog responded with narrative frames. Then chefs and artists (Alhäuser, Clopath, de La Falaise, dilettantin produktionsbüro, Froelich, Frühsammer, Wiesner) were invited to respond to the chosen constituents with drafts of recipes. In this episode, we sought above all to vividly emphasize the variance of culinary design practices as aesthetic practices while also visualizing the roots of the gustatory experience in biographically informed memories. The *discourse* chapter (Bonino, Bröcker, Knecht, Martinez, Vilgis, Wiesel) highlights the extension of cookery to other cultural domains. A key thrust of the *perception* chapter (Dollase, International Gastronautical Society, Studer, van der Meulen, Vilgis/Käsmayr, Waldenfels) is to foreground aspects of enjoyment and aesthetic perception as opposed to the customary social discourse framing of "health, sustainability and ethics". Among other things, the stress will be placed on exploring phenomenological aspects of the gustatory and its close links to other levels of sensory experience. This volume is concluded by a full bibliography on the subject. We included all references of the contributions, which are of a general interest in view of the culinary turn topic. If a reference is short cited within the contributions, the reader will find the detailed title in the full biography at the end of the book.

The present volume sets out to try and highlight the differences in the approaches derived from theory and practice and thus also to treat the two as equally valid. Over and above the afore-mentioned chapters, a number of images are scattered through the book (Kobe Desramault, Lucky Peach). We want in this way not only to emphasize the key role that the iconic and the visual play in the current discourse on the "culinary turn" (e.g., the different publications on theme brought out by Phaidon Press or in magazines such as "Alla Carta" or in food blogs such as My New Roots, Julie's Kitchen), but also take the perspective of aesthetic practice to offset the predominance of linguistic approaches to the subject.

Should this volume manage to reach readers in a broad variety of disciplines and areas of society and succeed in fostering dialogues across all dining tables, cuisines, museums, restaurants, desktops, libraries and digital networks, and if it moreover triggers debate, discourses and contradiction, then it will have achieved its objective.

Nicolaj van der Meulen/Jörg Wiesel, February 2017

Introduction

Nicolaj van der Meulen and Jörg Wiesel

The kitchen and cooking have emerged as important differentiated cultural fields in the 21st century. Alongside their important role in the natural and nutritional sciences, they are also in the focus of culinary studies, design, art, gastronomy and agriculture. The heyday of issues of nutrition to which this attests contrasts with the "crisis of food"[1] some have discerned and an increasing divergence between nutritional wishes and nutritional realities.[2]

Recent artistic approaches respond to this paradox with cooking and food projects. Unlike the "Eat Art" movement or the use of foods in the context of artistic works, since about 2004 a number of artistic positions have arisen on the line dividing art and design, agriculture, gardening and gastronomy. The discussion now hinges not on a more limited understanding of "food in art" but on broader issues of food, cooking, agriculture and nutrition.

There is an interesting equivalent in more recent gastronomy to this new turn from art and design toward cooking and eating: By way of advancing "Nouvelle Cuisine" and "Molecular Cookery", a culinary practice has evolved that focuses on "regionality", "seasonality" and "culinary traditions", and it has already been labelled "Nova Regio Cuisine".[3] It derives from an analytical study of rural areas and the interest in turning nature into something you can cook at a broader level by means of special cooking techniques. Chefs such as René Redzepi and Stefan Wiesner run their own archives and laboratories to this end. Selection processes, transformations of materials, and the scope for contingency when developing recipes all point to culinary "experimental systems".[4]

On 20 February 2014 Swiss Confederate Councilor Johann Schneider-Amman opened the touring exhibition "Wir essen die Welt" ("We eat the world") in the Confederate Polit-Forum; the successful show can still be viewed. Organized by HELVETAS it addresses the themes of "enjoyment, business and globalization" and discusses the changing socio-political

---

1 | Kimmich/Schahadat: 2012.
2 | Rudolph/Bassett: 2014.
3 | Dollase: 2014.
4 | Rheinberger: 2001.

relevance of nutrition. At almost the same tie, several exhibitions explored the question of healthy nutrition (Vevey in 2015; Marseille in 2014-5; Linz in 2014-5; Cape Town in 2016) and the importance of eating and food in art and design (Eindhoven in 2013; Wolfsburg in 2013-4; Bergisch Gladbach in 2014-5). The success of TV cooking shows, food trucks, elaborately designed cookery, gastronomic and culinary books and blogs,[5] the growing significance of the kitchen as a design task (through to the "Moley Kitchen" in the age of IoT) and the ever greater attention paid to celebrity chefs given the status of artists, all point the great social interest in nutritional habits and the alimentary practices of preparing food.

Hypothetically, one could speak of a *culinary turn*, although the strong public interest thus expressed in questions of cookery and eating, as well as the discussion of central social questions such as sustainability, health and nutrition contrast with the "crisis in food" some have diagnosed.[6] In numerous countries there is evidence of growing dissatisfaction among consumers with their own food and the quality of life, which can be attributed to external constraints (flexibility, mobility) and the wish in society for healthy nutrition, as covered by the media.[7] Complete nutrition such as "Soylent" (and the related discourses) are one expression of this crisis. They strip citizens of any personal responsibility, but come with the price of purely physiological *intake* bereft of any culinary enjoyment. Assuming a *culinary turn* politics and society face the paradoxical challenge of balancing the strong wish for a creative and joyful culture of food with the crisis in nutritional realities and the hunger for pragmatic solutions.

The wealth of magazines,[8] columns, blogs, books and TV shows devoted to things culinary is a strong indication for the virulent debate in contemporary culture on issues of nutrition. This also reflects the swiftly changing culture of cooking and nutrition – in a medium- or genre-specific way. Swiss writers Dominik Flammer and Sylvan Müller have studied the "culinary heritage of the Alps", not only analyzing how individual farmers, breeders, fishermen, cooks and restaurant owners contribute to maintaining culinary diversity, but also considering cross-border "taste" as a response to a hard-to-define need for "genuineness, credibility and authenticity".[9] In Pippa Lord's Foodblog "Sous Style", people present the dishes they create in their own homes. In Despina Stokou's blog "Bpigs" (2009) recipes are posted for the illicit participation in a dinner for Matthew Barney and Elizabeth Peyton. Chef Mina Stone has together with artist Urs Fischer developed a cookery book called "Cooking for Artists"

---

5 | Selby: 2012; Redzepi: 2013; http://www.arthurstochterkochtblog.com; www.derultimativekochblog.com; http://www.whatkatieate.com

6 | Kimmich/Schahadat: 2012, p. 7; Wilke: 2005, p. 7; Dell'Agli: 2009.

7 | Rudolph/Bassett: 2014, pp. 1 f.

8 | King/Williams: 2014.

9 | Flammer/Müller: 2013b, pp. 10, 16.

that was then distributed through Gagosian Gallery.[10] In "Artist's Recipes" a year later artists brought out recipes they authored attesting to their primary or secondary passion for cooking.[11] Through these and other publications, cooking and eating can be read as aesthetic practices that offer models of subjective identity we can adopt if we want. Magazines such as "The Gourmand" seek to bond with art and design when, for example, presenting Berlin restaurant "Themroc" (Manuel Schubbe) under the heading of "Sculptures Don't Eat"[12] and relying photographically on an aesthetic that corresponds with the profiles of the social media. The above series of publications could be continued at will and leads to one of our initial questions: In what way do art and design now communicate the transformation of culinary and convivial structures and what specific contribution do they make to current debates on food and cooking in society?

Within the above-mentioned development, cooking and food can be construed not just as everyday practices but also as aesthetic practices. Starting with the "Manifesto of Futurist Cooking" (1930), the Eat Art concepts developed by Daniel Spoerri et al in the 1960s, and the doctrine of the "Art of Cooking" developed by Peter Kubelka from 1978 onwards, countless positions have emerged that investigate food not only as an object of representation (still life) or representational material, but explicitly as edible representational content.[13] One famous example would be Rikrit Tiravanija, who uses the museum space as a kitchen and a place for social encounters, and thus contributes to a debate on the "relationality" of art.[14] Expressions of the opening of the traditional concept of the artwork through eating would not only be the restaurants run by Daniel Spoerri (1968) or Gordon Matta-Clark (1970), but also the shared eating projects more or less directly integrated into the artistic work as promulgated by artists such as Tobias Rehberger or Olafur Eliasson – without clearly being distinguished from "lifestyles" (monopol, 2014). Berlin-based Icelandic artist Olafur Eliasson recently brought out a cookery book that shows his team in conversation with chefs such as Alice Waters and René Redzepi.[15] A few years earlier, chef Ferran Adrià presented his concept of molecular cuisine at documenta 12 (2007).[16] Artist Dieter Froelich tabled two books, "supen" and "Topografie der Gemengsel und Gehäcksel" that are both aesthetically and conceptually lucid examples of how historico-critical effort and contemporary culinary practice can bond beyond all disciplinary boundaries to form an aesthetic practice – in a conceptually well-designed book.[17]

10 | Stone: 2015.
11 | Jahic/Röthlisberger: 2015.
12 | Teasdale: 2012.
13 | Autsch: 2015; Lemke: 2007a.
14 | Stahl: 2011; Bourriaud: 2002/2009.
15 | Eliasson: 2013.
16 | Lemke: 2007a, p. 31.
17 | Froelich: 2010/2012.

Countless artistic positions are currently to be found straddling the unclear terrain between ecological farming, social projects, design and curating and interfacing art and cookery. Unlike most of their predecessor movements in art history, these projects end in the bellies of their guests. Food is no longer representational material or subject matter, but the object of reflection on nutritional cultures that evolve in the act of tasting. Thus, Swiss artist Sandra Knecht explores the political and cultural conditions of possibility for "homeland" in a transferred and converted barn called "Chnächt" (Swiss German for "Knecht" = servant). "It's Sunday again" (a German pop song of the 1970s), she serves her guests gustatory perspectives on a home world and regionality and explores the political, ecological and cultural conditions for these. As primarily temporary installations (pop-up restaurants, food trucks) other artists investigate political relationships (conflict kitchen), less frequented spaces (SCU Yamada Studio), position themselves on the interface to farming culture and the rural world (Dimity Jones, Ayumi Matsuzaka, soil culture) or address issues relating to waste and food waste (WastED, Zur Bleibe, Wildbolz, Valentin Beck/Adrian Rast). In the process, specifically traditional artistic questions such as "being touched" by art (dilettantin produktionsbüro, International Gastronautical Society) are examined under new conditions. On the one hand, so we propose, from the artistic perspective the critical enquiry into cookery and food seems especially appealing as a means of linking traditional artistic maxims such as the triad of movere, delectare and docere to contemporary issues of nutrition. On the other, in the interaction of art/design and cooking, the narrow confines of art are abandoned so that a description of these activities as an aesthetic practice seems to be an appropriate angle to take.

NOVA REGIO AND REGIONALITY

The culinary and gastronomic paradigm of the early 21st century in the field of cookery/food is that of an autochthonous cuisine that derives from culinary traditions and is seasonal in thrust: It has come to be known under the term Nova Regio cuisine and René Redzepi has identified it as the cuisine of tomorrow.[18] In consultation with Redzepi, former master chef at the *Noma*,[19] Jürgen Dollase has defined the semantic characteristics of Nova Regio cuisine. Here, the consistent implementation of regionality and seasonality form the main agenda. What is quite literally close at hand in the region (and was often previously not used as food) becomes the precious resource that chefs seek to use. The goal of Nova Regio cuisine is, for example in the cooking of Stefan Wiesner (CH), not to use only the nut, but the whole tree and thus significantly improve the criteria of sustain-

---

18 | Redzepi: 2011.
19 | Redzepi: 2010/2013.

ability and diverse tastes.[20] Nova Regio cuisine techniques draw here on inter-culturally adapted cookery methods for effect[21] and on the insights of molecular cooking[22] and food pairings[23]. The Nova Regio menus rely on discerning recipes and high-grade ingredients and can not least be understood as visual and culinary representations of usually rural worlds. Chefs such as Elena and Juan Mari Arzak, Andoni Luis Aduriz, René Redzepi, Magnus Nilsson and Stefan Wiesner typically adopt a conceptually reflective approach that translates in exemplary fashion current issues of nutrition and culinary culture (sources of ingredients, regionality, sustainability, cooking techniques) into recipes.

As mentioned above, Stefan Wiesner's gustatory method bears special consideration in this regard: He analyzes and archives the currents in contemporary cooking such as regional cuisine, Nouvelle Cuisine, Cuisine Naturelle, Cuisine du Marché, Euro-Asian cuisine, Mediterranean cuisine and molecular cookery. In this context, he also emphasizes a reflection of social aspects such as species-appropriate farming and fishing, human nutritional policy and nutritional methods based on dietetics.[24] Wiesner attributes his "culinary aesthetic" to a creative method derived from Alexander Skryabin's compositional techniques and his synesthetic "visualization of music and art"[25].

Despite the potential Nova Regio cuisine has as regards new nutritional issues and their political implications, the criteria used bear studying a little more closely: First, how consistently are the product criteria of regionality and an organic methodology practiced, in particular with the view to internationally adapted cooking techniques? The *Noma* restaurant for example, which was voted best in the world in 2010, 2011, 2012 and 2014 (Restaurant Magazine Top 50), cooperated with the *Nordic Food Lab* platform which transposes international cooking techniques onto regional ingredients. Second, in what way do the afore-mentioned chefs develop a knowledge of taste and developments in taste given their emphasis on the autochthonous? Founded in 2009, the *Basque Culinary Center* in San Sebastián is an international college for chefs attached to the private university in the Basque capital that takes its cue from this approach and has featured an International Advisory Commitee (with Adrià as its president) which brings together chefs such as René Redzepi (Denmark), Heston Blumenthal (UK), Michel Bras (France), Alex Atala (Brazil), Yukio Hattori (Japan) and Enrique Olvera (Mexico). Despite their respectively different cultural and gastro-historical origins, all the chefs who aspire in San Sebastián to develop the future of food share a focus on experimentally reflecting on

---

20 | Dollase: 2014.

21 | Redzepi; 2010/2013; Gilmore: 2012; Wiesner: 2011; Aduriz: 2012.

22 | Vilgis: 2007; Adrià et al.: 2014.

23 | Blumenthal: 2002; Caviezel/Vilgis: 2012.

24 | Wiesner: 2011; Mepham: 1996; Lemke: 2007b/2012.

25 | Wiesner: 2011.

the 350-plus smell receptors and their roots in the human brain. Third, what artistic staging practices and concepts are adapted in order to reposition the practice of cooking beyond some crafts understanding of the discipline? Ferran Adrià, former master chef at the *El Bulli* restaurant outside Barcelona, revolutionized cookery and food world-wide with his gustatory and gastro-aesthetic innovations in the field of molecular cooking. Fourth, what significance do the paradigms of "regionality", craftsmanship and "cultural heritage" have in an age of globalization, migration and digitalization? Where is the interface to a paradoxically nationally-defined hipster community that proves to be highly sensitive to the conservative preservation of traditions? To what extent does an insistence on regionality and local trade routes lead to an undesired narrowing of culture and the open abandoning of cultural achievements? Thus, Tobias Moorstedt recently remarked: "A cosmopolitan consumer will thus buy olives from Morocco and not from a burn-out therapy farm in Breisgau. A cosmopolitan consumer knows that tomatoes from Spain may possibly have a better eco-balance than local vegetables. [...] A cosmopolitan consumer is open to ideas and things that are alien in order to advance, and also advocates precisely this being possible for people in other places."[26] Moorstedt's position seems to be as self-evident as that of the growth critics. The question is less whether you vote for or against regionality and more how you can interpret regionality in a way that can be deployed productively in economic, ecological, political and aesthetic terms without imposing limits qua doctrine. It is obvious that paradigms rely on confessions of principle. And it is equally obvious that such confessions are prone to intrinsic contradictions: "See: with lovers, When they start to confess, How soon they tell lies."[27]

PERSPECTIVES ON REGIONALITY AND SUSTAINABILITY IN LIGHT OF SOCIOLOGY AND CULTURAL STUDIES

Starting from Simmel's study of the constitution of community through eating (1957) and the structuralist examinations of the relation of nature and culture in food,[28] detailed fields of research have arisen on the social implications of food and nutrition. Although at an early date there was discussion of the humans' so-called "omnivorous character"[29] and their dual membership of nature and culture, sociology has tended to focus

---

26 | Moorstedt, T. (2016): Local Hero. 'Aus der Region'. Der Kauf lokaler Produkte und Dienstleistungen ist zum Hipsterbekenntnis geworden. Doch der neue Provinzialismus macht die Welt nicht besser, sondern unter Umständen nur dümmer, in: *Süddeutsche Zeitung*, no. 241, October 18, p. 11.

27 | Rilke, R. M. [1910] (2009): Song "'You, whom I do not tell", in: *The Notebooks of Malte Laurids Brigge*, tr. Michael Hulse, Harmondsworth.

28 | Lévi-Strauss: [1964] (2000); Douglas: 1979/1988.

29 | Fischler: 1990; Emmison: 2003; Johnston/Baumann: 2007.

primarily on questions of the social or family structuring of eating[30] and differentiation through it. By contrast, more recent developments as regards essentialization ("natural", "genuine") and the aestheticization of cooking and eating seem to not have been studied much.

Social attention to food not rarely articulates a wish for physical well-being, for sustainability and for social distinction. Products have, under the labels of sustainability, health and genuineness, become a trend focus in nutrition, and a socio-political task.[31] Filmmaker Valentin Thurn summarizes the content of his own new documentary film "10 Billion. What's on your plate?" (2015) as follows: "The most important thing is that basic food supplies must come from local farms" (on German TV show "titel, thesen, temperamente", May 29, 2015). The prehistory of the development that distinction has less to do with delicatessen meals from abroad and more with sustainable regional produce hinges on the *Slow Food* movement of the 1990s as one of the driving forces behind growing regional organic food.[32] The idea is to overcome the contradictions people experience between the nutrition they want to have and the reality by boosting the consumption of regional and natural products.[33] In this context, the growing success of the *Urban Gardening* and *DIY* movements bears mentioning as regards producing food in a way that interfaces between social focus and high-tech production methods.[34]

The contradictions between a cultural identity based on regionality and a socially and educationally desired inter-culturality have not yet been solved in terms of social sustainability.[35] Given the complexity of the relationship between nutrition (production) and cultural identity and the related historical dimension[36] the pragmatic definitions of regionality (e. g., a quantitative limit to 50 or 100 miles, sustainabletable.org) seem neither sufficient nor productive.

While aspects of the sustainability of nutrition (global vs. local food production, ethically appropriate approach to animal husbandry, "green revolution", protection of arable land) form a key focus of research in interdisciplinary Food Studies,[37] often "naturalness", "regionality" and "tradition" are

---

30 | Barlösius: 1999; Kaufmann: 2006.

31 | Hayn et al.: 2005; Rudolph/Bassett: 2014.

32 | Pence: 2002; Waters: 2010; Barber: 2014.

33 | Rudolph/Bassett: 2014.

34 | Clausen: 2012; Stierand: 2014; Cockrail-King: 2012; Baier/Müller/Werner: 2013. The question of the different concepts of urban gardening relates to aspects of this work and, to the extent that it directly touches on artistic works on cooking and eating, will be considered here. An extensive examination of this field would exceed the bounds of the present project owing to the slightly different focus.

35 | Wierlacher/Neumann/Teuteberg: 1993; Brunner et al.: 2007; Hirschfelder et al.: 2015; Parodi et al.: 2010.

36 | Hall/Gössling: 2013.

37 | Gastronomica Journal; Miller/Deutsch: 2009.

seemly presumed to be the stable variables of a good nutritional practice.[38] "Naturalness" is taken as a secure horizon of meaning, without reflecting at the same time on the paradox given the long since disenchanted state of nature.[39] Trailblazing in terms of the educational and communicative strategy are the Revis Project (2003-5), the European Food Literacy Project and the Harvard University Food Literacy Project, which seek to nurture an understanding for a transformative, alimentary practice and its relationship to agriculture, cooking and nutrition. Here, the need for interdisciplinary collaboration on issues of nutrition and culinary studies are laid out.[40]

As ethnologists, Ulf Matthiesen and Bernhard Tschofen site the stronger attention in regional cuisine and the "constitution of regional cultures of nutrition"[41] in the discourse on globalization. In light of the "re-regionalization of the European food and beverage cultures" Matthiesen defines the rediscovery of regional cuisine not as a "*counter*-movement against the dynamics of Europeanization and globalization", but as "their strict complement".[42] This goes hand in hand with a focus on rural spaces, as products made regionally using artisanal methods.[43] Matthiesen and Tschofen view the greater attention to regional cuisine critically: They place the reference to regional culinary arts in the context of the *terroir principle* and think it advances the myth of the interaction of the earth, climate and species. However, this myth, they say, rests in great part on the imagination that construes the reality of the rural regional countryside not as a product of an "historical and current agricultural regime"[44] and likewise not as the adaption of concepts that stem from elsewhere.

PHILOSOPHICAL PERSPECTIVES AND ANTHROPOLOGICAL THEORIES

Taste has always played a subordinate role in the classical doctrines of the senses and the debate on the hierarchy of the same as regards the issue of aesthetic experience and knowledge. It belonged, for example in the thought of Thomas Aquinus, to the sensory organs that first need to be nurtured. Bernhard Waldenfels attributes the lack of philosophical consideration of the sense of taste to its link to primary needs: Meals and beverages have the character of being necessary for survival (see article in this book). In Classical Antiquity and Modernity, the enquiry into nutrition

---

38 | Kneafsey: 2010; Betsy et al.: 2010.
39 | Rückert-John: 2010.
40 | Wierlacher/Bendix: 2008.
41 | Tschofen: 2007, p. 25.
42 | Matthiesen: 2005.
43 | Waters: 2010.
44 | Tschofen: 2007, p. 41.

and the culture of food, starting with Hippocrates, Epicurus and Claudius Galenus, centered on aspects of balance and dietetics. Both the ancient doctrines of ethics and early Christian theology think of food and drink in the context of moderation, bodily harmony, renunciation, asceticism and sacrifice. Under such conditions, a diversity of taste and an intensity of culinary pleasure seem precarious in terms of both morals and health.[45] This ethical take on and tabooing of gustatory enjoyment is seeing a renaissance in recent discourses.

An explicit historical reassessment of nutrition and the related efforts to establish cookery as an art started with Christoph Wilhelm Hufeland's reasoning on macrobiotics[46] and thus first came into its own in the early and mid-19th century,[47] whereby in particular Vaerst's outline of a gastrosophy distinguished healthy and ethical nutrition from Brillat Savarin's "gourmet doctrine"[48].

A "gastrosophy" that took its cue from ethical, political and health issues has in the last 20 years made substantive contributions to a "philosophy of food". On the basis of philosophical traditions, Harald Lemke and Kurt Röttgers elaborate a philosophy of cooking and eating that is consistently geared to questions of "practical reason", of the political and ethical.[49] Röttgers proposes a "critique of culinary reason" as a "post-Kantian menu of the senses": As a supplement to or compensation for the non-existent fourth Critique, Röttgers reflects on the cultural implications of cooking. An aesthetic foundation of cooking, so Röttgers, would originate in cultivating the senses. He thus adds an aesthetic dimension to an ethically structured discourse. Harald Lemke places his concept of gastrosophy clearly in the context of politics, ethics and morals. His "ethics of food" discusses the philosophical history of the alimentary and the culinary and ends, borrowing from the Frankfurt School, in a "critical theory of good food". In his "politics of food" Lemke seeks to integrate fields as divergent as global starvation, nutritional sovereignty, political gardening, and slow food. In this gastro-ethical approach, sovereign citizens who have successfully undertaken the program of gastrosophical education, define their right to "good food".

What is striking about the philosophical discourse is that an emphatic aesthetic definition of the culinary arts and the diversity of taste actually only occurs marginally or as a social taboo,[50] in other words essentially *ex negativo*. Pleasure and culinary diversity are, like *fast food* suspected per se of being unethical and unhealthy and inserted into an action plan of

---

45 | Endres: 2002; Diaconu: 2013a; Lemke: 2007b.

46 | Pfeifer: 2000.

47 | Rumohr: [1822] 2010; Brillat-Savarin: [1825] 1979; von Vaerst: [1851] 1975.

48 | Lemke: 2007b, p. 375.

49 | Lemke: 2007a/2012; Röttgers: 2009.

50 | Lemke: 2012.

"should, may, can" without in the process reflecting on the justifications for moral principles.[51]

Against the backdrop of philosophical debate and the intentions of aesthetic practices of art and food, elaborating an aesthetics of taste as regards aspects such as enjoyment, hospitality, community and touch would constitute a project in its own right. In the center of studies of the community at table, on orality[52] and on gastrosophy, in particular the element of physiological and metaphorical touch by the gustatory forms a relevant lacunae. Presumably there are special conditions for this. Chefs, artists, gastro-critics and physicists point from different angles to the fact that taste and aroma can have a specific complexity,[53] texture, temperature, pictorial status, spatiality and temporality[54] that can only be accessed by "culinary intelligence"[55]. It is becoming ever more apparent here that concepts of cookery and enjoyment can be addressed with exact scientific definitions.[56] The hypothesis would be that an elaboration of touch by taste from the viewpoint of cultural studies and philosophy cannot be undertaken without differentiated observation and analysis of aesthetic practices.

There are above all two relevant methods for elaborating on a "touch by taste" alongside contemporary artistic/design-based and culinary practices: 1. Starting from Iris Därmann's (and here she follows Simmel: 1957) definition of the company at table as the constitution of community,[57] Bernhard Waldenfels has devised the initial basis for a phenomenology of food and drink, emphasizing, in light of Marcel Mauss among other things the importance of the "gift": Food is characterized as something that from the outset has to do with others[58] and affords an opportunity to "ingest" the other culturally.[59] "Tasting" constitutes the touching of the Other. In this context, secondly, the element of the transformation of sustenance into enjoyment, energy and content is key: Following Richard Wrangham's lead, Michael Pollan has pointed to the importance in human evolutionary history of cooking sustenance[60] which will be discussed in greater detail in the following article on the image of the plate (see van der Meulen).

Given the simultaneity of rising attention and the crisis of food and nutrition one can talk of a *culinary turn* that shows how central questions of society today are discussed in the form of questions of nutrition, preparing nutrition and the food culture. The editors of this volume assume that

---

51 | Wilk: 2010; Hofstadt: 2009; Hirschfelder et al.: 2015.
52 | Kleinspehn: 1987.
53 | Vilgis: 2007/2009; Vilgis/Vierich: 2013.
54 | Dollase: 2014.
55 | Dollase: 2005/2006.
56 | Vilgis: 2014.
57 | Därmann/Lemke: 2008.
58 | Mauss: [1923/24] 1990; Waldenfels: 2008/2010.
59 | Möhring: 2012.
60 | Pollan: 2013.

where they interface art and cooking offer respectively unique models for a sustainable and enjoyable culture of nutrition. At the points where they intersect one can detect a shared interest in social issues, in the specific practices of the experimental transformation of commodities, in current questions of sustainability and communication. The goal of this book is to identify the coordinates where art and cookery meet and assess their potential for current social questions of cooking and eating.

Kitchen

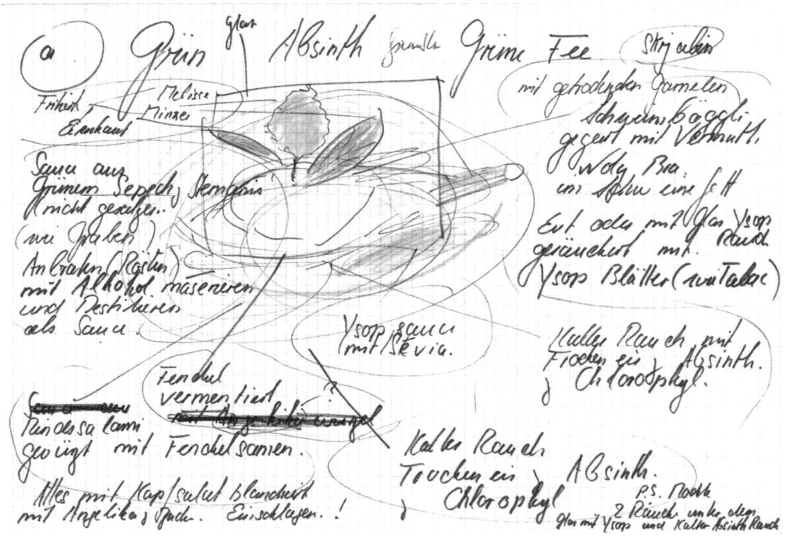
Grün
Absinth
Grüne Fee
Melisse
Minze
Sauce aus
Ysop sauce mit Stevia.
Fenchel
Kalter Rauch
Absinth.
Chlorophyl

Fig. 1

Avant-garde Natural Cuisine

Nicolaj van der Meulen, Jörg Wiesel and Stefan Wiesner
in Conversation on Cooking as Aesthetic Practice

Fig. 2

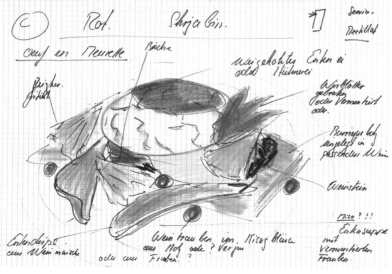

Fig. 3

Nicolaj van der Meulen and Jörg Wiesel: *To start with, let's talk about your approach to cooking. How do you create a recipe, and a gourmet menu in particular? The way you work seems related to certain methods employed in design and the arts. Can your way of cooking be termed concept cuisine?*

Stefan Wiesner: A traditional understanding of cooking often views chefs as creating their dishes arbitrarily or by following their intuition. One example of this is color cuisine. It involves cooking by color, ingredients are chosen according to their visual qualities. Another problem is that while chefs might learn a lot about their craft at culinary school, they often don't question what they have learnt. Chefs often lack the courage to do their own thing. They want to stand out from the crowd, but they don't dare to. I would prefer to tell stories, express something and question the status quo. My thinking and my action may be childish or naive at times. It often requires explanations. Through my way of cooking I gain knowledge of nature, art and the sciences, because for each menu I look at a particular topic. And this always brings a learning effect with it.

To me, the message of a menu is key. While in the past I created menus and then gave them a name afterwards, I do things the other way around now. I need the idea and the concept to be thought-out first. So in this way, "concept cuisine" does fit. I begin by asking myself what I want to express with a menu, which subject matter I'm interested in: a clock, a building site, Dada. Then I create the menu on the subject – with my one condition always being that everything I use should be as regional and seasonal as possible. In the past I focused on perfumery and scent – my second book was also written in this context [Avantgardistische Naturküche, 2011] – I travelled the world, and brought tree bark, resin and essences back from wherever I went. Recently I have become a little more calm and concentrated, I am returning to my own roots. The mind needs to be sated in order to return home.

On the other hand, logical and aesthetic deliberation also brings you closer to the arts. You move away from the craft you learned a little. But having perfect command of your craft is a prerequisite, on which it is then necessary to build through expressing inner, personal aspects. This holds as true for architecture as it does for graphic design. And this is what I try to convey when teaching the arts and design students I work with at your University. They shouldn't imitate but develop. It works exactly the other way around in the catering trade: a chef goes to work with Andreas Caminada, and a few years later he will cook perfectly – but exactly like Caminada. It takes years to free yourself and develop something of your own. Some never achieve this and continue to create Caminada cuisine, while others manage to incorporate their own personality. In my eyes it is only when this happens, when the chef's own personality shines through, that you encounter a true dining experience and real culinary art.

NvdM/JW: *You said that you want to express something through food. That isn't a given for many people, seeing as just seventy years ago people in Germany* *and Switzerland had to worry about where their next meal would come from and how to make rations last. When going to a restaurant in the sixties and seventies, people actually just wanted to have a good meal, which also meant: satisfying their hunger. When you say you want to express something through your cooking then there's something else at stake, this isn't about feeling full or eating tasty food. What do you mean when you talk about "expression"?*

StW: Of course food is primarily "life" in the sense of "survival". This is still a part of our culinary daily life. Well-cooked, fresh, organic everyday meals are of course very much desirable. In restaurants more so than at home things like hospitality, the presence of other diners or a special atmosphere conjure up a sense of pleasure and contentment – this holds true even for fast food restaurants. I want to raise the bar in my restaurant in this respect. It should be as though my guests were going to the theatre or to see an opera. I want to take them on a journey to another world. The food might be thought-provoking, causing them to think about what they've just eaten, or conjuring up a memory, maybe even one from their childhood. Discoveries in the field of neuro-gastronomy are interesting to me in this context. It investigates how food can trigger certain memories or feelings. Scents can even have this kind of effect by themselves. I am looking into this at the moment. I create four menus per year, which means that I can't delve into the topics involved as deeply as I would like to. What is the case instead is that I investigate a topic, then I process it and convey it in the way I understand it. I assimilate existing knowledge and turn it into my own, which is why I like to call myself a charlatan. You could also say I turn it into art, because what exists can be modified. The ancient Greeks for example considered there to be four elements and the Chinese had five. Why not combine all of them and turn them into six elements? I have included ash once more, because it stands for the mineral element and we all return to ashes. That is how I interpret myself, with truth or untruth or simply with naivety. I also look at spagyrics, at holistic thinking about the body, mind and soul for the purpose of healing. And I practice spagyrics – however, my motive doesn't lie in healing but in bringing these principles to the realms of cooking and eating.

JW: *Where does the urge to incorporate knowledge from the most diverse of disciplines come from? That's rather unusual for someone like you, who has learnt their trade as professionally as you have.*

StW: I probably have a predisposition of some kind towards it. Not every chef is interested in, or inclined to, put knowledge into practice and listen to their inner voice. My species will probably die out sooner or later or become involved in other disciplines, for example in art, which I also feel very close to of course. If I was a carpenter rather than a chef I might be creating the same kind of art, just using wood.

NvdM: *Was there a turning point for you, at which you noticed that there was a transformation in the way in which you cook, away from how you approached cooking before and towards the discovery that you can do something else with cooking than fill people's stomachs and create good menus – namely, express something with these menus and tap into a range of topic areas and investigate them?*

StW: This realization really crystallized over time. It began to happen unconsciously and became more and more deliberate as time went by. I now work towards things I would have done intuitively in the past in a much more purposeful way. Previously I would let myself be led by my gut feeling when creating menus. With time this became more professional and ambitious. When I cooked Scriabin in mystical harmony in the color key I realized I was going too far. No-one except for classical musicians was able to comprehend what I was doing. So I aimed to make my food accessible to all once more, amongst other things through employing smaller harmonies. The harmonies in a menu are created using taste and texture. In the past they were much bigger, but nowadays they are smaller, which makes them easier to understand. If you create a harmony with fifteen or twenty components it always works out, because you can blur everything a little. This is where things are currently headed: dishes contain so many components that you've actually enunciated an entire menu on a single plate. Reducing things to a few harmonies makes it simpler and easier to understand, but more difficult at the same time. That's the "monotypic" culinary art I strive for, creating harmonies out of five or six elements. They might be easier to comprehend but they also require more skill because they force you to be precise.

NvdM: *Which role does what is generally called "holism" play for you? You say that actually it isn't just the apple that's interesting in terms of fruit but the entire tree. Why do we need to take a more holistic look at the apple?*

StW: This is always about the interplay between body, mind and soul. As a child I arranged tins of food in the cellar in pretty ways and burnt cardboard boxes and packages in the heater. I thought that people who had fresh vegetables in their basket were poor and those who had cans were rich or well-off. And so I stopped off at a whole range of different stations as a chef too, from truck stops on the Route Suisse to pajama parties to country nights, I cooked Spaghetti à discretion for the entire family for eight francs. It was only when I wrote my first book [Gold Holz Stein, 2003] that I actually realized what I was doing. The chemist Markus Zehnder first made me aware of the fact that I am engaging in spagyrics, for example through employing incineration. The press called me a Paracelsus, and I didn't know who that was. In the end, the dose makes the poison, and I began to look into these topics and employ particular techniques more deliberately. I only realized as I was doing it that this was my own interpretation of spagyrics – just not in the homeopathic sense, of course. Eventually I touched upon a wide range of subject fields. For example I cooked Paracelsus in the planet. And the planets themselves are in the metals and in the plants. The moon for example is silver and has whitish growths. The sun is yellowish and has red plants and is associated with gold.

So I broached many topics, the most recent of which was monotypic culinary art, which, in the sense of a narrow mode of thinking, asks where and with which neighbors something grows, which animal occupies itself with what. This includes, amongst other things, the singing trees, which communicate with one another, as well as what is happening inside of them and what they yield for us: their leaves, fruits, woods, juices, tars, bitumen. Birch tar or coal for example that is distilled into vinegar. Those are building blocks, which I have collected and finally unified to form a key.

JW: *So you proceed from the technical knowledge you gained in your training as a chef and take this as the basis, and this is joined by a great interest in approaching other fields, communicating with these and using the structures you have learnt in connection with them, such as for example with music and a composer like Alexander Scriabin.*

StW: Exactly. But it can be Leonardo Fibonacci's arithmetic, too. This in turn could provide the formula for a spice mix. Or if we were to look at the golden section: It exists both in the human body and in our architecture. Everything is connected in this way; it ensures proportions are balanced and harmonic. The same principle can be employed in the kitchen, too. Architecture can be found on our plates, in our chairs and tables. An architect works in a similar way I do, we are very much alike. And this finally holds true for all those working in the creative industries; the way we think is the same.

JW: *In the context of our research at the Institute for Aesthetic Practice and Theory we are also interested in the fact that you don't merely let the other art forms you're interested in stand for themselves, but instead allow a third entity to arise out of the encounter between your culinary art with music, architecture or even the agricultural sciences – a third quantity, which you communicate to your public, your guests or students. Would you agree?*

StW: That third element you refer to is the heart, it's love. When you're eating, you can listen to yourself, to your own awareness, I think that's what it is. Food and art give rise to a sense of contentment that we all strive for. Art shouldn't stir up aggressions either, despite there being those who might provoke them. In my opinion what the combination of culinary art and other disciplines ultimately create are a sense of pleasure and love.

NvdM: *Earlier, we spoke of the notion of a concept. Concept implies that a lot of ideas are generated, developed and categorized beforehand, before the actual implementation takes place. There were various different trends in painting,* *such as for example Impressionism and Expressionism, which generally tried to circumvent the conceptual and communicate directly with the empty canvas. For other movements the things happening in the artist's head beforehand were decisive, and their implementation was nothing but an organic continuation of the preceding thoughts. I would ascribe your practice to the latter. The end product, which can be experienced and received, is important – but so are the thoughts going into it before, as they ensure the harmonic balance in the end product.*

StW: I agree. The thoughts always come first; putting them into practice is actually the easiest part. When I clear my mind for what I want to express, a perspective opens up that allows me to see it. I can draw from every magazine, every TV program in this way. I write it down, order it and then I turn it into the story, the menu. When I have all of the elements I need I can write it in one day.

NvdM: *You are essentially a gustatory architect. In relation to his work, Le Corbusier spoke of the "promenade architecturale", which refers to the architectural design choreographing the experience which occurs when walking through the building. You pass through Le Corbusier's structures and in doing so you experience architecture as a unity.*

StW: Something similar applies to the succession of dishes in the menus I create. It's possible to puff up a single course and enhance it to the extreme, but this tends to just confuse the guests. In my opinion a menu needs peaks and depths, has to be made up of new things, tried and tested aspects and even primitive ones. It has to address all senses in order to tell a holistic story. You could say a menu leads you through different rooms, and you take them in one by one. My strength seems to lie in being able to envisage such a succession of rooms and, if needed, tear down some walls, fill the space with new furniture and change the lighting – I can even change from an interior perspective to an exterior one. I have a good imagination: I dream up a lot of things when I'm cooking or writing. And if there's something I don't quite like about what I'm doing, I'll take the thought and my writing material to bed with me and work it out overnight. I tend to have the solution the next day. This meditative procedure does have a bit to do with white magic. Magic necessitates a great imagination, if you meditate enough it lets you pass into a second body, the astral body, which allows you to fly, walk on water or through the fire. If I have been to New York once I can travel there in my mind whenever I want, look at houses and shops and sit on a bench and look at the people walking the streets there.

NvdM: *Do you also see this as a gustatory journey?*

StW: Of course I do know how shrimp tastes and I can imagine saffron. But obviously it doesn't work in the way that I can actually smell all of these scents with my nose or really taste them. You can certainly also use books as an aid. But with a good imagination you can let your mind wander into a petrol motor and all the way to the cylinder. You can watch the cylinder go up and down. And the drive shaft. You can see that in your imagination.

If you have a large enough imagination the possibilities are endless. If I go into the forest with students, I ask them to look at nature very closely, for example at how a tree is composed, with its bark and lichens, or at the interplay of colors. These observations and realizations can be useful in many contexts; you just have to translate them. What's important is being more open, more conscious, and turning what you've perceived into something that is your own. This doesn't mean you're not allowed to copy, but you should create interpretations rather than straight copies. But why not take ten architectural structures you like and blend them into one?

JW: *It seems very interesting to me that you have always attributed a life force to the materials and textures you work with as a chef. You meet a piece of wood, a seed, a flower or a piece of meat almost as though on an equal footing, you read them as subjects.*

StW: With the plants and animals I use in my cooking, I try to incorporate the place in which they grow or live. This might mean combining the snail's eggs with the plant and the fish with the algae that surround it in nature. But there's nothing wrong with thinking about this in a contrary way, for example bringing the Alpine goat together with the wolf of the sea. The thing that is the most important to me in all of this is doing it purposely. If the chain of thought that forms the basis is not coherent and elements are combined willy-nilly, I can't stand for it. I did, for example, look into the Chinese and Greek theories on temperaments at the suggestion of a student of mine. This led me to create a menu with six courses, each of which is attributed to an element: air, fire, water, earth, wood and metal. I noticed that you can find the elements wood, metal, glass and water in many wellness restaurants, which are of course places were guests can lean back and relax. This led me to the realization that it makes sense to cook with these elements too and thereby create a connection between eating and the way we live. The most important thing for a human being is his cave, whether this is a hole in the mountain or a modern home, as well as the presence of fire and water. Those are very important elements, which most people like to have around them.

NvdM: *Let's speak about some of your drawings, in which you design your menus, in this context of elements.*

StW: Interestingly those have totally slipped my mind. In the course of my examination of monotypic cooking I very strongly projected my thoughts into the menu and mulled it over many times. This was followed by a phase of sickness during which I was somewhat removed from the work I had done previously. This meant that when I later did put my ideas into practice

I made many mistakes. If I had mentally revisited the menu before imple-menting it that wouldn't have happened. It is essential for me to take some quiet time to myself at some points during this process, where no one will ask anything of me – and sometimes this can take two or three days. Of course this isn't always easy for the people around me.

JW: *How do you communicate with your coworkers? Do you show them your sketches?*

StW: Yes, I make sketches and give them to my crew, sometimes these also feature menus or recipes. My team is strong enough for its members to grasp my ideas through spoken dialogue only, without me needing to actually formulate a recipe. I only write down recipes for the more complex foods, such as bread or sausages.

JW: *Your sketches suggest that you conceive dishes visually from the very start, in terms of using different colors and already considering the way you want to present these to your guests.*

StW: Yes, in part, but I remain flexible in this respect because ultimately it boils down to the materials I end up using in the dishes. Sometimes you have to compromise, for example if the original idea would create too much work for the chefs. In the end it has to be possible to serve the menu – it has to be doable. You can't stretch to the point where things need to be fried, cooked or served with such extreme precision that even the last second matters. It's about finding a consensus that works for 25 serving guests, too. The experience the chefs bring with them plays an important role in this sense. And you essentially don't need to reinvent the wheel: a crème brulée is a brulée, a parfait is a parfait, a glacé is a glacé, and bread is bread. Of course you can change the ingredients, add something or leave something else out, freshen up an old recipe or include new elements, but essentially everything already exists in nature, and nature provides you with rich pickings. In the German-speaking part of Switzerland you are disadvantaged to a certain extent because people are less "animalistic" in terms of food. In the Ticino and the southern European countries people don't mind being able to taste the animal in the dish. Here it's more difficult to serve certain foods; you always need an alternative to dishes with innards or blood.

NvdM: *Does including meat and the animalistic aspect play a role for you in terms of a holistic view?*

StW: Monotypic cuisine assumes a ratio of 1:10 when it comes to animal and plant-based ingredients. It would actually have been one of my objec-tives to serve less meat and more food based on organisms belonging to the vegetable kingdom here at the restaurant Rössli, too. However, the monotypic menu I created reflects that this did not correspond with what the guests want. At least we offer more vegetarian courses than we used to, which is certainly justified and should be a maxim to follow in everyday life too. I find the flexitarian approach – of eating little meat, but good meat when you do – very sensible. But I do see meat as being part of the human diet. To me, it is definitely a part of it.

JW: *This also relates to a very important point in our publication on the 'Culinary Turn'. Do you get the impression that the culinary knowledge guests bring to the table when they eat in your restaurant, but also in other places, is strongly influenced by ethical, political, cultural or religious issues? Until a few decades ago it was of primary importance to know how one should behave at the table, as this was a marker for a person's social standing in society. Nowadays, it seems much more important to know what it is you're eating. Have you observed this shift, too?*

StW: Much has fundamentally changed in terms of the food we eat, and in Germany, Austria and Switzerland this has tended to be for the worse. The southern Mediterranean countries are still very interested in taste, but here, a lot of people will simply eat roasted chicken and nothing much else. Yet despite this it is of course still the case that guests come to my restaurant very much anticipating a new taste experience. In the end of course the experience and the sensations they take away from menus I create are subjective. I prefer not to ask my guests about it too much, because then I would receive answers that confuse me. The same holds true for the development phase of a menu. Even the question concerning the meaning of a single detail will have a manipulative effect on me. But after I finish writing the menu I'm open for questions and ready to listen to input. When you serve something you have developed you have to begin by watching and listening. Do the guests eat it? Do they eat everything? What is the undertone?

NvdM: *We are under the impression that two aspects are currently of importance: on the one hand, many people seem to want to taste something new and explore the world through their sense of taste. But our capacity to perceive flavor seems untrained, and somehow also dulled. The sense of taste plays a special role because what you taste you usually then ingest, making it a part of yourself. It tests: is this good for me? That also explains why food is such an important topic for so many people. But then there is another facet to this: Through your way of cooking, you take us on a path – and we are really very much only at the beginning of that path. I imagine that we face your dishes in a similar way people approached paintings by Kandinsky or musical pieces by Schönberg in the early 20th century. Until recently, our tastes were very much shaped by standardized flavors – for example through the use of Aromat[1]. Your way of*

---

1 | Swiss produced seasoning mix consisting mostly of monosodium glutamate, a flavour enhancer.

cooking opens up new taste experiences, which simultaneously carry in them the memory of something we previously knew.

StW: This corresponds with the idea for the new menu I am developing based on concepts found in neuro-gastronomy. The ability to smell is regarded as the oldest of our senses; humans can perceive thousands of tastes and smells and in contrast to animals we can also understand these. This concerns a vast field which can be studied in depth. I did try out many things subconsciously in the past, but at the time I couldn't find an explanation for them. This is what I am aiming to do now. It is possible, for example, to conjure up memories from early childhood – and smell is very important in that phase: after all, mother and child are able to recognize each other by smell. Society, economy and school cause us to un-learn this earlier ability; as small children we are much more responsive to tastes and smells. I plead in favor of a return to child-like thinking, towards a thinking that is led much more strongly by the instincts.

On the topic of "standardized tastes": Aromat, monosodium glutamate and umami are dead. They take away all of the rough edges a dish may have, so it may be consumed without thinking. However, the realization that it is boring to eat like this, and that feeling full alone is not truly satisfying, is gradually taking hold. To speak in harmonies: Schnitzel, French fries and lemon are a boring triple harmony. The pleasure lasts for about three bites then you merely gulp the food down until you feel full. Skill in cooking lies in creating harmonies that make eating the entire dish a pleasure. In order for it to be perceived as light by the tongue, the chef has to work magic with acidity, piquancy, sweetness and bitter flavors. The latter is especially important, because the bitter flavors make the food better and the harmonies more coherent – yet for a long time, they were frowned upon. Bitter flavors help you make out the individual components more clearly. Umami on the other hand flattens everything out. The Swiss love Aromat and Maggi, it's difficult to wean them off these. I see eating as having a lot to do with education and style. The higher classes used to have more style when it came to food, and this made them healthier and live longer, while the lower classes had to content themselves with simple, unhealthy food; and they died earlier.

JW: *You really do provide aesthetic experiences. And I don't mean this only in the sense of experiencing something "beautiful", but in the sense of a holistic atmospheric encounter. We are looking into this new interest in food. After all, it's possible to perceive a painting by Kandinsky with your entire body. This means not just looking at it, but entering the painting with your body – not in a metaphorical but a literal sense. It's also possible to physically absorb a text by Max Frisch. Your menus are ingested in an entirely new way. – What would you say, why does the young generation post selfies of their visits to restaurants on Facebook, why do they take pictures of their food, of their Schnitzel and fries or their salads? People show images of what they eat to the entire world. What are they communicating in doing so?*

StW: I believe this to be a backwards step. The mobile phone is turned into a second brain, one that people almost rely on more strongly than on their instinct. This results in the instinct atrophying. Funnily enough, there's often talk of over-aging with respect to gourmet cuisine. You tend to find older, often affluent guests in restaurants with 18 *Gault-Millau*-points, but very few 30- or 40-year-olds. In our restaurant on the other hand the audience is very mixed, we have many young guests. The oldest generation however doesn't come at all, because it still feels more at home with traditional, opulent gourmet cooking. Opulent means expensive and expensive signifies good or special. But this is slowly changing. A contemporary chef is likely to assume that it is possible to create a wonderful dish by using nothing but garden lettuce. You can fry, distill or ferment the core and the inner and outer leaves; you can dry them or turn them into granules.

NvdM: *You already mentioned that regional ingredients play an important role in your kitchen, alongside seasonality. Do the processing methods you just listed also stem from the region, or do you draw from the diversity of all human culture?*

StW: Molecular cuisine has opened up many avenues for us and also given us freedoms. Old techniques such as sterilizing foods were suddenly up to date again, as were materials such as nitrogen and dry ice. I already used distillation beforehand. Working with xanthan gum was a great revelation for me, as this makes thickening cold liquids possible. But at the same time we have also produced new directions ourselves, for example working with a wrought iron oven that can heat up to 1200 degrees Celsius, or working with fire, charcoal and wood. That's our turf; it's an area where we're ahead of everyone else. Much of it has a regional basis: distilling, using fire and wood coal. And deep-frying has also emerged as being a reliable method – but we now deep-fry entirely different foods to the ones treated in the past – herbs for example.

NvdM: *The same holds true for fermenting. While in our latitudes people used to ferment silage and white cabbage in the past, we have now tapped into many different possibilities.*

StW: Of course on an international level the different cooking cultures are blending into each other. For my first book I already fermented carrots after the oriental method, and at the time I was the only one doing so. It's a shame we didn't follow this up more closely. Today, the Nordic Cuisine is a forerunner when it comes to fermenting, the Dutch celebrity chef Ron Blaauw also works with it. At the moment we work with the bubbler [vaporacid cooker] a lot, for example in order to poach fish using formic acid. We worked with ants even before René Redzepi started cooking; by placing gauze on anthills and working with it or placing eggs in there and so on. The *Gault-Millau* guide then reported I was divorced from reality and it was impossible to understand my methods, so I forgot about most of it. But now

I'd like to pick up on these techniques once more. When I read negative reviews – amongst other things I was criticized for cooking stones – I put the method in question aside for some time. I feel hurt by criticism.

NvdM: *In the same way artists are hurt if they venture on new paths and are met with ridicule. But at the same time it is also a compliment.*

StW: In order for me to pick something up again I first need self-affirmation, I have to know I am strong enough. We invented the bubbler and I'm certain others have already picked up this technique too, they might even overtake us in using it. This happens to us time and again. We might be the first to do something, but won't necessarily remain the best at it. I would need a few employees like Rebecca Clopath, who want to work in the laboratory every day. In our current involvement with neuro-gastronomy I also need three or four chefs who are ready to carry out intensive studies. At the moment I work by myself and that's also why I sometimes find myself on thin ice. Which is why I call myself a charlatan: I enter a particular area and talk about it in my menu, even if everything isn't always entirely well-founded.

Anthropocene Kitchen

Joachim Krausse, Reinhold Leinfelder and Julia von Mende

At the beginning of the third millennium, three unconnected news opened up an entirely new perspective on the human condition and at the same time on the image humankind has of itself as a species. The first decisive news was derived from the data of global demographics: The 21st century marks the first time that a majority of people lives in cities. Urbanization seizes the former agrarian societies and is becoming universal, its global momentum follows that which industrial countries experienced in the 19th and 20th centuries.[1]

The second groundbreaking news was the result of the anthropological research conducted by a group headed by Richard W. Wrangham, according to which the use of fire for cooking and the consumption of cooked meals took the evolution of humankind out of the hominid development stage. The effect of cooking on our physical and social constitution primarily made this animal into what we call the human.[2] According to the theory, as a universal cultural technique cooking is not only a cultural, but also an anthropological matter.

The third news suggests a reformulation of the era in which we live: Given the numerous indications that "in the coming millennia the climate on the planet will significantly diverge from its natural development" and that this divergence can be attributed to human activity, the geologist Paul Crutzen proposed that the current geological era be no longer classified as Holocene, but rather as Anthropocene.[3] In 2008, the Stratigraphic Commission of the venerable Geographical Society adopted this position itself and confirmed the classification 'Anthropocene' as the term for a geological period, in which the human species has become the dominant geological factor.

---

1 | In Germany, for example, the ratio of urban to rural population was reversed between 1870 and 1930: Whereas in 1870 two thirds still lived in the country, in 1930 two thirds of the population were already living in cities. This reversal had considerable consequences for the way people lived and their relationship with the environment. With regard to the momentum of the global urbanization process see WBGU: 2016.

2 | Wrangham et al.: 1999; Wrangham: 2009.

3 | Crutzen: 2002, p. 23; Leinfelder: 2012; Waters et al.: 2016.

The activities conducted by humans that are triggering changes on Planet Earth are as extensive as they are profound, they affect all living beings, all eco-systems, the entire human interaction with nature and ultimately its own habitat. What was nature has become an artefact – and this manifests itself in the Anthropocene on a planetary scale and in an all-embracing meaning.[4]

However, in the process of the transformation of the planet into an artefact it has become so evident that the life-preserving systems are extremely vulnerable that neither experts nor a majority of politicians now seriously question the need for a "rethink", in particular with regard to energy and climate policy.[5]

Indeed, the directions for action resulting from the data compiled by climatologists, geologists, biologists etc., which at least resulted in political decisions being made, do not go far enough to bring about concrete changes in behavior; they are by their very nature top-down processes, which miss the mark if not underpinned by bottom-up processes. This too is now undeniable and is reflected in what researchers into the Earth's system call the "bottom-up/top-down estimation of vulnerability". By this they mean "the collaboration between scientist and experts, who provide information about affected regions, areas, and population groups". This also embraces an estimation of adaptability, e.g. "the question of how quickly and how greatly policies and human behavioral patterns can in general be changed"[6].

It is noticeable in the way that scientists put things that their field of action amounts to advising policy makers on scientific matters, and that with regard to the last point in particular, i.e., the possibility of behavioral changes, there is great uncertainty. However, an actual bottom-up approach would have to involve all those who are meant to change their own behavior and in particular those who of their own accord wish to change their behavior.

---

4 | Anticipating this, US architect, designer and inventor R. Buckminster Fuller (1895–1983) came up with the metaphor of the Spaceship Earth, for the operation of which there was no instruction manual. "Lack of instruction has forced us to find that there are two types of berries – red berries that will kill us, and red berries that will nourish us. And we had to find out ways of telling which-was which red berry before we ate it otherwise we would die. So we were forced, because of a lack of an instruction book, to use our intellect ..." Buckminster Fuller, R. (1969): *Operating Manual for Spaceship*, Carbondale, Ill., pp. 52–53; see Krausse, J. (ed.) (1998): *Bedienungsanleitung für das Raumschiff Erde*, Dresden/Amsterdam, pp. 249–255.
5 | This is documented by the fact that on April 22, 2016 in New York 170 countries signed the Paris Agreement on Climate Change. See *Frankfurter Allgemeine Zeitung* (2016), no. 95, April 23, p. 5 and Sommer, J./Müller, M. (eds.) (2016): *Unter 2 Grad? Was der Weltklimavertrag wirklich bringt*, Stuttgart.
6 | Mastrandrea, M./Schneider, S. (2011): Vorbereitungen für den Klimawandel, in: *Das Raumschiff Erde hat keinen Notausgang*, Berlin, pp. 11–59, here pp. 52.

In other words, it is less about generating acceptance or even about implementing a previously prepared program than about impetuses and invitations to sample and test new possibilities that are less onerous for oneself, for others, and for the environment than those to which we have become accustomed in a largely ready-made existence. It is worthwhile going along with the involvement of individuals in the major transformation process, as ultimately the overall effect we experience as a crisis for the global regeneration system is made up of the thousands of trivialities in our everyday life. Nothing speaks against beginning to rehearse this social contract so needed for a *major transformation,*[7] with minor divergences from regularity, in the kitchen and at the dining table.

TRACKING DOWN EVERYDAY ACTIONS

To this end, we must first set out to track down everyday actions. Only by studying them first can adaptations to actions be introduced on the basis of intuition and participation.[8] The approach adopted by the 'Anthropocene Kitchen' project in the 'Image Knowledge Gestaltung' excellence cluster at Humboldt University in Berlin is the result of the recognition of an apparent gap between academic findings and the imperatives for action by policy makes derived from them on the one hand, and the change in habits on the part of the population at large on the other.[9] With the term 'Anthro-

---

7 | WBGU (2011): *Welt im Wandel – Gesellschaftsvertrag für eine Große Transformation*, main expert opinion, Berlin.

8 | The trail illustrated the intuitive user behavior that is governed by the choice of short routes. Ever since the 1920s, research into the emergence of "desire lines" has been the subject of urban and transport planning (see Throgmorton, J./ Eckstein, B. [2000]: *Desire Lines: The Chicago Area Transportation Study and the Paradox of Self in Post-War America. The 3Cities Project*, available online at: http://www.nottingham.ac.uk/3cities/throgeck.htm [accessed on May 28, 2016]). As in studies by Frei Otto and his SFB 35 research group in Stuttgart, nowadays computer simulations of the emergence of beaten tracks are being used (see among others Helbing, D. [2013]: *Verkehrsdynamik: neue physikalische Modellierungskonzepte*, Berlin) in an attempt to gain new insights into human behavior. In planning the term "trail" is associated with participation and self-organization processes and as such in literature is repeatedly associated with Christopher Alexander's work. It serves as a metaphor for informal actions in response to formal structures that do not correspond to the needs of individuals or entire groups. See among others Nichols, L. (2014): Social desire paths: a new theoretical concept to increase the usability of social science research in society, in: *Theory and Society* 43/6, pp. 647–65.

9 | Currently conducting research on the basic 'Anthropocene Kitchen' project are Karl W. Grosse (architecture and design), Alexandra Hamann (media design), Jens Kirstein (geology), Joachim Krausse (design theory), Reinhold Leinfelder (geology and geobiology), Julia von Mende (architecture) and Marc Schleunitz (biodiversity,

pocene', a geological measure that embraces millions of years is associated with the kitchen, a place where everyday actions are conducted, in which day by day decisions are made as to what is served.

With foodstuffs from all over the world, the kitchen is the end of the route for global logistics and production chains. Resources are put to use here, the Anthropocene takes shape here in everyday practices. Cuisine and the kitchen are reliant on the availability of certain natural resources in its environment. As such it is dependent on global flows of goods on trade routes that provide an infrastructure – from foodstuffs and cooking utensils to elementary resources such as water and fire – while at the same time exerting a not to be underestimated influence on global changes: e. g., the disposal of waste water and the return of different wares to the natural cycle. Thus the kitchen assumes the role of an important hub in the era of the Anthropocene, it is link between a home and the outside world. At the same time the development of human culture is very closely linked to changes in the kitchen.

TASTE AS A PREREQUISITE FOR BEING ABLE TO MAKE DECISIONS AND TAKE ACTION

This culture also includes tasting and trying food before it is actually consumed. In this prelude to a comprehensive appropriation and assimilation process taste, which always includes smell, is called upon as a sensual decision-making authority to form an initial opinion about edibility, wholesomeness and tastiness of food and drink. The previous knowledge collected over generations and the handing down of empirical know-how on foods that vary tremendously locally and regionally always form the basis of every type of cuisine and every dietetic and culinary culture. However, as the latter do not consist solely of the preserving of proven traditions, but rather over the course of the cultural history of cooking and eating are also prepared to consider new foods and dishes previously unfamiliar (such as potatoes, tomatoes, pizza and so on), the formation of taste is also decisively involved in the acceptance of such innovations. The driving forces for food novelties are shortages, migration but also tourism. In the process of cultural learning the mouth assumes the function of an individual laboratory in which testing is practiced. Curiosity is the driver. However, the willingness to cross the "disgust threshold" when trying unaccustomed items such as eating high-protein insects and larvae, something not usual in our regions, can be learned and is involved in forming the sense of taste. The latter is essential for developing an ability to judge whether something is good for us or not. It is the precondition for spontaneous, but also consid-

evolution, ecology). Until 2015 involved in the base project were Stephan Barthel (geography), Philipp Oswalt (architecture and urbanism) and Anne Schmidt (architecture and urban design).

ered and correct behavior as regards our physical wellbeing. Only then can benevolent and responsible action be performed on a larger scale.

In the course of industrialization these opportunities for taste formation have been lost. In the supermarket foods are often packed so we are unable to smell them, and are quite literally "homogenized". Processing of milk plays a pioneering role here. "Branding", "labeling", certification or sell-by dates relieve us consumers of the decision on whether something is good for us or not. Nutritional styles intended to increase efficiency whether with regard to body shape or weight, work performance, or time saving have come to replace food choices guided by sensual considerations.

Cultural appropriation processes, which to date took up the time of an entire generation have accelerated alarmingly and are increasingly subject to short-lived fads for self-improvement. Thanks to an ever-expanding choice, a mass of information, and mobility our taste is seemingly also going global. That part of our nutrition that can be sensually experienced now occupies an ever dwindling part of the global chain of influences that today constitute our kitchen metabolism and our eating behavior. However, the fact that we are unable to experience the connection between individual everyday actions and global impact represents one of the key problems in the Anthropocene. It is important to first analyze these systemic connections and then to form a picture of them.

EVOLUTION OF INDUSTRIAL, URBAN KITCHEN METABOLISM

One aspect is the realization that the kitchen space has altered from a place of production to one of consumption, and that it is closely networked with the city. After all, while until industrialization the house formed the focal point of actions involved with human nutrition, the use of fossil forms of energy produced new forms of households.[10] The switching over of the fireplace from wood to coal and the introduction of iron stoves and oven about 250 years ago, followed the shifting of water sources from the outside (wells and water pumps on squares, streets and in courtyards) to the interiors of houses. Finally, thanks to a pipe system it moves into the home itself, i.e., into the kitchen, then the toilet and bathroom. The same applies to the waste water system. An innovative kitchen metabolism asserts itself, with whose developments the causative conditions for the Anthropocene are established. The pipe system for water becomes a model for supply household with gas, while electrification of the kitchen and household in the 20th century will also follow an existing pattern.

---

10 | This transformation is the subject of five films in the series "Küche, Stube usw. Geschichte der Arbeiterwohnung" by Jonas Geist and Joachim Krausse, WDR Cologne, 1978, and the three films "Das Neue Frankfurt 1925-30", ibid., 1985, as DVD edited by Christian Hiller, Joachim Krausse, Philipp Oswald, Filmverlag abso-lutMEDIEN, Berlin 2015; see Krausse: 1992, pp. 56-60.

All the pipe systems connect kitchen and household directly to large, industrial, external utility firms. The disposal of waste, water and feces via a canalization system running through towns and cities is the decisive measure against the city epidemics of the 19th century. This is followed by organized rubbish removal and the creation of "urban hygiene". From now onwards households are connected to an urban supply network. With the emergence of the food industry food preparation moved to a large extent outside of private households. The increasing delocalization and relocation of food processing coincides with limits to the individual means of tracing back your own behavior and ultimately exerting an influence.[11] Simultaneously, the urban supply structure with its interfaces penetrates private households and the kitchen.

PARTICIPATION, POPULAR MEDIA AND INTERACTION

But in order to examine our habits and open up intuitive options on the tracks of the everyday, we feel it is necessary to do away with the division between the production and communication of knowledge and to avail ourselves of popular means of communication. One of our approaches for analyzing and visualizing the complex interlocking of local, regional and global factors is to develop a specialist comic-based co-design. This gave rise to the academic specialist comic *Die Anthropozän-Küche*,[12] which describes the current status of the global food situation together with its cultural, social, resource-related and geo-political embedding using drawn individual stories with a view to possible future courses of action and relies on the dialog as the format to connect the everyday behavior of the real protagonists from ten parts of the world with scientific data. Amongst other things, we discover, for example, in the case of the 75-year old Kelema Mutawa from Uganda, that within a generation the provision of food (prosumption, supermarket), the equipment of the kitchen (cooking place located outside the home, gas stove in the house) and the type of preparation (use of various fossil energies) can alter completely. The participatory, intercultural specialist comic project is interdisciplinary in the sense that the scientific research comes in particular from questions directed at the protagonists (What do you eat? Where do you shop? Do you know where your food comes from? How is food integrated into your everyday lives? What social role does it play? What is a simple, favorite dish?), and the storyboards were then developed jointly by scientists, communicators, protagonists and artists and the intercultural nature of the project was also

11 | Barthel, S. et al. (2014): Privater Haushalt und Städtischer Stoffwechsel – Eine Geschichte vor Verdichtung und Auslagerung Berlin 1700–1930, in: *Arch+ 218, Zeitschrift für Architektur und Städtebau*, Aachen/Berlin, pp. 92–104.
12 | Leinfelder et al.: 2016. See also http://anthropocene-kitchen.com and Leinfelder/Hamann/Kirstein: 2015.

to be expressed in the various styles of portrayal used for the individual chapters by the artist from the respective countries and regions.

Regaining sensory self-control over your own consumption of resources in the kitchen is another solution explored by the research project. Knowledge and lost knowledge about the human metabolism are visualized by graphic descriptions of the process chains involved. The omnipresent image of resources that are seemingly always available in any quantity should also be corrected in light of newly acquired experiential patterns. In experiments with a lab kitchen that is currently being assembled, among other things, data visualization of the interfaces and the relations of user actions are being analyzed. The goal is to underscore options for action that lead to a sensitive approach to consumer goods.

IDEAL TYPES FOR PATHWAYS TO THE FUTURE

Let us now conclude with another form of path that concerns us in the 'Anthropocene Kitchen', that of the ideal types for pathways to the future. When designing future regional or global worlds and addressing the issue of nutrition there are not one but numerous options. It seems sensible to outline these in potential ideal-type pathways to render the potential more comprehensible. The future design of nutrition could take an alternative path, be it reactive, sufficient, bio-adaptive or high-tech.[13]

A *reactive* solution would be to boost productivity by relying on technology, simultaneously enhancing efficiency and lowering the impact on nature. Greenhouse gas emissions would need to be controlled by separating the carbon dioxide and storing it, and new or now resistant vermin combatted by new pesticides.

The *sufficient* pathway, by contrast, would entail basing nutrition as exclusively as possible on regional, seasonal products, consuming far less meat or opting for vegetarian or vegan food.

In a *bioadaptive* world, nutrition would be produced with as extremely low resource inputs as possible, meaning best of all with complete recycling. Examples could be hydroponics or aquaponics, or eliminating packaging or composting it entirely. Phosphates would be reclaimed from the irrigation and sewage systems. Insects, raised in a very resource-friendly way and their chitin shells could then be used for bioplastic production, could serve as fishmeal for aquacultures, and also play a greater role in human nutrition.

The *high-tech* pathway would lead to fully-processed and modular food composed with a view to optimal health, and might be created using 3D printers. Meat would be artificial and lab-grown. The requisite raw

---

13 | Leinfelder, R. (2016): Das Haus der Zukunft (Berlin) als Ort der Partizipation, in: Popp, R. (ed.): *Einblicke, Ausblicke, Weitblicke. Aktuelle Perspektiven der Zukunftsforschung*, Berlin/Wien, pp. 74–93.

materials would be produced using genetically-modified and optimized strains in highly efficient high-tech factories, best of all in the places where they would be consumed, meaning in the middle of the large cities in special high-rises, farm-scrapers.

This pathway system is intended to be as visionary as it is visualizing, a framework to practice openness, a zest for experiment and discussion of the unusual in a social process; they are already sketched out rudimentarily in the 'The Anthropocene Kitchen' comic. The actual nutrition futures will no doubt, depending on the regional, cultural and social context, be assembled from wildly different admixtures of these options that, to the extent that their systemic impact does not conflict with our planet's limits or with the goal of sustainable development, will hopefully guarantee a large or even larger regional and global diversity in food in future. It is therefore all the more important that the kitchen as well as the cuisine of the future does justice to the sociological context and to the inevitably reflective character of nutrition.

The Evolution of Kitchen Design

A Yearning for a Modern Stone Age Cave

Antonia Surmann

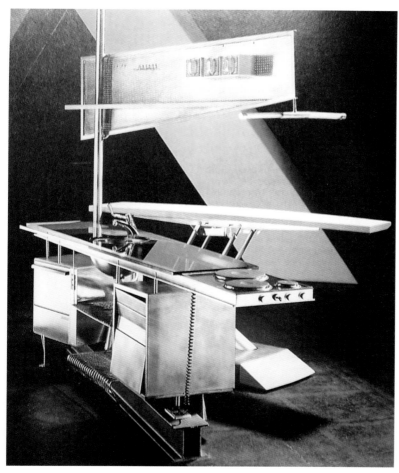

Fig. 13

Fig. 1

Fig. 4

Fig. 1 a

Fig. 5

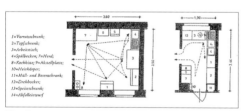

Fig. 2

Fig. 6

Fig. 3

Fig. 6a

Fig. 7

Fig. 11

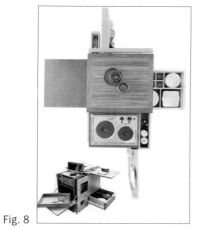

Fig. 8

Fig. 11 a

Fig. 12

Fig. 9

Fig. 10

Fig. 14

Fig. 15

"Inappropriate kitchen arrangements, often based on the furnishing of other rooms, are the cause of countless difficulties that lead to an excessive loss of time. The kitchen should be the workspace, the laboratory for the housewife, in which every superfluous bit of space and every inconvenient arrangement of the fixtures creates additional work in the long run. It must be a mechanism, an instrument. To the woman of the house, time should be too precious to put up with the inconveniences of old-fashioned kitchen management day in, day out."[1]

As early as 1926 a 1.90×3.40 m 'work kitchen' was developed that went by the name of *Frankfurter Küche* ['Frankfurt Kitchen'] which became the prototype for a prefabricated, standardized type of kitchen. But the streamlining of the work environment and the spatial dimensions of kitchens actually began in America. Catherine E. Beecher was the first to address the subject of kitchen design in relation to the issue of domestic servants in 1841. In an analogy to the rationally-structured organization of work in the industrial sector, Christine Frederick and Lillian M. Gilbreth attempted to transfer this logic to housework. They broke down the work processes here into the three fundamental steps involved, *preparation, cooking* and *cleaning*, and allocated these to the appropriate workstations of *store cupboards, stove* and *sink* in a purpose-designed arrangement aimed at making the work easier and more efficient. In addition to this, Catherine E. Beecher and Lillian M. Gilbreth championed the recognition of housework as a profession and the kitchen as housewife's workplace. This article examines the changes in kitchen design in the period from 1926 through to the end of the 1980s and demonstrates that residential building programs and social interests, along with wide-spread notions of society and roles, are reflected in the very design and use of the private working and living space that is the kitchen.

In Germany it was the changed image of women resulting from women's increasing employment that prompted the re-examination of housekeeping.[2] The recognition of housework as a professional role represented a trigger for a thorough review of the subject of the kitchen. Alongside the book published by Bruno Taut in 1924, *Die neue Wohnung, Die Frau als Schöpferin*[3] ['The new home. Woman as creator'], probably the most important work in the rationalisation movement in Germany was *Der neue Haushalt. Ein Wegweiser zur wissenschaftlichen Haushalts-*

---

1 | Muche: 1925, pp. 15.

2 | Schlegel-Matthies: 1995, pp. 149.

3 | Taut: 1924.

führung[4] ['The new household. A guide to economical housekeeping'] by Erna Meyer. The rationally structured household revolved around three premises: the ergonomically founded principles of saving time, energy and materials, the implementation of a functional and ergonomic aesthetic, and the demand for using technology in the household. Whilst initially it was primarily housewives' associations that picked up on the rationalization of the household, in 1924 architects began to follow suit. The new type of kitchen – a purpose-designed, functionally arranged workspace – was not however positively received by everyone in Germany. In the 1920s a widespread debate was sparked regarding which form of kitchen was better, the kitchen-diner or the separate 'work kitchen'. Efficient work kitchens were further developed and introduced on a grand scale as part of the residential building programs carried out by cities. Each city had its own 'kitchen planner' within its building department, so kitchens varied from city to city. There were kitchens with designs specific to Munich, Hamburg and Stuttgart. Whilst all these kitchen types have since been forgotten and no further concepts for work kitchens were put forward during the Nazi era, the successful model of the 'Frankfurt Kitchen' was developed further in the US, Sweden and Switzerland, with adaptions continually made according to the advance in technical developments. After World War II a modified version of the 'Frankfurt Kitchen' made its way back to Germany as a Swedish kitchen or American fitted kitchen. Even today, the 'Frankfurt Kitchen' has lost none of its significance in house construction.

Due to the ever increasing need for housing, a ten-year residential building programme was set up in Frankfurt in 1925 under the aegis of Ernst May as head of the Municipal Building Dept. One of Ernst May's core principles for the planning of mass housing projects lay in making housework more efficient. Thus, with a logical floor plan, rooms would be laid out in such a way that housework could be carried out with the least effort required. The architect Margarete Schütte-Lihotzky (1897–2000) was instructed to take efficiency in the carrying out of housework into account when planning and constructing these homes. In the Frankfurt residential building program, the kitchen-diner was considered not 'contemporary' enough and was replaced by a 'two-cell built-in kitchen and living room'.[5] Margarete Schütte-Lihotzky used the *Mitropa* catering company's kitchen design for the railway dining car of the time as a model. This kitchen made the preparation of five-course menus in a space measuring 1.97×1.83 m together with a pantry of the same dimensions possible (fig. 1: Floor plan of the *Mitropa* dining car kitchen; 1a: View of the *Mitropa* dining car kitchen). These spaces would see two people preparing food for up to 80 passengers in a relatively short time. What's more, these two spaces totaling 7.12 square meters also contained drinks, crockery, cutlery and glasses. In the *Mitropa* kitchen, Margarete Schütte-Lihotzky saw a purpose-designed workspace that implemented the savings in terms of the ground a user needed to

---

4 | Meyer: 1926.
5 | May: 1928, p. 118.

cover and the movements necessary for completing their tasks with the utmost logic and consistency. She attempted to transfer this approach to the private household.[6] However, this did not mean that Schütte-Lihotzky wanted to change the way housewives cooked. First and foremost, she wanted to create a logical arrangement of workstations in order to achieve efficiency in the cooking process and the ground covered during the work.

During the 1920s, proponents of the work kitchen came to see the kitchen as the center for housework as a laboratory[7], factory[8] or workshop[9]. As a consequence, investigations were carried out for the work processes in the kitchen in line with business management considerations in a process similar to that of the Taylor system, with various jobs in the kitchen timed using a stopwatch. The aim was for the size and the shape of the kitchen to maximise savings in terms of the steps necessary and the distances to be covered. The evaluation of the results revealed a long, narrow space 1.90 m wide and 3.40 m long to be ideal (fig. 2: Steps saved in the 'Frankfurt Kitchen' [right] relative to a conventional kitchen [left]). The kitchen structure was adapted to suit essential work steps. The outwardly ventilated food cupboard was located on the left, next to the worktop positioned in front of the window. To the right of the work station was the sink unit and the crockery cupboards with glass doors along the longer wall. The sink adjoined a worktop under which there was a food cupboard with drawer-containers. This was followed by a cupboard for pots and pans and the broom cupboard in the corner. The three-flame gas cooker with oven and the stove were arranged on the opposite side (fig. 3: 'Frankfurt Kitchen' by Margarete Schütte-Lihotzky). The aisle of the kitchen was 0.90 m wide. The narrow aisle meant there was less ground to cover between one side and the other. A wide sliding door led into the living and dining area. In order to remain true to the principle of short distances outside of the kitchen too, the distance between kitchen and dining table was set at three meters. The 'Frankfurt Kitchen' was the first fully-equipped work kitchen to be implemented on a large scale for Frankfurt's housing development programme. It was to provide the housewife with a workplace comparable to that of her husband in terms of its function and quality. The kitchen thus became a mono-functional room, a workspace for an individual person. What was however forgotten in all of this, was that previously the woman had carried out her cooking and kitchen duties in the presence of her family and/or her children, from whom she was now separated. In the 'Frankfurt Kitchen', supervision of the children and communication with other family members was no longer possible. At the same time, the streamlining of the household was linked to the desire to expand the woman's individual scope for freedom. But where was her individual scope for freedom here? Not really in private pleasures or in supervising children

---

6 | Lihotzky: 1927a, p. 157.

7 | Lihotzky: 1927b, p. 121.

8 | Anonymous: 1925, p. 19.

9 | Ibid.

after working in the kitchen, but rather in other productive activities like working outside or inside the home. Housework was part of a function-alization process that aimed to effectively exploit women's productive abilities. The design of the 'Frankfurt Kitchen' was indeed based on an emancipatory approach, but ultimately this demand could not be imple-mented as the crucial characteristic of professional occupation – remuner-ation – was not part of it. Without this, there was still pressure on women to work and thus to carry a double burden. The work kitchen as a spe-cialized workspace for the housewife was not simply something marginal and interior-design-related, but rather it related to the general social trend towards the functionalization of people (at the workspace and in the home) to the benefit of social systems. Furthermore, it became a paradigm for the interpenetration of the capitalist world of work and the private home environment. The efficiency euphoria evident in the period of the Weimar Republic is however no true indication of the reality of housework at that time, as the poor financial situation meant most working-class households could not afford to install the 'new kitchen'.

As a result of a different view of womanhood in the National Socialist period based on a new image of 'motherliness' and family, the model of the independent, working woman was replaced by that of the housewife and mother. Construction of large-scale apartment blocks in cities was initially halted in favor of smaller settlements and apartments on the city outskirts or in villages. These new private homes boasted a living and kitchen area at least 14 square meters in size. In general, it can be said that kitchen planning for small-scale settlements and apartment buildings both in the Third Reich and the Weimar Republic was carried out inconsistently. Both kitchen-diners and separate work kitchens were planned according to the region.

Kitchen research in Germany came to a halt in the 1930s due to the ideo-logical changes taking place. However, American and Swedish institutes picked up on the German kitchen research of the 1920s, and the 'Frankfurt Kitchen' in particular, and developed further. Thus the further advanced 'Frankfurt Kitchen', now known as the 'Swedish kitchen', became the ideal fitted kitchen during the post-war period.

The Cologne Furniture Fair of 1950 was the launch pad for the first German built-in kitchen for serial production. The kitchen dresser, until then a primary feature, was replaced by overhead cupboards and floor units that could be set up independently of one another. The fridge, oven and sink remained separate units up until 1956, when they were finally brought together under a seamless stainless steel surface. In the early 1950s worktops were made of linoleum, which towards 1955 was replaced by a plastic-coated surface known as Resopal, namely Formica. Whilst the design of kitchen furniture was initially limited in terms of shape and color, with angular shapes and grey, white and black tones dominating, from the mid-twentieth century onwards manufacturers began offering curved kitchen furniture and a wider spectrum of hues ranging from bright colors to pastels. It was with the new Formica worktops in particular that a harmonious overall impression could be achieved that was in keeping with the general look of the kitchen. Kitchen spaces, devised as areas for work first and foremost, were thereby given a personal touch. Serving hatches and breakfast bars were soon also integrated into the kitchen, facilitating social interaction inside and outside of the room itself. This represented the onset of the disappearance of the work kitchen, without functional processes losing out however. The 1950s thus saw kitchen design change in technical, aesthetic and social terms over the course of the decade. The models sold in 1957 no longer exhibit any similarities to the kitchens manufactured in the beginning of the decade (fig. 4: Kitchen at the beginning of the 1950s, WKS kitchen by the architect Sep Ruf, fig. 5: Kitchen in pastel tones, about 1955). Within the decade the development of technology and electricity, as well as colors and materials, brought forth a new style that has been integral ever since. Although a new style was developing, the ergonomic set-up of workstations as developed by Margarete Schütte-Lihotzky did not change.

Through into the 1960s, the most important work and design criteria were effective use, ergonomic improvements and demands in terms of hygiene. It was only towards the end of the 1960s that design criteria based on psychological considerations and a more attentive view to social interaction were incorporated into kitchen planning. Warm colors and faux-wood decoration were combined with breakfast bars and table areas and shelves were incorporated, breaking up the closed kitchen units and heralding the tentative beginnings of a kitchen oriented towards greater "liveability" and communication (fig. 6: Model *Majestic 500* by Nieburg Küchen, 1966, fig. 6a: Kitchen units with pine decoration, 1974). The 1970s saw the continuation and culmination of this trend. Simple, rustic wooden kitchens were offered alongside colourful kitchen units. It was primarily alcove shelving that emphasised the overall look of kitchens with what, in the 1970s, was considered a homely character (fig. 7: Wooden kitchen in a rustic design, 1974).

The sterile fitted kitchen, once a workspace for one person, lost its supremacy and was gradually replaced by a 'cosily designed' kitchen-diner. Alongside the improvement of the warmer colours and decoration and the curved, more scattered wall units, this coziness was achieved primarily through the incorporation of an eating area, which once again made communication and shared work in the kitchen possible.

In parallel to conventional kitchen planning, however, innovative and visionary planning was also underway. During the period between 1968 and 1973, this was known as 'kitchen ideas for the future', with research initiated by chemical companies and kitchen manufacturers independently of one another. These 'innovative kitchen designs' consisted of concepts not designed for mass application and use, yet nevertheless kitchen companies picked up on individual elements and put these into practice. Specific ideas from this time that can be considered innovative are kitchen trolleys and, most significantly, kitchen islands. Whilst the kitchen trolley *cucina minima*, designed in 1964 by the Italian designer *Joe Colombo*, will already be familiar to many, having earned its place in certain museums, the kitchen islands designed by British designer *John Heritage* and by the Swiss firm *Novelectric* around the same time have largely fallen into obscurity (fig. 8: Mobile kitchen trolley *Cucina minima*, Joe Colombo, 1964, fig. 9: English kitchen island *Masterplan*, John Heritage, 1963, fig. 10: *Novellipsenküche*, by Novelectric, 1965). This may be due to the fact that the kitchen island was precisely the one idea that was immediately picked up on by manufacturers and further developed as part of their kitchen ranges.

The 'visionary research work' for the 'kitchen of the future', specially commissioned by kitchen companies, made clear that kitchen manufacturers were also addressing the prevailing themes of the time, such as space travel and the momentous event that was the moon landing. The innovations in space travel, the small dimensions of a space ship and the limited, yet efficient living conditions associated with this were transferred to kitchen technology. Thus the main function of the kitchen was focused, for example, on heating up ready-made meals and not on actual cooking. The technological advancement that was microwave oven was introduced in 1967, after a ten-year period of development. By that point it had already become foreseeable that frozen foods and ready-made dishes would become ever more important due to women's employment outside the home (fig. 11: Model *Experiment 70* by the designer Luigi Colani, Poggenpohl, 1970, fig.11a: Model *Typ 1*, by Bulthaup. 1970). Whilst the ideas about future kitchens were oriented on the one hand towards technological developments, on the other hand there was also a focus on the design of the spatial relations and dimensions. In parallel to the dissolution of the status of homemaking and thus the work in the kitchen, at the beginning of the 1970s designers simply got rid of the kitchen as a space. Instead, the kitchen became a mobile module, which could be opened up when in use, and slotted away and stored in a corner when not needed (fig. 12: Model by Haas + Sohn KG, 1972). During this time kitchen design focused more strongly on time-saving than on the culinary arts.

Due to the new lifestyles emerging in the 1980s, which were characterized by a changed image of the family, alternative living and partnership arrangements among unmarried couples and single-person households, the types of use of living and kitchen areas and ultimately the pleasure in eating also changed.[10] From now on, more value was placed on fresh and seasonal produce. There was also a greater desire to prepare European and non-European dishes, as well as to cook together in the family or with friends. In order to meet this demand, kitchen planners began shifting the kitchen back towards the heart of the home. This also now included a particular focus on conceiving kitchens as decorative objects of prestige rather than pieces of 'equipment' in the home (fig. 13: Model *Mal-Zeit*, Coop Himmelb[l]au, 1987–1989, fig. 14: Model *Eroica*, Alberto Rizzi, Rossano Didaglio, 1990). With the dissolution of the traditional image of the family in the late 1980s, streamlined kitchen planning faded further into the background. Kitchen manufacturers now took new lifestyles that placed

---

10 | Flaig/Meyer/Ueltzhöffer: 1993, p. 75.

different demands on the kitchen into account. The kitchen as a spatial unit all but disappeared. Where possible, it was integrated into the living space: an island worktop made it possible for people to prepare meals together, and many kitchen cupboards and drawers were replaced by stands with shelves and panel systems made of stainless steel. Furthermore, the combination of electrical appliances made of stainless steel with matching kitchen units in metallic hues gave kitchens a professional look (fig. 15: Kitchen model from 1989). The kitchen and the work and smells within it were now a subject for presentation and not something to be hidden as had been the case from the 1920s right up to the 1960s.

While in the 1920s the focus had been on freeing women from unnecessary and monotonous work, combined with the recognition and acknowledgement of their work as a profession through providing women with their own workspace within the home, ultimately what remained of the idea of modern, efficient housekeeping was merely the functional and clean work processes. The concept of the kitchen as an anonymous workspace for an individual has not prevailed. In fact the opposite has been the case: the kitchen has once again become the heart of the home, it has become the social hub and central point in which cooking can either be equally important or, due to work commitments, subordinate to the social togetherness and the shared mealtimes and work that go on there. The kitchen has once more become a meeting point for family and friends. Just as in ancient times people would sit around the fire as the source of food preparation, today all people, be they families, married couples or simply housemates, likewise come together around this source. And what is more: the kitchen is not merely a hub for the fostering of social togetherness, rather the shared activity and experiences in the kitchen facilitate and shape this social communion.

The Kitchen of the Future

Somewhere Between Sci-Fi and Social Design

Hanni Rützler and Wolfgang Reiter

> "If all art forms were to disappear, the
> noble art of cooking would remain."
> (DANIEL SPOERRI)

It is well known that in the world of Star Trek the "kitchen" consists of a single device, the replicator, which in the 24th century, when addressed, dished up any meal requested within seconds and spares the crew of the Enterprise cooking and washing up. Unlike the practical, but from a culinary point of view somewhat unsatisfying inventions of the early 21st century – for example the liquid food *Soylent* and the food powder *Bertrand* – which are intended to replace traditional meals completely,[1] the replicator enables any object, the atomic structure of which has previously been recorded or programmed, and as such food and meals, to be replicated, in other words reproduced. In the Star Trek world there is therefore no need to drink nutritive solutions, swallow pills, or stir powder to make a mash in order to subsist. You still can eat.

The replicator would also, for example, be able to recreate a retro-menu with several courses à la Eckhard Witzigmann, the "chef of the 20th century"[2], in the space of just a few seconds. To some extent at least, if we are to believe the critics of replicator technology living on the Enterprise, who complain that synthetizing meals at molecular rather than quantum level is the reason why replicated meals taste worse than "real" food.

People living in the 21st century, who are eating ever more convenience meals that are industrially produced according to adapted recipes

---

1 | These and similar "foodstuffs" promise to completely meet our nutritional requirements, i. e., they contain all the nutrients the human body – according to present-day medical science – needs to function properly. With a diet of means such as these, the social component of eating plays just as little a role as culinary aspects.

2 | Alongside Witzigmann, only three other chefs have to date been awarded the title "Chef of the Century" by the renowned restaurant guide *Gault Millau*: Paul Bocuse, Frédy Girardet and Joël Robuchon.

for classic dishes and which are just heated up in the microwave at home or in the office, know full well that replicating comes nowhere close to the original. Providing you have some knowledge of cooking and are not totally dispassionate about it, veal goulash prepared from scratch will always taste better than one that has been industrially replicated. Nonetheless, almost all answers to the question of how we will feed ourselves in the future primarily suggest technological solutions which will replace cooking or at least make it radically easier. The vision of tomorrow's kitchen is of a high-tech-laboratory, crammed full with talking refrigerators, self-cooking stoves and sous vide appliances controlled by smartphone, which just as much take off our hands the work cooking always entails as the sensual experiences handling food can involve.

THE KITCHEN PARADOX OR HOW CONVENIENCE FOOD MAKES THE NEW DESIRE TO COOK POSSIBLE AT ALL

At the same time trend researchers and dietary sociologists are saying that cooking is reinventing itself, that young people in particular are standing over pots and pans again, spending hours strolling round and buying from weekly markets and helping out in communal gardens, so as to be able to prepare their meals using genuinely fresh produce.

The apparent paradox of the increasing need among lots of people for the sensual experience of cooking and eating, although ever more ready and semi-prepared meals are being sold disappears quickly if we appreciate that it is the triumphant march of convenience food, the microwave, the dishwasher and fast system catering itself that is creating the conditions for this new desire to cook, bake, and preserve. Liberated from the tiresome task of daily cooking to feed the family, which women in particular saw themselves subjected to until well into the 20th century, it was not until the beginning of the 21st century – in a society geared to individualization and self-realization – that a passion for cooking was able to develop again. For cooking that did not serve to feed mouths every day, but that is a counter to de-sensualized computer work, is a social event, as a tool for performance accomplishments and social distinction.

With this change of cooking's function, our kitchens are changing too. Whereas until into the 1990s the lounge was a showpiece that spoke for us, nowadays we often express our identity through the kitchen. It is the place that says who we are or want to be. As such, design-wise it has long since not been enough for it just to be a functional space that serves the preparation of meals under as effective conditions as possible. Nowadays it should also be fit to express our personality: Our status as connaisseurs or our conscience with regard to resources and the environment, our passion for cooking or health awareness, our down-to-earth attitude or extravagance in culinary matters.

The kitchen is also becoming a multi-tasking space, where people work and make phone calls, do homework and discuss projects; even in homes with a conventional footprint, in which there is often insufficient space for the kitchen in its new role. Because even if with changing lifestyles the way homes are divided up into classic, one-dimensional functions (cooking here, eating there, working here, learning there, watching TV here, resting there, bathing here, sleeping there) has become anachronistic, the size of kitchens is not automatically increasing. This applies not just to old buildings. With regard to new housing as well, the growing cost of homes and increasing awareness of the environment have reversed the trend: Whereas over the past decades homes became bigger and bigger, the number of square meters per person is now falling and will in future continue to do so, first and foremost at the cost of spaces intended to serve a single function. For this reason the kitchen will once again become multi-purpose, communal space: lounge, workspace, and playroom, for which it also needs totally different "kitchen furniture" that is fit not just for cooking. Innovative engineering makes it possible to integrate the hot plate in a desk or transform a desk into a stove[3] (fig. 1–3). Furthermore, at the flick of the wrist furniture with greater flexibility can make space for other activities, and smart new kitchen appliances not only save space, but also make cooking easier and more productive, such that on the side you can work on your laptop, help your kids with their homework, or play.

Fig. 1

Fig. 3

Fig. 2

---

3 | Functional cooking tables, which at the same time can be used as a hob, dining table or desk, and as such as a communication and multimedia information zone, no longer feature only in theoretical designs (http://www.moritzputzier.com/the-cooking-table, accessed on Nov. 21, 2016), but are also included in the ranges of well-known manufacturers of kitchens and kitchen appliances such as Miele and Bulthaup (http://www.mega-kuechen.ch/bulthaup/news-bulthaup, accessed on Jan. 26, 2016).

As a Social Event Cooking Inspires Design Ideas, Which as Social Design Go far Beyond Mere Object Design

Tomorrow's kitchen will not only integrate nature and engineering symbol-ically. It will become a place where food is not only stored as well as possible, prepared, and eaten, but also cultivated and the organic waste recycled for further use as compost or biogas. Several good reasons speak in favor of this: Ecological and health-related ones, just as much as less (at least perceived) dependency on the food industry, but primarily the pleasure of gardening and experiencing nature (fig. 4). And because vegetarian cuisine in particular produces a lot of organic waste, engineers and designers are searching for efficient, resource-saving solutions for the "waste problem": Though ideas such as the bio-converter kitchen island for producing the gas for cooking from waste produced in the kitchen are still future dreams, they are an indication of the way things are going.

Fig. 4

In future, changed eating habits and diets will influence how kitchens are designed and fitted out. Whereas microwaves and deep fat fryers fit the bill superbly for convenience food, when it comes to vegetarian and vegan cuisine there are totally different requirements in terms of fittings, work areas, and appliances: in most cases, more ingredients have to be cleaned, washed, and chopped up, more space is needed for sprouting glasses and more and better storage containers for spices. And, of course, there ought to be room for a grain mill and a climatic cabinet, in which herbs and lettuces can be grown regardless of the season.[4]

---

4 | In collaboration with a professional chef, Austrian designers have designed a model kitchen for vegetarian cooking (www.vooking.at, accessed on Jan. 26, 2016). Numerous start-ups, as well as established companies are working on indoor gardening concepts, which will make it possible to grow herbs, shoots, and vegetables in small kitchens as well (see for example https://grovelabs.io/, accessed on Nov. 21, 2016).

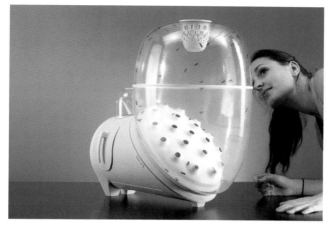

Fig. 5

Fig. 6

Fig. 7

Whether another piece of equipment that is currently getting a lot of hype – the 3D food printer – will be the rage in the kitchen of the future will depend on whether it is able to trigger innovations with regard to eating and diets. The first, soon to be ready for market products – e.g., the 'Bocusini' by the German company Print2Taste GmbH, which is explicitly being advertised as a "plug&play food printer" are targeting playful uses: Decorating Grandad's birthday cake with sugar lettering in his 8-year old granddaughter's handwriting, serving mashed potato shaped like an octopus with tentacles and bulging eyes, or draping intricate marzipan patterns over an ice cream dessert.

Of greater interest in this respect is the approach adopted by the British designer and researcher Susana Soares, who in the course of her 'Insects Au Gratin' project[5] "feeds" the 3D printer with basic products that are not exactly commonplace in our diet, namely insects, which are turned into flour and mixed with cream cheese before coming out of the printer as high-protein decorative "biscuits". Not least of all the project is a reminder that it is often only new technologies that make valuable basic products out of available resources. Just as the invention of the combustion engine once created a meaningful and profitable use for oil, for which apart from as fuel for petroleum lamps there had previously been none, the 3D printer could make it possible to use a readily available source of protein in the the human diet; even for those of us who do not exactly relish the idea of biting into a locust or eating mealworms. The first devices suitable for breeding insects and mealworms at home and thus turning the kitchen into a protein production plant that will cover our own needs are now ready for series production, and will be available during the course of 2017.[6]

Apart from the technological advances, the kitchen of the future opens up a totally different social perspective that goes beyond families and households: Pre-arranged communal cooking in large neighborhood kitchens, in corporate communal kitchens, in which cooking becomes a regular part of team building activities, or in commercial communal kitchens, of which until late 2015 Jamie Oliver ran the successful prototype in the form of his 'Recipease' in London's trendy Notting Hill district. These kitchens are not primarily about food intake, but about the experience of cooking and eating together. In them it is not meals that are replicated, but rather a human practice that goes back thousands of years.

5 | See www.susanasoares.com/index.php?id=82, accessed on Nov. 21, 2016.

6 | The products "Farm432" and "The Hive" (fig. 5–7) were developed by the Austrian design studio "Livin" and are currently being produced in Hong Kong (see http://www.livinstudio.com, accessed on Nov. 21, 2016).

La Brigade de Cuisine

Carolyn Bahar for Lucky Peach

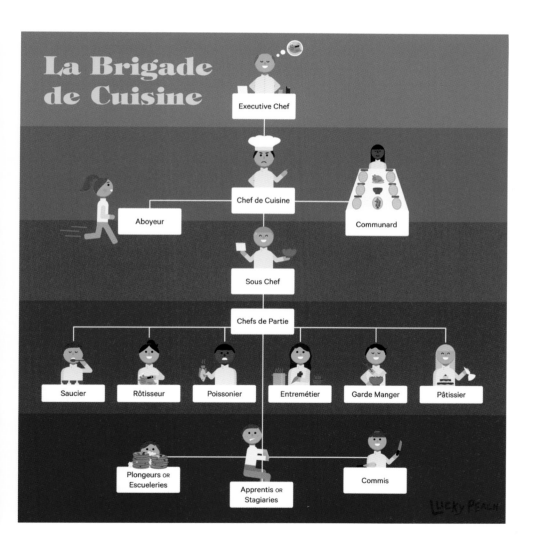

Kitchen Culture

Iliana Regan

My kitchen is my home. The people I work with, over time, become my family. I think about the future of my staff, restaurant, and industry.

I am 36 years old. I have been working for myself for the past eight years seemingly without any break. I have run my own kitchen for six years and my own restaurant for close to four.

I am about to open two new restaurants. It is important for me to have an environment that I want to be in. This is where I spend all of my time and when I am not within the walls of my restaurants, I am thinking about what has happened and what is going to happen.

Since the opening of Elizabeth I have exponentially grown and evolved. In the beginning, having come from or working closely to kitchens that were a bit harsh, that is how I was. I could be mean-spirited, yell, become frustrated quickly. When it was my ass, name, livelihood on the line, yes, I was going to yell. But I found I was yelling because I did not know how to communicate effectively. Each day was a rat race to get things done, to even find our bearings. I have forgiven myself for this because for my first restaurant, my little small business where I run all departments, it was a lot. Most people might have been pulling out their hair too. However I found that my lack of knowing how to communicate effectively was a direct result of my inability to organized myself. I could not stop to explain what I wanted or needed from my chefs because I was too busy trying to keep my own mind in order. I still have these days but today I have more insight on to be able to better address the situation rather than blow it up. I cannot speak for other chefs while I am certain each is exhausted. I do not know why we think this being harsh, crude, mean-spirited or yelling is effective. I have had a few employees where it worked but it was not sustainable. After a few days they were back to their same old selves and no amount of my push was going to get them to do things the way I needed them done. I have learned that I have to hire kids who want to learn, have their own sets of ambitions and driving forces. When I hire chefs I tell them I am not going to yell, while it is possible and I do, it is not the norm. I tell them I am not going to breathe down their neck. I tell them I will give them the tools to make food for Elizabeth and make it well. That we will work, learn, and grow together as a team. That I will present the standards I expect but I am not going to chase after them to hold them. If they do not I will know and they will not have a place in my home. It is very simple. The chefs who excel in my walls are chefs who are ambitious, can see the opportunities I am placing before them. They can see that Elizabeth is small enough that if they want to learn every possible thing they can.

Kitchens are always going to be full of seekers. It is an interesting breed of humans that are drawn to this industry, particularly the back of the house. We are wild, queer, nonconformist. The long hours keep us off the streets and out of trouble. It has been my mission to give my crew tools for the future no matter where they end up or what they do. They will learn how to care about what they are doing, not for me but for them. They will pay attention to the smallest of details. Be present. Act like adults. Be obedient. They will learn how to read attitudes and learn how to nurture the good ones. They will become teachers.

I do not know if this has any difference on whether it is a male's or a female's perspective. All I can say is: Elizabeth is my home and at times, these are my kids.

Production

Plates

Kobe Desramaults

Three Theses for Increased Enjoyment

Holger Stromberg

First: We Are What We Eat – Listen to Your Body

As a chef I have for years now been passionately addressing the topics of eating, savoring, and health. Nowadays eating is a matter of course in that we eat every day – but what we lack is knowledge about it. In times of excess food in the Global North, eating has, to a certain extent, become a pursuit that involves chewing and swallowing something or other, without exactly knowing what you are actually eating. And as part of an activity that is crucial to life. Please do not get me wrong: I do not think you need to busy yourself with eating around the clock – unless you do so professionally – but even then, believe me, you occasionally do something different as well. But if you have to eat, and it is so important for your body, a good mood, and first and foremost your health, then you really should also pay attention to what you are putting down your throat. You can see where I am going here. I want you to think about what you eat. You make sure, perhaps, that you drive a safe car, have a fantastic plasma TV in the lounge, or shoes by whoever in your wardrobe. You see to it that only the very best will do.

And if need be, you do not mind splashing out either. So when it comes to things that are not that important, it is OK. But it would be great, and this is a big concern of mine, if we were all to behave the same way with our diet. The world would be a whole lot healthier and nicer, believe you me.

Nowadays I very much appreciate that because, like so many of my fellow chefs, at the tender age of 30 I was confronted with the unpleasant consequences of a burnout. I was looking in the mirror one day and no longer recognized myself. OK, I had worked hard (too hard), and achieved a lot. But in one fell swoop I came to realize that if you are not healthy, all that means nothing. As a child I was overweight for a long time – thanks to the delicious Coke I drank by the liter, yes it was a trend even back then. Today I no longer am, but my joints can still remember when I was. Perhaps every one of us needs to suffer somehow in order to discover a personal philosophy with regard to eating and nutrition. That is why the subject of nutrition, product quality, and health is so close to my heart, and so for myself, and not just because I see to the culinary well-being of top-flight sportsmen, I underwent a development process; after which I now see myself as a nutrition coach.

If people were to spend just two minutes a day thinking hard about nutrition they would learn the key nutrition A–Z in the shortest of time. They would begin to realize why they cannot get out of bed in the morning if they eat pasta in the evening, or why after a fatty lunch they feel sluggish in the afternoon. Armed with this knowledge they begin the most exciting stage of their life. If you know that healthy food consists of protein, fats, carbohydrates, vitamins, and minerals, you will never again pick up any of those brightly-colored packages that promise youthfulness and fitness, but actually contain only rubbish. The packaging is often more expensive than the content, which I find incredibly perverse. And it gets even worse: people still resort to using products such as these, because knowledge about a healthy diet is no longer passed on in families. Instead of being large families we have become single or two-person households. In past times your grandmother would cook with you, and told you what to look out for. Nowadays people buy ready-meals with flavor enhancers and preservatives. All this began with the industrialization of the food sector, when edible goods began being produced in factories and laboratories. For a long time, manufactured foods were the height of chic. Glutamate was even used in top kitchens; my father, who is an excellent chef and in the 1970s used to cook for pleasure-seeking passengers on luxury cruise liners, worked, for example, with flavor enhancers just because everyone else did, and it was the thing to do. Nowadays armies of scientists spend their time investigating the effects that additives such as these have. The complaints they can cause range from what is known as Chinese restaurant syndrome to allergies and suspicious intolerances, which make carefree eating difficult. Only: Thanks to a resourceful food industry, artificial products nowadays (unfortunately) have their firm place on our plates. There is industrially made bread, cheese alternative, substitute ham, artificial yoghurt blends, brightly-colored carbonated drinks.

Whenever I go to the supermarket I take a magnifying glass with me and read the small print. If I am not familiar with something, I do not buy the product. You do not have to eat fast food, nor in an airplane do you have to eat the bar of chocolate just because the friendly member of the cabin crew forces it into your hands. Just think about what it will do to you.

We need to become choosy again. For this reason we have to start off with children, and begin where habits are formed and knowledge discovered. We need nutrition teaching across the board, but we should not teach the classic nutrition pyramid. That is not enough, because each and every person is an individual, and genetically totally different. Which is why our diet has to be individual as well. What is important is to explain to our children is what is good for what, and what has which effects. The pyramid says, eat lots of fruit and vegetables, but some people cannot eat fructose. I am one of them. Nor can I eat asparagus, as I am genetically prone to gout. If I ever eat a hearty portion of asparagus and drink one or two beers with it, my foot really hurts and my fingers become stiff. Your body tells you what it wants. We just have to learn to listen to it. I am convinced that we all have culinary intelligence. It is in our instinct, some things you forget with time, especially if you are attuned to one-sided taste experiences. But you can learn to taste things (again). I experience this in my work with schoolchildren. They have a basic interest – as if they instinctively know the important role diet plays in life, even if at home they never or only rarely get served fresh produce. On children's day I set up what are known as eating stations so that they can taste the quality and try different things. Just how great the uncertainty they have learned is, sounds like this: "I cannot eat that, I have a gluten intolerance, a lactose intolerance, etc." Now it is by no means for me to doubt a medical diagnosis, but I do think that this increase in health disorders that have something to do with eating could well have something to do with a lack of intuition. Lots of children no longer learn to listen to their bodies. What is more, they grow up on products full of additives, which for their part can be detrimental to healthy bodily functions. But if we teach children that fresh, tasty products are best, and show them what they can do with them, then we are surely on a better, healthier track. Just ask yourself, what you are really worth to yourself, beginning your appreciation process with the most important daily activity (alongside breathing): eating. Eat what is really tasty, and not what pretends to be.

SECOND: COOKING IS A MATTER OF SENSORY APPEAL

Every one of us has a different sense of taste. Some people's is very keen, some have a sensitive nose and are able to detect the slightest differences in aroma, while others again who can, well, just about distinguish basic flavors. You can develop your sense of taste simply by getting to work at the chopping board and the stove yourself and then going along with what you do next. Smell, season, taste. A ready meal never smells the same as when I prepare exactly that dish using fresh produce. Favorite dishes are also stored deep down in our memory. Smells accompany us our entire life, we associate feelings with them, good and bad. For this reason, our sense of taste is so fundamental. Just think of the smell of freshly baked bread or freshly grilled fish on your last vacation, of a really good piece of cheese.

I once had a guest who, after the meal, thanked me enthusiastically and said: "You just cooked me the dish of my life." And his greatest wish was to be able to enjoy it (zander fillet on pistou risotto and black pudding) again and again. It does not work that way though, as every freshly prepared meal has its own magic, its own flavor. And that is the opposite of the monotony you get with pizzas, pastas, and other industrial produce, which always taste the same, and which are sold as food.

But cooking is not just about ethereal senses such as smell and taste. When cooking you can, indeed must taste, and touch things. Your sense of touch is called for. You can feel the outside, consistency, the shape and the texture of a product. Some products are a joy just to touch. Do the self-test. What does an eggplant feel like, the outside of a peach, a bushel of basil, the yeast dough you are kneading? Does it remind you of anything? Does it make you happy? And it smells so good: It is all so aromatic, fresh garlic, chopped herbs, sun-dried tomatoes, fresh bread, melted butter, strawberry jam. Enjoy all the different aromas when preparing and cooking food. Experience how they change as you cut and cook them. That often happens unconsciously, intuitively, and anyone with a little experience of cooking can tell from the aroma whether a dish is perfectly seasoned. Ah, delicious! Keep on having a taste as you go along. Taste the difference between raw and cooked, roast and boiled, sour, salty, bitter and spicy. There are incredible differences. Feel taste, aromas and textures in your mouth. A new world opens up.

Consciously or unconsciously, however, our experiences, certain familiar patterns, habits und paragons play an important role in how we eat. Basically, the way our taste develops is determined by culture, in other words: What individual taste experiences do I have in the course of my life, what gives me the greatest pleasure? It all begins very early on: From developmental psychology we know that babies and small children, provided they are healthy and of normal weight, have a good sense of being hungry or replete. They know by nature when, and most of all what, they would like to eat. In scientific jargon this is known as somatic intelligence. Children rely entirely on their body sensations. They look forward to their food and abandon themselves fully to eating. They do not do so by the by, but wholeheartedly, employing all their senses. Just watch any tiny toddler eating an ice cream in summer, oblivious to everything. If you let children follow their own personal eating rhythm and give them fresh, high-quality products, they sometimes eat more, sometimes less, develop preferences and taste, stay healthy and cheerful and develop a strong immune system. With time they adopt new habits; the children grow, and go to school, where they might possibly have lunch. At home there are certain rules and eating rituals (or not, as the case may be). In any case, this way, over the years, they become familiar with a form of eating behavior that as adults it is often not that easy for them to change. Changing one's own eating behavior, for example if you want to lose a few pounds or just feel fitter and more efficient, means replacing your previous habits with new forms of behavior. You have to practice this, which takes time and patience, and generally speaking it only works if nothing is forbidden and you enjoy it. We now know that a balanced, varied diet that is adapted to your needs, combined with physical activity, is the key to a long and healthy life. That is the one thing. The other is that what we eat, and which foodstuffs, also impacts our physical and mental health, our efficiency, our feelings and thoughts, our self-esteem, relationships and our environment. What is extremely important is that the topic of eating should never be a compulsion, but rather should enrich our everyday life in a positive, creative way.

On the way to what today is something very close to my heart, indeed a vocation, I got a lot of inspiration from my parents' cuisine. I come from a long-established family of restaurateurs in the Ruhr region, where cooking still had something archaic about it, and was defined by rural everyday life. I can remember butchering day at home, a major event in the year. The butcher would come round and slaughter the pig that had been slowly fattened over the course of the year. He certainly knew his trade, never put a foot wrong, working in a manner that was calm and collected. The whole family was there to watch this impressive event, after all it meant nothing less than that an animal was losing its life in order to provide us with delicacies even during the winter months. My Grandmother stirred the blood in a large pot, and we all helped make the sausages. We then hung the dry sausages beneath the roof. On days like this we processed everything from the animal that for a whole year had lived a normal pig's life and had been able to grow at its own speed. Back then we learned instinctively that meat is a delicacy, and on this particular day each and every one of us showed the animal their respect. We, i.e., my Grandmother, my aunties, who also helped, all worked with the greatest of concentration, gladly, and with gratitude for the precious thing we were given there. A love of food. That was one of my most memorable experiences. Then there was my father of course, an outstanding cook. He kept on hitting the mark with his culinary creations and had a gift for preparing even small dishes in such a way that they just looked good and at the same time tasted incredibly good. He was a fanatic in terms of taste quality, had an outstanding sense of smell, cooked regional and crossover dishes, as he had learned as an apprentice and working on the cruise liners. In our region as well he would cook rather "exotic" dishes such as lamb or venison, which he himself did not eat at all. But with his senses alone he was able to conjure up a true feast with them. I have always loved the gastronomy "milieu" and the search for perfect flavors, new flavors. In earlier days I occasionally used to get hay fever – anyone who suffers from the allergy knows how tedious it is, especially for a chef, who then cannot smell anything. I learned to use my eyes, to recognize consistency, recognize the right time for the right spice. In this respect cooking is a holistic experience.

THIRD: COOKING AND EATING ARE SOCIAL ACTIVITIES

Try striking up conversation with others about eating. You will discover that there is hardly any other similarly stimulating topic of conversation about which you can exchange personal experiences. There is something deeply vital but at the same relaxed about eating and savoring food (unless, that is, you cook for a living, things can get a bit hectic then), and it one of the nicest things there is. But low key, in the evening after work, with good music and a glass of wine in the kitchen or for your beloved, cooking puts you in the limelight or brings you down to earth, and at the same time clears your head. All provided that this cooking does not end up in hyper-ambition, as it does with many an aspiring cook, then things can indeed become very stressed. Basically, our attitude to cooking has changed quite a lot over the past few years.

Cooking well, and with fresh produce, is always possible, and without you feeling that you are spending all your time in the kitchen. Consider conjuring up something there for yourself and your loved ones as your personal chill-out time. And do not be scared of getting all those around you involved. If you do the cooking, you definitely do not need to load the dishwasher or lay the table ... And cooking is a cultural virtue. In this respect the French are way ahead of us, cooking and savoring good food being part and parcel of everyday culture for them, something they live out even in the smallest and simplest of kitchens. But I notice that there is a lot happening here in Germany as well. Awareness of natural foodstuffs and a cooking as a creative everyday craft is on the up. As a lifestyle attribute, cooking has been trendy for years now. Basically though, cooking is one of the most archaic human activities and arts there is, something mankind has been doing for millions of years. In the beginning women and children went foraging, while men hunted game and fish; they all then prepared what they had found and caught and together, sitting by the fire, consumed it. Over the course of time cooking became a science based purely on experience. If you investigate the foodstuffs you are using more closely, you will also notice that in a culinary respect you can learn something new every day and with every dish. Preparing meals with carefully chosen fresh produce nurtures responsibility for yourself and other people. At the same time, you become more discerning with regard to flavor and quality, which increases your self-confidence and self-esteem.

Better than a therapist: Cooking is a very social matter. Cooking for other people means doing something for other people. Cooking defines encounters and opinions we have of one another. It has to do with esteem, affection, love. You are worth, or at least ought to be, feeding yourself and the people you love high-quality products. It is good for your well-being, your health and efficiency, and for a good mood, because eating not only sustains your body, but also your soul. The better the ingredients you use are – and I do not mean caviar and Kobe beef (even if it is delicious) – the more esteem and care you are showing yourself. It need not cost a fortune, but first and foremost requires attentiveness when shopping, and good planning. You will then simply begin to enjoy cooking as you get started in the kitchen. With regard to planning: Always make a menu for two to three days. Get inspiration from good cookbooks (these are available for beginners as well) and write a shopping list.

I want people to abandon their fear of haute cuisine. For a long time, knowing how to cook was treated as something secret. But if we want to improve a food culture we have to share this knowledge. I want young people as well to be interested in my food. Our school system offers nothing that amounts to genuine nutritional science in the form of sensual, intuitive experience. On top of which, a booming food industry with its single flavor does not make it easy to impart this basic knowledge, which is part and parcel of a good life. Children in particular are the victims of this system, and they are also aggressively wooed with products that no longer have anything to with food in the literal sense. Plus nowadays, in times of mobility and flexibility, a large family where people cook and eat together, hardly exists any longer. And in small families as well, in which both adults work, the ritual of eating meals together does not take place.

My parents both worked as well, but our great aunts always prepared breakfast for us children, before we said grace and talked about what was on the agenda for the day, and what we were eating. I know that we cannot bring back these "olden days", but we can nurture rituals such as eating meals together. They bring people together, slow things down, get rid of stress. Here too I am seeing a trend reversal and think that the discounters will soon have had their heyday. On the one hand that has something to do with the popularity of cooking, with TV cookery shows, as well as with our knowing more about good health. The small supermarkets with a more individual, and in the case of fresh produce vegetables, fruit, and cheese a regional range of products, are catching up. You can support this trend by starting to shop in smaller stores and at farmers' markets. That will benefit not only the suppliers, who will be able to continue producing high-quality goods, but you too. In this respect I am, however, decidedly of the opinion that just like the work of the farmers, without who there would be no genuine food or natural products, that performed by smaller food manufacturers, who know exactly what they are producing, and do so with love and craftsmanship, must also be worth something again. To a certain extent that must, and can be reflected in the price, because foodstuffs are valuable. After all, we eat them. And in this context, if need be I get personal advice and valuable tips when shopping, or find out where the products I am putting in my shopping cart come from. You should be worth feeding yourself and the people you love high-quality products. It is good for your well-being, your health and efficiency, and for a good mood.

Previously, the definition of food was "a means to survival"; nowadays it should rather be defined as and indeed regarded as "a means of prolonging life". For this reason I call for practical nutritional science to be a permanent feature of school curricula, because we are living in an era in which knowledge of foodstuffs and a healthy diet are no longer sufficiently passed on in families. Furthermore, considerably more findings about healthy eating are available to the current generation. We should exploit that.

As you can see, eating and drinking are far more than the mere ingestion of nutrients in order for the body to function more or less properly and our mood not to hit rock bottom. Eating and drinking has a lot to do with sensors, emotions, and perception in general. With flavors, aromas, and with whether we like what is on the plate in front of us. If you allow it to be, cooking is always an experience, it stimulates all the senses and breaks up your daily routine in the pleasantest of ways. Learn to listen to your stomach again, and handle products instinctively. You do not need to be an expert to know about food. Cooking is an art you master through experience.

The Mind's Eye and Palate

Daniel de La Falaise

Fig. 1   Fig. 2   Fig. 3

At the turn of the last century, Auguste Escoffier divided kitchen tasks into a brigade system and ever since cookery has been taught in a way that prioritizes replication. This model has swayed the balance and dominated the changing face of kitchen and shopping habits, with people delegating the refinement of taste to a projected greater "other". The recipe must be repeated! This constraint has merit when you are called upon to serve a banquet to a precise and exacting rhyme. A chef expects his brigade to snap into action at his command, and perform a perfected trick. The professional kitchen is a vertical hierarchy; maintaining standards is imperative to survival. Obedience holds the group in formation. This is less essential at home. A school of replication – however faintly imposed – is diminishing for it curbs instinct by devaluing individuality and creativity.

I did not go to culinary school. Rather, I come from a long line of cooks and gardeners, and so was initiated at an early age, spending time with my family in both kitchen and garden, planting, harvesting, tasting and cooking. When I ascended to the world of the professional kitchen, I became apprentice to a great chef and mentor whose refined ways of doing I was able to glean, and over time, adapt to my own rhythm. This afforded me the tools to communicate a vision I had sensed but not had the means to execute in childhood. By the time I had a kitchen under my own jurisdiction, my approach to cooking had metamorphosed into a rolling form of structured improvisation. The menu was ever evolving, to reflect the transiting seasons. Primed with an awareness of who is to be fed and an understanding of the ingredients at hand, the cook's objective is simply to resolve how to optimize the vitality and nutritional integrity of raw materials. Peremptory recipes in this context are a hindrance. They clutter and intellectualize what is essentially a sensorial journey.

Taste is experienced with the taste buds upon the tongue, whereas flavor, an altogether more ephemeral and volatile affair, is experienced by the olfactory glands and the nose. The aspiring cook should encourage taste to lie subtle and clean, and flavor to flower and gently stimulate the palate. For both cook and gourmand, sensory references to perfectly ripe produce act as guide and trigger to the imagination. These references serve to crystallize cookery into a sensory vision that operates in two realms simultaneously: the outer reality of the produce available, and the inner potential of your imagination to compose menus in harmony to your mind's eye and palate. The more connected you become to the inner realm, the more capable you become as a cook. You dare to improvise. The challenge is to maintain a minimum level of curiosity and to have fun whilst you are doing it.

A child's palate is a blank canvas and instinctively open to opportunity, eager to explore and curiously graze, all whilst curating a sensory flavor bank that, once acquired, serves as a companion for life. The quality of a sensorial reference is determined by a lottery of sorts – by birth, hemisphere, altitude, and the capacity of parents to cultivate their children's senses. Once savored, natural produce at the height of its season is ingrained as a sense memory upon the palate. Ripe fruit seduces the eye, then the nose, and tastes just as it smells. The equivalent seduction tactics court our senses across the comestible realms. Those who benefit from the archetypal assets of a given ingredient innately skip a step ahead. They are equipped to improvise and strategically adjust their cookery according to the quality of the ingredients before them. Those lacking precise sensory references must perpetually reinvent the wheel.

A cook needs to be both disciplined and free. There is no shortcut to mastering basic skills. Haste is not the answer; rather time. Cooks who dash about chasing the moment rather than owning it are prone to upsetting the rhythm of things. Better by far to learn to execute a task gently with care. In time it will become a reflex, a device at your disposal. Cooking should be like a dance. If you can be disciplined enough to cook to the potential of your skills, tools, and raw materials, there is very little that cannot be done. The broader your skill set, the freer and more confident you are to give sway to your imagination. In turn your cooking comes to be shaped and formed by your senses. The ideal is to visualize and savor the potential of produce in your mind's eye, then to consolidate sensory marvel and nutritional sustenance. Cooking is shaped by vogues of humor, hunger, and inspiration. The ingredients and the method chosen with which to cook them are ever liable to change. A cook's every gesture has its own intrinsic sensory justification. Given the same ingredients, any two people will execute an individual sequence of controlled actions and deliver quite distinct results.

When curiosity, preparation, and opportunity converge in the kitchen, the way forward is to improvise. To live by your senses, in the moment, all whilst focused upon converging food to table with the very minimum of transformation. The golden law of improvisation is to say "yes" and then "adjust". This becomes possible when awareness fuses with understanding to reveal a breadth of options that lead to your goal. In short to improvise is to maintain both a bird's eye view and a sharp and clear super objective, juggling as you go the duality of internal and external stimuli that define your approach.

Let the menu come to you; survey season and occasion for guidance. First consider who is to be fed: the young, the elderly, the hardworking, the idle, strangers, kin? The who, why, when, and where of it reveal pointers as to *what* to cook. Each atmosphere has its own quality of hunger and informs the choice of produce. At market, with your audience in mind, react to the produce before you. The seed of an idea will emerge, and slowly but surely a menu befitting the occasion suggests itself. When composing menus, I draw upon sensory references – garnered from a lifetime of grazing – that act as triggers to colors, flavors, textures, and tastes that stand timelessly fixed upon my palate. These sensorial references in turn unmask a host of natural synergies – simple associations of flavors that when eaten together transcend their individual qualities. Think: melon and cardamom, tomatoes and lovage, eggs and ginger, asparagus and tarragon, rabbit and sage, grappa and coffee, wild strawberries and flowering mint. It is the vitality an ingredient projects that guides and informs the cook how to best use it. When you apply method to ingredient, you are free. You discover the ingredient before you and you intuitively decide how best to proceed, even if that means to leave well alone and celebrate the ingredient raw, just as it is. The kitchen is a theater for instinct.

Ambitious restaurant cooks aspire to legitimacy. They are concerned with "a standard of gastronomy", often at the expense of pleasure. This quest for what has been by consensus deemed "perfection" is a reflex that requires individual skill, but it is hardly the way to cook at home. A grazing stroll through an orchard or an herb garden offers vitality and stimulation to rival a dozen courses of high gastronomy. Ideally, a meal should commence with the last breath of an ingredient soon to be over, consist in majority of ingredients at the height of their season, and conclude with early pickings of the next glut to come. In this way, the food shared at table becomes a celebration of a place and a moment in time.

The spike in public interest that food and cookery are enjoying has been deftly grasped upon by the industry; food preparation is the topic, though its provenance rarely the focus. Dietary choices have increasingly become an outward manifestation of social aspiration. Eating organic is a badge worn, yet often inquiry is arrested in development. Organic yes, and produced where, by whom, and all importantly – how? Too few of the players teach us about soil and water and sustainable models of production. Between the World Wars, when soil degradation was taken seriously, there was a glimmer of hope; visionaries such as Rudolph Steiner with his concept of biodynamics strove to address farming practices that would restore, maintain and enhance ecological harmony. As ever, a brave band of independent producers prevails, folk standing tall and farming by natural methods, fighting for a sustainable future – individuals who understand and respect Mother Nature's delicate capacity for growth and renewal. As people find themselves increasingly disconnected from seasonal ingredients and the sources and methods of food production, the more dulled their senses become. Their knack for seeking out what the body needs is eroded.

The day the aspiring cook knows his seasons and has equipped his mind's eye and palate with the sensory flavor bank that is nature's larder, a spark is lit. He hones the basic skills of sourcing and caring for produce, and he begins to use his tools as extensions of the mind's eye. Cookery then becomes a joyful journey of discovery. One becomes familiar on a seasonal, sensual and textured level with the wealth of natural synergies that occur between the disparate realms that make up nature's bounty. Once you have mastered roasting, simmering, emulsifying, and are aptly extracting the vitality and essence from the ingredients at hand, then perhaps you are ready to cast aside the shackles of replication and improvise. Food should be fun. Cookery with a disciplined backbone becomes so. A window opens up to a land of instinctive improvisation where there are no rules – only what one aspires to taste.

Saving Diversity

Béla Bartha

For over twenty years the ProSpecieRara Foundation has been working to preserve, expand and promote the diversity of crops and livestock breeds in Switzerland and Germany. During its more than thirty-year history, the organisation has prevented 29 endangered animal species from dying out, alongside collecting and protecting thousands of crop species. It now preserves these in various collections in private gardens and on farms. This form of protection of genetic resources is generally referred to as *in situ* conservation, i.e. preservation in either the wild, in the environment of the species' origin, or on the farm or in the garden, whilst so-called *ex situ* conservation involves the preservation of plants in the form of seeds or plant parts and of animals in the form of sperm, eggs or embryos kept in a frozen state in gene banks. The *in situ* preservation enables animals and plants to adapt to new circumstances, but also to remain visible and tangible to human beings.

How ProSpecieRara Got Cooking

When it comes to conservation work in the garden and on farms, sooner or later you inevitably discover that it can only be sustainable if the purpose of the fruits, crops or animals are part of the conservation strategy. Thus, alongside reaching enthusiastic gardeners and farmers, there is an increasing need to appeal to consumers so that they can understand the close correlation between their consumer behavior and the preservation of diversity in our crops and livestock. This is not always an easy task. How do you make it comprehensible that an endangered species can only survive if we eat its meat or use its products? An apparent paradox, but something that can be easily explained with a change of perspective: Why should the farmer rear cattle if nobody is interested in their milk or meat? Products marketed under the ProSpecieRara label frequently stem from varieties or breeds whose use and processing in the kitchen are not immediately apparent to the general consumer. These products do not always speak for themselves on the store shelves, and require further product information alongside normal labelling, for example on their processing and cooking characteristics. So who better to convey such information than a chef?

The professional angle a chef takes – with regard to preparation, taste and the composition of a huge variety of factors in creating an overall experience to be served on a plate – should actually be part of product development and thus also a part of the breeding or cultivation work. Despite this, no practical examples where a chef has been involved as an expert in a specific breeding program spring to mind. Cooking characteristics and taste-related properties are still tested by the same research institutions that also examine the agronomic properties of a breed. If these scientific processes are however linked to excessively rigid specifications, there is a risk that the creativity of chefs will not be taken into account. If, for example, we take the carrot variety known as 'Küttiger Rüebli' and judge it merely on its taste properties as a raw food or test it for sweetness as a cooked food only, then we fail to do it justice. A creative chef very quickly comes to the conclusion that its highly accentuated carrot taste develops best in combination with other flavor components. In aiming to achieve a satisfying culinary experience it is not the individual vegetable components on the plate that are crucial, but rather their combination with other vegetable varieties.

One can assume that most of today's tomato, pepper and zucchini varieties never encounter a chef throughout the ten-year process of development they have to undergo. They are therefore never able to prove their culinary advantages before being eliminated from the cultivation process altogether.

THE WAY OUT OF THE BREEDING DILEMMA

Before breeding programs concentrated merely on transferring individual properties from one plant to another, there was a prevailing notion that the breeder must develop a particular approach whereby he or she gradually formed an idea of what the result of his or her breeding activity should ultimately be. If we are to look at the tremendous diversity that this now seemingly outdated concept of breeding facilitated, then it becomes obvious that it was geared towards satisfying aesthetic and culinary interests rather than purely agronomic ones. One thing that has not changed since: the breeder always has a specific objective in mind and his outlook is always directed forward towards this objective (greater yields, better resistance to disease, longer storage life etc.). Anything new that develops in the field during the course of the breeding work and does not correspond precisely to this objective is then selectively bred out. It is rejected. This procedure is part of the very essence of breeding work and is called selection. That which has been bred out is irretrievably lost if the rejected plants are not preserved in the meantime. If one now assumes that during the breeding process crucial selection criteria have been forgotten, then one has to argue the case for a reversal, and re-examine the former local and traded varieties developed in previous centuries using new selection criteria. This is only possible, however, if these are still available in various private and public collections. It can be assumed that here and there hidden culinary treasures are still to be found. So why continually search for new, exotic experiences when there is so much that is new and undiscovered in the old?

This not only relates to a loss of taste diversity, but also applies to varieties of plants for garden or balcony use, and thereby also for all purposes away from the mainstream, meaning those not related to large-scale commercial cultivation. It is to be feared that many potential market segments, primarily in the specialty area, no longer play a role in the selection of new varieties and therefore are not taken into consideration. If we want to bring more variety and diversity in terms of flavor to the plate once again, then various interest and user groups should be consulted into the breeding process. Breeding should not merely be a task for specialist breeders, farmers and processers, but should involve representatives of various social groups. Breeding work that is consistently participatory in nature could go far beyond the close cooperation between farmers and breeders considered progressive today. Breeding, i. e. the pursuit of a vision, represents a broad-based social task (community breeding).

To put it in different terms: social "shared cooking" should be much more broadly defined and ought to go far beyond the conventional framework of eating together. It should begin as early as the field or even in the breeding laboratory. Who sits at the dining table during development is crucial to quality of the result in terms of flavor and variety.

How Can Variety Be Brought to the Plate?

Bringing biodiversity to the plate is a challenge, because today's production conditions tend towards the opposite direction. If one wants to offer vegetables of appealing quality and at a reasonable cost and price, then it is essential to produce a certain quantity. When we talk about the production chain, we initially think about the producers who grow, harvest and sell the vegetable for the market. The seeds the producer uses for this, however, generally do not come to mind. Yet this constitutes the crucial bottleneck in terms of a varied, regional and authentic range of varieties. The producer must be able to make up for investments in both infrastructure and in the work involved in preserving variety and in the production of the seeds entirely through the sale of such seeds. This can only be achieved where a critical quantity of seed can be sold per variety. It is worth considering here that generally, for any specific variety, the market volume of the whole of Switzerland is too small for all this work to be refinanced through the sale of seed. It may be that the reality and the chef's desire for exclusivity stand in each other's way here. However, a good chef will be capable of compensating creatively for the practical constraint that leads to a finite range of varieties in the market.

So what contribution can art make to the improvement of variety on the plate? None, if we are to assume that artistic creativity cannot be exploited for a specific purpose. Yet this is precisely what is frequently done. Art works are exhibited in restaurants in order to create a pleasant environment. Skillfully executed craftsmanship, good taste and styling are equated with artistic creativity. Restaurant critics elevate chefs to the level of artists and talk about the high art of cooking. The terms 'art' and 'cooking' are currently excessively used in connection to the extent that they are now almost inextricably linked. This absorption doubtless lies in the essence of art, and yet time and again it is artists and philosophers who manage to position themselves against the flow of economic and results-oriented pressures and dependencies and thus to develop a new view of things.

For me personally, it would be lovely if the result of a coming-together of producer, chef and artist were not the achievement of any product whatsoever (new variety, new breeding strategy or a new menu), nor mutual exploitation to serve a particular purpose, but rather that each gain insights for their own area of work from the communication taking place here. A shared meal would then become a symbol of the exchange of a huge range of philosophies that enrich and inspire one another on the basis of a shared experience. Here it is both chef and artist who nourish the source of inspiration with their ideas and their creativity.

Sustainable Food Systems

Bernadette Oehen and Robert Home

Eating is essential to all people on the planet. Food maintains life, health and wellbeing. Most of us do not produce our own food, but depend on others for our food supply. This food can come from near or far and can be heavily or lightly processed. The ingredients, which are the raw materials for food, have to be produced somewhere and we, the consumers, often have little or no idea about whether the ingredients are produced in a sustainable way.

People are ever more concerned with how their food is produced and processed. These concerns are driven by reports in the media about healthy and unhealthy food, scandals about food safety, and also by scientists. Steffen et al., the IPCC, the IAASDT and Rockström et al. among others have all been sounding the alarm that the global ecosystem is in a precarious state.[1] They have identified key processes that regulate stability and resilience, and all are relevant to the provision of clean, affordable and accessible energy and an adequate supply of food.[2] Increased greenhouse gas emissions, pollution of soils and waters, and loss of soil fertility and biodiversity put this in danger. Industrial agriculture production of food, feed, fibres and, increasingly, energy (biofuel and biogas) is one of the drivers of the anthropogenic pressures on the global environment.[3] These industrial agricultural systems depend on external inputs, such as synthetic pesticides, fertilizers, precision technology and information to maintain their productivity for a price that is acceptable on the international markets.[4]

---

1 | Steffen et al.: 2015; IPCC (2013): Climate Change: The Physical Science Basis. Contribution of Working Group I to the Fifth Assessment Report of the Intergovernmental Panel on Climate Change, Cambridge/New York; IAASTD (2009): International Assessment of Agricultural Knowledge, Science and Technology for Development, in: *Agriculture at a crossroads: Global Report*, Washington, D. C.; Rockström et al: 2009.

2 | Steffen et al.: 2015.

3 | IAASTD (2009): International Assessment of Agricultural Knowledge, Science and Technology for Development, in: *Agriculture at a crossroads: Global Report*, Washington, D. C.

4 | Murphy et al.: 2012.

Despite stable, or even increased productivity, the current form of industrial agriculture is not sustainable: not only for its negative environmental impact but also because it is failing to healthily nourish the people in both developing and developed countries.[5] The human health results are problems related to malnutrition such as obesity or stunting. To understand this, we need to have a closer look at the current global agri-food system. We see four categories of actors: the input suppliers, the international grain traders, the food processors and the food retailers. Consumers and farmers are buyers and therefore do not belong to the system.

In addition to the grain traders, almost all of the actors in the agri-food systems are well known international companies, such as Syngenta and Monsanto (input suppliers); Unilever, Nestlé, and Kraft (processors); and Aldi and Tesco (retailers). In the shadow of these companies, the trade with commodities is dominated by four big traders – Archer Daniels Midland (ADM), Bunge, Cargill and Louis Dreyfus, collectively referred to as 'the ABCD companies'.[6] They are key players in the countries exporting wheat, soybean, maize, rice or palm oil, which are Argentina, Australia, Brazil, Canada, China, Indonesia, Malaysia, Russia and the USA. These companies are highly diversified and integrated vertically. As a result, they not only trade grains, but also provide the external inputs to produce the crops, such as fertilizer, pesticides and seeds. Their size and power give them access to investments and, more and more, access to land.[7]

The ABCD have a long history of being the bridge between producers and the world's largest food processors and retailers.[8] In such a market, the competition among the companies is low and it is difficult for new actors to enter the market. The established companies control the prices, the access to farmers, and distribution. They appear to be stable and secure. Even if they were to disappear, the unsustainable way of food production could survive along with the idea, that farmers and consumers should be segregated from each other as far as possible.

To become more sustainable, the current system has to take into account, that farmers, including small holders, actually nourish 80 percent of the world population. This point was expressed in the International Assessment of Agricultural Science and Technology for Development (IAASTD) with the words, 'Business as usual is not an option anymore'. The United Nations Conference on Trade and Development (UNCTAD) put it even more dramatically in the title of its *Trade and Environment Review*: 'Wake up Before it is Too Late: Make Agriculture Truly Sustainable Now for Food Security in a Changing Climate'[9] or in Felix zu Löwenstein's book, 'The Food Crash': "Either we will feed ourselves organically in the near future,

---

5 | Hilbeck/Oehen: 2015.

6 | Murphy et al.: 2012.

7 | Ibid.

8 | Ibid.

9 | UNCTAD: 2013.

or we will not eat at all anymore".[10] In addition, these smallholder farmers are managers and guardians of an agro-ecological system whose long-term functioning and environmental health is imperative for sustained productivity and food supply.

Food from small holders is mainly traded local or regionally in short supply chains. Some of these farmers have maintained traditional and local seed varieties, which are well adapted to local conditions and are often ingredients in the regional cuisine.

However, a paradigm shift concerning eating is taking place. In a world, where food is perceived as unnatural; food production as destructive; food trade as unfair; and food processing as distrusted, producing and processing own home-grown food has become trendy. Cooking and eating authentic, traditional food has become a more and more important topic. New forms of cooperation between consumers and farmers in short supply chains have been developed. Of course the motivations might be different. For some, it is a way to transform the current systems and become independent from the food industries. Others want to be reconnected with nature or reconnected with their culture. These initiatives survive because the large players have no access to niche markets. Furthermore, they transmit additional values such as tradition, sustainability, fairness and, as should not be underestimated when food is discussed, health, pleasure, and taste. Perhaps the most interesting aspect is that farmers see the consumer as partners rather than just as buyers. Examples of such initiatives can be found in many countries, including Greece and Portugal, which have been hardest hit by the financial crisis, and China.[11]

A lot of know-how has been generated on the production side, and many methods for an alternative, sustainable forms of agricultural production have evolved. These alternatives include organic farming, conservation agriculture, agroforestry, permaculture, and integrated pest management. This rich body of expertise continues to grow. Pimbert sees a new form of agricultural production in these steps toward more regionalised agri-food systems: based on autonomy, prudent use of resources, and cooperation along the agri-food chain.[12] There are also changes on the consumption side. Safety, authenticity and quality are major consumer requirements when buying food and represent key issues for the European agri-food industry. Pingali points out that rapid urbanization and economic and income growth in Asia, combined with globalisation in which the urban middle class are increasingly connected worldwide, has led to unprecedented knowledge of what others are eating: at regional, national and international scales.[13] This change has led to new levels of experimentation, but also new expectations for quality and safety and an interest in the origin, authentic, and trustworthiness of food. The widespread knowledge means

10 | Löwenstein: 2011.

11 | Hilbeck/Hilbeck: 2015.

12 | Pimbert: 2009.

13 | Pingali: 2007.

that trends spread faster and wider than ever before, and can achieve a critical mass.[14]

Local and regional agri-food systems play a key role in creating spaces in which consumers and producers can interact face-to-face at markets, stores and in restaurants. They produce an arena of exchange that is imbued with more social meaning than conventional food retail and consumption spaces. However, these systems have to include all actors along the supply chain; from the farmers and how they produce up to the consumers and how they cook and eat.

A step that is often ignored in discussions about more sustainable and resilient food systems is the importance of cooking skills. In a similar development to farmers having come to completely depend on the inputs and information from the large agribusinesses, consumers are in danger of losing the skills needed to produce, choose, and cook food. Cooking needs teaching and training as much as do gardening and farming. When consumers are unsure of specific cooking techniques, or lack the confidence to cook certain foods, the easy option is to turn to convenience food.[15] Hartmann et al. investigated whether cooking skills are related to the frequency of consumption of various food groups, with results confirming what was suspected. Competence with cooking skills correlated positively with weekly vegetable consumption and negatively with weekly convenience food consumption.[16] To gain skills in cooking means to learn about food, so we can assume that this correlation may be causal and that cooking skills may help people to make healthier food choices by eating more vegetables.

Food is absolutely central to human life, but eating and cooking are about much more than just nutrition. The culinary turn goes beyond cooking and appreciating. The choices we make have implications on global sustainability, on our health, and on our autonomy.

14 | Ibid.

15 | Caraher et al.: 1999.

16 | Hartman et al.: 2013.

Consciously, but Not Knowingly

Dominik Flammer

There is deeply rooted lack of regional awareness among restaurateurs and chefs in the northern Alpine region, like an innate inferiority complex with regard to any culinary influences from elsewhere. Be it in Switzerland, Austria, or southern Germany. It is so deep that at best they dare to offer domestic Tyrolean gray cattle as a *carpaccio,* and faintheartedly put on the menu as *panna cotta* the cream sourced from cattle that graze freely in meadows. They might well wrap domestic zander in some wooly pig fat from the neighboring organic farm, but on the menu they call it *fish saltim-bocca.* They then at best naively put a geographical allocation in front of the dishes, so as to pretend to guests from the area as well as tourists that there is something regional about them. This takes the form of: *Allgäu brassato*

with olive tapenade or *Aargau Châteaubriand with curry and orange-flavored butter.*

That said, they have long since been aware of the fact that guests and tourists not only long for genuine regional specialties in the mountains at home, in pretty Alpine inns and in shady beer gardens, but are also increasingly looking for them on their plates and on menus. This is something that up and down the country gastronomic circles, chefs' federations, and tourism associations have been eagerly discussing for years on panels, and at seminars and symposiums. However, pure laziness and wrong regional awareness then frequently result in nothing more than ridiculous pseudo-regional strategies, whose regional character is mostly limited to a few images of the local countryside on the menu. In fact, particularly shrewd restaurateurs think they are doing justice to regionality by buying New Zealand lamb and Argentinian beef loins from the local butcher and then plugging them as "chef's-style".

Awareness alone is not enough if there is a lack of knowledge. Or if one does not have the courage to adapt obsolete and long since outdated chefs' teaching curricula to new circumstances, to offer chefs further training, and to strengthen collaboration between regional agriculture and domestic restaurateurs. And this way to stand up to the ineffable campaigns staged by tourism bureaucrats aimed at elevating supposedly national cuisines to a leading position. There is, however, no "Swiss" cuisine, just as much as there is no Austrian cuisine and no German cuisine. What there is are regional cuisines, which for all their overlapping are clearly different from one another in terms of diversity and range.

Not that this knowledge has not long since been available: over the past two decades innumerable organizations put enormous efforts into systematically and thoroughly putting the necessary foundations in place; knowledge which, through the globalization and industrialization of the food industry, in particular in the second half of the 20th century, had to a large extent had disappeared. Through their work, organic organizations, the slow food movement, fruit and vegetable growers and associations dedicated to the preservation of bio-diversity such as *Pro Specie Rara* in Switzerland and *Arche Noah* in Austria have played a major role in revitalizing the existing, regionally so different diversity. Botanists and chefs who are enthusiastic about natural produce have made us aware of the unique diversity of edible wild plants again. And for years now books about patios at home, crop plants, the range of cheeses and the abundance of fish have been at the top of bestseller lists. Markets specializing in regional produce are springing up all over the place, attracting thousands, at times tens of thousands of visitors; leading the way slow food fairs, *Pro Specie Rara* markets, *Bio Marché* and *Authentica* trade fairs, cherry and chestnut markets, Alpine cheese markets and fruit fairs.

Although the large retailers and discounters have long since recognized the re-emergence of regional foodstuffs and cuisine, their nationwide strategies make it difficult for them to adopt a credible approach to it. Only produce that as it were is available all year round and is consistently good quality finds its way to the supermarket shelves. Lots of hospitality and hotel chains that operate across the country are using 'Swissness' campaigns to try and jump on the regional cuisine bandwagon. Even at the breakfast buffet though, this regional image is limited for the most part to bread and at best marmalades, while visually slices of Leerdammer cheese, packets of Kellogg's cereals and Nutella sachets are still dominant.

Especially in Austria and Switzerland, but also, for example, in German-speaking northern Italy and Germany's Baden-Württemberg region, top chefs have assumed a leading and important role in the rediscovery of regional diversity, not least because for a culinary elite, top-class regionally defined cuisine has emerged as a new status symbol. Nowadays top chefs are increasingly acquiring modern kitchen popstar status, and they enjoy a lot of media attention, which very much accelerates the revival of regional diversity.

Heinz Reitbauer, for years now the undisputed no.1 among Austrian chefs, successfully puts this regionality into practice with his unique creativity but without determined dogmatism: although he only works with regional ingredients from producers he knows, he does not shy away from using new sorts of chili from his vegetable farmer for his culinary creations, not to mention the citrus fruits from his Viennese orangery. Thanks not least of all to Reitbauer, Austria's cooking elite has long since come together under the umbrella of the country's Chef Campus. Together the top chefs are very successfully adopting an approach that gives their fare a diverse regional image.

In Switzerland too, a handful of young chefs has recognized the benefits of a regional focus. With increasing success, and Nenad Mlinarevic, for example, showing the way; he works in the Park Hotel in Vitznau on Lake Lucerne, and since 2015 has only been using domestic produce, which in 2016 earned him the title of Swiss Chef of the Year. At first sight Mlinarevic may well seem more radical than comparable fellow chefs, because with the exception of coffee and cocoa he does without exotic spices such as pepper, nutmeg, and cloves. In exchange he is helping local traditions and those that were thought to have been lost along the way, find their place in cooking again, from Cornelian cherries to rosehip oil and whey caramel to whitefish roe.

And nonetheless Mlinarevic pursues an undogmatic approach, is curious and cosmopolitan. And proves in the process that regional awareness is anything but restrictive: Like Reitbauer he too works with curious local farmers who above all are eager to try something new, and who sometimes supply him with Amaranth flour or with South American herbs, with which they experiment; as, two hundred years ago farmers in these parts began experimenting with potatoes from the New World or one hundred years ago local vegetable farmers began growing tomatoes.

The fact that gastronomy – and this by no means applies only to top cuisine – makes its mark primarily through regionality, is not only due to a traditional or indeed new variety of produce. Rather, it is primarily due to the faces and the stories behind this diversity. And only those who ignore the history of our diet fear allegiance to traditional dishes and produce, because like never before, innovative producers and farmers are ensuring not only that the old diversity is preserved, but that a growing diversity that is for ever renewing itself emerges. Put in more simple terms: only thanks to old apples do new varieties appear.

The elite of young Swiss chefs has recognized this principle: Fabian Fuchs from L'Equitable in Zurich prepares the regional organic produce he uses precisely and accurately, such that his restaurant is now almost always full booked. And with cookery that focuses exclusively on home-grown produce and her unbridled curiosity about regional discoveries Rebecca Clopath, a chef from the Graubünden region of Switzerland has emerged as a guest chef who is much in demand. In Austria, polished concepts and the skillful use of the bio and product diversity in their respective regions have long since put chefs such as Andreas Döllerer in Gölling in the Salzburg region and Josef Floh in Langenlebarn in Lower Austria very much in the top flight.

In the aspiring luxury hotel business in new Swiss tourist spots, Swiss chefs were once the first outside France to learn and indeed advance the sophisticated craft of erstwhile French top chefs. During the culinary globalization stage as well, chefs from the Alpine region have long played an important role worldwide. But since, with the molecular renewal of cooking techniques, the Spanish in particular have laid the foundations for a new awareness and with a concept geared to sustainability and biodynamics involving only regional cuisine the Scandinavians are admittedly now in a leading role, the attention Alpine cuisine attracts has dwindled. Not least of all because the, by comparison, great economic success of mass Alpine tourism has made the hospitality trade sleepy and induced a comatose state as far as its will for renewal is concerned. That said, of all European regions it is this diverse cultural area in particular that in the future has the greatest chance of positioning itself as a culinary stronghold, because nowhere is there greater diversity than here at the heart of Europe, where for centuries influences from the north and south, from the west and east have all come together. Influences that have become blended, that have remained here and yet have advanced individually from valley to valley. There are still thousands of varieties of fruit, hundreds of wild plants that are suitable for cooking but for the most part still not used, dozens of unique animal breeds, innumerable sorts of bread from incalculably diverse Alpine grain traditions. And not least of all, of course, a wide variety of processing and finishing techniques still nurtured by an almost unfathomable range of butchers, distillers, cheese makers and confectioners.

In order to assume a leading role here, the hospitality trade, like agriculture, must continue to concentrate on the existent diversity. And it must do everything it can in order, together with all the powers that be in regional tourism marketing, to focus on its peculiarities instead of getting entangled in an interchangeability competition on the level of a rating wrangle. By, to repeat yet again, banking more on faces and stories.

In future, menus will then read something like this: Rampion salad with roast beechnuts and a pine shoot and vinegar vinaigrette with camelina oil. Or: Lake Zurich zander marinated in barberry juice with crispy Jack-by-the-Hedge seeds. Or perhaps: Fillet of Murnau-Werdenfelser beef on a wood sorrel jus with spelt dumplings and 'Haferbirne' pear slices.

Because despite all our wanderlust, all our curiosity about foreign cuisine and all our belief in the fact that anything can be globalized ad infinitum, there is one thing we should not lose sight of: Almost everything can be exported or imported – skills, commodities, talent, and technology. But not regionality. Because it can only be experienced in a credible, sensual manner, where the countryside and agriculture, people, culture and cuisine interact. We cannot for eternity just abandon this finding to cheese fondue served in Alpine inns by staff wearing traditional costume and to the sound of cowbells and Alpine horns.

Concept

Morsels

Samuel Herzog

PRE-TEXT

Everyday an enormous amount and variety of vegetables, spices, cereals, meat, fruit, and fish pass through our hands and across our palates. What interests us most is whether we like their taste, how they can be cooked, and how they affect our health. What they cost, and how they can influence our social standing is perhaps also of importance. It could well be that we have a particularly loving relationship with this or that piece of food that passes between our lips, something that generally speaking has much to do with our associating it with memories of our childhood or vacations, love affairs, and victories. Even we are constantly surrounded by these 'morsels', we mostly have very little to say to them – and if we have to describe the many forms of delight they give us, we always end up saying more or less the same thing.

All of this perhaps also has something to do with the fact that nowadays there is an abundance of food in the Global North. We no longer have to endure hunger. Language, however, occasionally serves to replace something, to make something otherwise missing, that we long for, present through words. When we are hungry, our imagination comes up with representatives: Sentences one can chew and phrases from which the meat juices spray. In plentiful times we can save ourselves effort such as these. But are we also not lacking something if we simply take all this food for granted?

Since 2013 Samuel Herzog has been working on a series of articles, in which some of these 'morsels' are elevated to the role of protagonist for a moment and taken seriously in a concentrated way. It is do with deceleration and viewing individual pieces of food in a manner that is as amateurish as it is narrow-minded. And it is also about trying out a new form of reflection on and writing about these 'morsels'. The articles are written on the back of, to some extent ritualized concentration on the particular object for a limited period of time – and it goes almost without saying that where possible they are begun when the author has a certain feeling of hunger in his belly.

HEAD OF A PIG

As an amateur cook you sometimes just reach your limits and are really put to the test by the food you want to prepare and taste – in particular of course if it is your first time. That was the case with my first (uncleaned) lamb tripe which, turning up his nose, the Turkish butcher handed over the counter to me in a small plastic bag. My first black salsify party had existential traits as well – me thinking after preparing several kilos that as fate would have it the world would start sticking together in my kitchen. My first whole shark also presented a problem in that the next generation gushed from its stomach on to my kitchen table – three baby sharks the length of a pencil, which looked as if they were praying. I could also tell you a few stories about durian fruit, or the fermented fish I tried to clean in a Norwegian lake ...

To date, however, the biggest test of my culinary belief in the good was my first whole pig's head. I had explicitly ordered "as small a head as possible" from the butcher, as it is always best to start off modestly with new dishes. When I noticed that the sales assistant did not have the strength to hand it to me over the counter, I began to have misgivings. A gloating smile on his lips, the packet he finally managed to push towards me over the floor of the butcher's, weighed almost ten kilograms. I had some difficulty securing it on my bicycle's luggage rack and cycled extremely carefully, having no wish whatever to see it sliding across the road in a bend.

At home I freed the head from the blue plastic and heaved it on to the kitchen counter. There was something strangely natural about the way it lay there, pointing its snout up and allowing its ears to hang in the sink. Its eyes had already been cut out in the abattoir. I felt as if there were a speech bubble hovering over its skull with the terse sentence: "I am dead!" A pig's head like this is not a butchery masterpiece, as no bones are removed, and nothing is saved. All you do is take a sow and saw through it behind the ears – job done.

I initially planned to immerse the head in salt brine for a few hours – to get rid of the snot from its nose (or to rid myself of the idea that its snout just had to be full of mucus). Because I did not have a pan big enough, I hauled the animal to the shower, where I put it in a garbage bag and poured salt and water in, thus giving it a modest bath.

I actually intended braising the head on a bed of root vegetables in the oven for several hours. But that way the tray would not fit in the oven, so I removed the vegetables and slid the large, imposing piece in on its own, it to my mind looking somewhat undignified. I left the kitchen to fetch a few bottles of red wine from the cellar. When I returned I was hit by the smell of burnt flesh and the kitchen was full of black smoke. I threw open the window, then the oven door. The heat had caused the head to swell, and the snout had got wedged in the upper heating coil. In order to be able to get the tray out of the oven again I had to cut the animal's nose off and then scrape it off the oven with a spatula.

I thought it was all going to be festive and nice: a whole pig's head, braise for hours, repeatedly basted with wine and fat, bright golden on a bed of carrots and parsnips. The reality was far removed from this ideal. I had invited all my friends to this "pig's head" – and was now glad that an unusually high number of them had sent their apologies. There were ultimately three of us sitting over the severely mutilated and slightly charred head – what an undignified end, what a sorry sight.

There is no other way to put it – my very first pig's head was a culinary disaster. It was more than a year before I dared tackle this part of the animal again – and this time a different butcher actually sold me a small head weighing just 1.7 kilos that also fitted in my pan. I gave it all my attention for an entire evening, turning it into a 1.3 kilo terrine that I was so proud of I would have liked nothing better than to parade through town like a

trophy. So reaching your culinary limits does serve a purpose after all –
even if it is only to give a pig's head a dignified send-off.

CHARD

I hate chard – and this has always been the case. Even under the pretty
name of silverbeet it conjures up the most disgusting of thoughts in me –
the color of its stem is reason enough to leave it well alone. When Cara-
vaggio created his 'Entombment of Christ' in 1603 he chose chard-white – a
color that is entirely discarnate for being so bright, yet still somehow green-
ish-grey – for the savior's deadest parts, thereby leaving no doubt about
the complete lifelessness of the depicted body. Maybe he even picked the
color of chard to allude to the fact that he essentially did not really believe
in the Resurrection at all. Recently, chard with red and yellow stems has
increasingly been the flavor of the week; but this does nothing to change
the dread this vegetable is able to induce – this colorful display is mere
window-dressing, for in all truth, all chard is pallid and death-like.

As a child I ate basically everything and a lot of everything – which
did somewhat worry my parents; for example when I, and this was long
before the onset of puberty, was dead-set on ordering a second andouil-
lette at a French country inn. My younger brother was my polar opposite
in this respect – the list of things he would not eat was so long that at
times he himself lost track. He was particularly averse to vegetables and
specifically to spinach. This likewise distressed my parents, who tried to
persuade him to ingest at least a minimum amount of vitamins. One day
he impressed me at lunchtime with a deed hardly inferior to the miracle of
the seven loaves and fishes: Forced by our mother to eat just a little fork-full
of spinach, he vomited about a liter of bright green mush onto his plate.

Up until that point I had never quite understood why some people
detested any foods whatsoever. But at that moment I realized that these
revulsions were not really about taste, color or consistency after all, but
simply about having your life in your own hands, about being able to
fashion the space of your own body as you saw fit. And in that moment I
realized what an immense deficit I had – I who ate everything suddenly felt
like a creature without a will of its own, a child without qualities, nothing
but a rag without character.

That was the hour of chard. Today I can hardly reconstruct why it was
chard in particular that fell from grace – it is possible that I had previously
exhibited a certain reluctance towards this legume. But from that moment
onwards I refused to let chard in any shape or form anywhere near my
body – and I did so successfully. If I was invited for dinner somewhere
later on, I proclaimed, not without a certain sense of pride, that I would eat
"everything – except for chard". If I was occasionally asked why I did not
eat this specific green I would always supply the same, highly differentiated answer: "I hate it!" The formula behind my fiery anti-chardism could
possibly have read: "I do not eat that – therefore I am."

Over a quarter of a century passed without my coming into contact with chard. But then one day I signed a fateful contract – with an organic farm that promised to supply me with seasonal vegetables on a weekly basis. It was a pact with the devil – because, as I would soon find out, the veggie-subscription consisted almost entirely of spinach and chard. First I turned pale, then I tried exorcist curses in order to expel the abhorrent stalk from my life – but nothing worked. I was able to gift the legume to my neighbors and friends a couple of times, but eventually, the day came.

The first bite was so terrible it made me gag in parts of my body I had not even known existed. The second was no better and the third – well, to my terrific horror I had to observe that the vegetable suddenly lay in my mouth like a delicate, pleasantly scented green, aromatic and tasting like an amalgamation of spinach, carrots and beetroot, with a distinctive end note that was both bitter and sweet at the same time, and sometimes also agreeably sour. Should I have vomited it onto my kitchen table in order to salvage my independence? I did not do so, for too weak was I. On the contrary – at the next arising opportunity I stuffed some raw chard into my mouth, which, in fact, you should not do too often as this may lead to kidney stones (due to the so-called oxalic acid, which also makes raw chard somewhat less palatable). The herbaceous, bitter and heavily earthy aroma seemed so profound and multi-layered to me that it unexpectedly reminded me of a very old pinot noir – and it continued to have an effect in the mouth, changed on my gums, assumed all kinds of fragrant flavors, becoming exotic-fruity, then turnip-like, fleshy-bloody, withering marshy landscape, pinewood, dune. Had there not also been the fierce, furry after-taste drying out the mouth, that scratchy over-acidification of the pharynx and the esophagus, my kidney stones would have rejoiced.

Since then I know that chard is a profoundly evil, abysmally low vegetable. Which is why I attack it with my longest kitchen knife at every opportunity. I cut its sallow spine from its green body, roll its leaves until I hear its ribs bursting, dissect it, let it sweat in fat or in the oven and finally strangle it with oil, lemon, white sauce.

There is no need to shout it from the rooftops – humankind's true avengers have always operated undercover. If I am invited for dinner anywhere nowadays I have a new formula at the ready: "I eat everything except for large sheep's eyes" – in the silent hope that nobody will be deterred by my words.

LIME

I was in love. And as such highly attentive to the flavors of the world I was still unfamiliar with. He was called Matthew and was the son of an English-German couple that moved to our neighborhood one day. He had blonde hair, like me, but his blue eyes shone through long slits. His skin was fair and waxy and looked as if it had been formed by air and light. His voice was soft and melodious, restrained like his light brown cords and clear like his impeccably ironed shirts.

I loved him because he was handsome and because I sensed that he was the cause of a new feeling I was experiencing. And I was convinced that I could get something from him, something special, that had something to do with the big secret surrounding him – or was it just me shrouding him in it? Matthew was seven years old, just like me – but he had already lived in Japan, South Africa, England, and Brazil. He was used to being a stranger and had a gentle melancholy approach to things, as if they were always about to disappear.

I was in love, and whenever I saw him my face began glowing. I had an enormous thirst. All I ever thought of now was him, I adapted my way to school to suit his habits, I waited for him, I skulked around his house, I verily lay in wait for him. I had, however, no idea of what I actually wanted to achieve, of what I had in mind. And my uncertainty was probably also a reason why no real friendship was able to develop.

One day Matthew pulled a small, bright green fruit from his trouser pocket, and without saying a word handed it to me. I had never seen anything like it before: "Is that a green mandarin?" I asked. He smiled, bringing his eyelids closer together to form even narrower slits; nonetheless it seemed as if a new shadow were passing across his face.

I carried the fruit home as if it were a treasure, locked myself in my room, sat down on my bed and moved the green ball through my hand. Its skin felt smooth and waxy, its aroma seemed strange to me and reminded me a bit of the eucalyptus sweets I sometimes sucked. Ultimately I tried to peel it – and was a little perplexed by how difficult it was to separate the thin skin from the light flesh. Today I can no longer exactly say what impression the fruit's aroma made on me – all I know is that it seemed excitingly strange to me.

When, the following day, I went past Matthew's house again, two men were carrying a flower-patterned sofa through the garden to a big truck. Matthew and his parents had already left. I have absolutely no memory of how I dealt with this first major loss in my life – the removal men with the flowery sofa are the last mental image of this love story.

At the time limes were hardly known in Switzerland – in any case not among the people I associated with. Yet many years later, when I tried my first caipirinha, Matthew's pale face reappeared immediately – and with it the memory of the rare glow the boy had brought into my life. Since those early years I have cut open thousands of limes und used them in all sorts of ways in my kitchen. And yet the greenish, resinous, rosy, lilac-like aroma of the fruit, its salty acidity and its dry sweetness keep on reminding me of Matthew and his farewell present. That is perhaps why even today the tiny fruit, which is only green because it is always harvested before it is ripe, has remained curiously foreign to me – exotic and full of undreamt promises.

Bay Leaf

"I do not believe in God – why should there be such a thing? Maurice said. He briefly swirled the Morellino di Scansano in his glass, sniffed it and shut his eyes: "Plums and shit", he mumbled.

"If there were a God after all", mighty Danilo said in a deep voice, "you would have to say, as would Woody Allen: 'I hope he has a good excuse'."

The two men laughed. I was travelling round Italy with Maurice Péfort in order to learn about what he called "eating properly". Maurice, who has written poems and essays about kitchen culture, spices, offal, wine and other things, was for many years my teacher when it came to matters of the belly – and is still a good friend today, one with whom despite his biblical age you can still get nice and drunk. For three days we had been staying with an artist, who owned a magnificent property near Grosseto, a magical wine cellar, and his even more enchanting wife, who was called Sarah and was an excellent cook. She had a slender, lithe-looking body, short, dark-brown hair, and eyes which were green like moss. I found the veins on her neck and on her arms, which my imagination followed well into her clothes, even more fascinating. She was considerably younger than Danilo, but about ten years older than me, which added spice to my desire.

"I do not believe in God, but I am convinced", Maurice pontificated, "that there is more to the world than its material being, that beyond fathomable reality there is still something unfathomable for which we have no name – but without which there would be no beauty in the world. It appears when we listen to music, look at paintings, at the fading sun that has just disappeared beyond the horizon."

"Or when we eat my wife's pigeon", Danilo added, while Sarah put a large pot on the table before sitting down next to her husband. It went quiet in the room – Maurice considered any form of conversation during a meal a "disrespectful bad habit". And his friends knew this, too. The light of a cool winter's day fell through the windows, while the air inside the home was filled with aromatic steam. A crackling fire was smoldering in the fireplace and all that could be heard from the people sat around the table was a quiet smacking of lips, tongues and teeth, as these nibbled the moist meat off the dainty skeletons with precision. I found it hard to concentrate on the food – the sauce's flowery freshness, interspersed with a few hints of camphor, seemed to me to be directly connected to Sarah's armpits. I did not just see skin touching skin in her delicate underarm fold through the transparent fabric of her blouse – I was positively in that space, lodged into her scent.

"The question simply is", Maurice had finished his pigeon, its bones now spread out on the edge of his plate like victor's laurels, "whether we are simply imagining all of this and the splendor of life really has no support in what we, for want of a better word, call reality."

"What exactly do you mean?" I asked – probably only in order not to remain completely mute.

"Well the big question clearly is: Does the poetic element reside in the world – or is this just a trick we play, a construction made up of words, sounds, brush marks, or in the worst case even just convention?"

Sarah cleared away the plates, and as she walked away from the table I saw that she was barefoot, she had evidently taken her shoes off during the meal. I could not drag my gaze away from these feet, their muscles seemed to dance for me, to call for me – before disappearing, much too quickly, into the kitchen. How I would have liked to help Sarah with the washing up, but I just did not dare follow her – maybe also because I realized that the two gentlemen needed me to be the audience of their little dispute.

"Does that even play a role?" Danilo now growled: "After all, we imagine colors too, and smells – without those phantasmagorias we would have no orientation. So why should we not also imagine something that lends our lives some luster and beauty?"

Sarah placed a bowl of pears in white wine on the table, then stopped behind my chair and placed her hands on my backrest. It was as though I could feel the warmth of her fingers, heated up from her work in the kitchen, on my neck. I froze.

"When I cook it is bay leaves in particular that are able to light a flame in the foods – without them, many dishes stay flat and without mystery", Sarah said, and I was now certain I could feel her finger tips on my skin: "It is impossible to describe or explain: but it is still very real to me."

The two men nodded. They evidently did not know quite what to make of Sarah's bay leaf intermezzo. It was only then that I realized that all of her dishes had indeed been cooked with bay leaves – the grilled liver in pig's caul, the pigeon braised in jus and now also the pears in white wine.

I was not used to eating extensive lunches – and on top of this I was barely able to follow the conversation between the two men. Sarah had vanished to the kitchen once more, so I lay down on the sofa next to the fireplace for a moment.

The sun was now hitting the windows horizontally and Sarah's body cast a sharp-edged shadow on the wall as she stood up straight next to the bed. I approached her, coming close enough to feel her breath on my face. My fingers slowly traced a blue vein of hers that flowed from her shoulder over the front of her ribcage like a river running wild, across her belly and past her hip bones to the top of her thighs. She sank onto the bed and I kneeled above her to kiss her neck, her mouth, her breasts. She smelled of nutmeg and eucalyptus, of cloves and green leaves – her sweat tasted sour in a fresh way and sweet at the same time. Now I felt her hand on my thigh and the tension my arousal created sent blissful shivers down my back and buttocks. But in the next moment I brushed the covers off the bed in an awkward movement and it was only then that I saw we were lying on a gigantic pile of bay leaves, which now fluttered off in all directions, dancing around us like blossoms – so wild I could suddenly no longer see anything at all.

I opened my eyes wide and Sarah's face was right in front of mine. She was kneeling next to the sofa and really did have her right hand placed on my thigh in a friendly way – while extending her left hand towards me with a cup of espresso. Maurice and Danilo stood behind her in their coats; they evidently wanted to take me on a walk with them. My member, erect from the dream, was pushing up against the textile of my trousers a mere five centimeters from Sarah's fingers, and I felt myself blushing with such vehemence that my head turned into a fireball almost instantly.

Over a quarter of a century has passed since that day in the Maremma. I use bay leaves in my cooking generously and often, in order to light a fire in my dishes – and sometimes Sarah, who died in a car accident a few years ago, stands at the stove with me as I do so, and I feel the touch of her kitchen-warm fingers on my skin, hear the blood rushing through her veins. The smell of bay leaves also reminds me of Maurice's big question, to which I still do not know the answer. Since those younger years I have however been haunted by the odd thought that there might be a connection between the poetic and the embarrassing – after all, both put a shine on the everyday in their particular way. And if the embarrassing is of this world, why not poetry, too?

MILK

I hated it – and for good reason. I had human nature on my side and the great minds of dietetics would without doubt have supported my cause. Admittedly, at the time I certainly did not yet think about whether such behavior was justified or not. I simply hated it, and if it somehow came too close to me, I screamed my head off.

Yet everything had started off so peacefully. I have no recollection of that time, but if I am to believe what is generally assumed, it must have been delightful to me to suck with my tiny baby lips from my mother's breasts something that I would many years later be introduced to by the name of milk. But like many a source of the good, the breast of breasts also ran dry at some point – and it became time to discover the rest of the culinary world.

If it is true what I was later told, then I pounced on anything I could get my hands on with a voracious appetite – including liquor-filled chocolates and cat's tails (an early influence indeed). I once also munched down a matriculation essay that my father had carelessly left next to my playpen. For the life of me I cannot remember whether I liked the taste of ink. But my young father was so worried about his future as a teacher that he gave the student top grades in order to cover up the embarrassing incident. Someone out there, born in 1948 or so, may thus owe his career to nothing more than my appetite. Who knows, maybe that student even became a writer and now occasionally asks himself whether it was all just a big misunderstanding.

To return to milk. As large as my appetite for all manner of things, including unspeakable ones, turned out to be (and I did not shy away from experiments that had to be reversed in the hospital) – if anyone came near me with a baby bottle, the force of my protest drove everything out the house that had legs or wings to carry it. My father even claimed it was me who pushed our hamster to suicide, as it suddenly stopped eating and was eventually found lying lifeless in its wheel.

It is hard to say whether my aversion had a medical basis or not. The greater part of the human population does, after all, slowly lose the ability to break down lactose even when being nursed and is then inherently lactose intolerant. It is only the peoples of North Europe, for whom dairy farming plays an especially central role, who have over time developed the ability to digest lactose as grown-ups, too. My origins lie with these tribes – but maybe it was precisely this which was the secret message behind my bawling: I did not want to be a Northerner with cheese-like, pale skin, thin blonde hair and stupidly blue eyes – and I would much rather have been born further south, where people do not scurry around with cold hands and numb toes for six months of the year.

Of course my mother tried everything she could think of to somehow make milk palatable to me – after all, at the time the white stuff was seen as indispensable for healthy growth. But all temperatures and aromas she employed to dupe me were in vein: I instantly recognized milk in any guise whatsoever.

At some point my providers laid down their lactase arms and finally left me in peace. In view of the fuss I kicked up when faced with just a few drops of milk, my entourage of course did not think to try out other dairy products on me, such as cheese or yoghurt. Not to forget that in those days, margarine was considered as being much better for you than butter and was most certainly regarded as being much more modern. Astonishingly, my parents did not even give me chocolate – although I now have an inkling that this might have been done, at least partially, out of revenge. So I lived happily for about six or seven years without any contact with the white enemy.

I only met with the epiphany shortly after starting school – it came in the guise of Master Ming. I was a strangely greedy child and skipped none of the many illnesses children generally catch – be it measles, mumps or rubella, all viruses felt completely at home in my body. I even wheezed through whooping cough twice. For which reason I often spent weeks in a small village up near the Brünig pass, where my grandparents would dote on me most wonderfully in their little holiday home. One day, as I was just curing myself of the last residues of meningitis, a small excursion led me past a building that reminded me a little of the kitchen at my school. This was due to the facade being covered in diverse metal instruments and large tools, the function of which defeated me. I stopped in front of the house in order to get a closer look at things. Suddenly, the door flung open. A thick cloud of white steam puffed towards me. And there he stood in the midst of it all: A white giant, with a shiny, silver liquid dripping off his armor and onto the floor. I was terrified by the sight of him. Frozen to the spot, I stared at this creature, convinced that he must be God the Almighty himself – or, failing this, the devil (my grandparents where quite religious). The man noticed that he had scared me and quickly disappeared into the interior of his house, in order to return, a short moment later, with a piece of cheese, which he thrust into my little hand with a serious look on his face. I knew cheese – after all, my parents and grandparents ate it on a regular basis – but it would have never crossed my mind to eat the pale stuff instead of the smoked sausage, salami or fish fingers, which, at the time, where my favorite foods. But what was I to do in that instant? After all, this was clearly a gift of the gods. I meekly put the piece in my mouth, convinced that something dramatic was about to happen. And it did. I perceived an intense burn on my mucous membranes and my tongue felt as though it had been paralyzed, like a salty, swollen rag. I think tears rolled down my cheeks at that moment. And the devil continued to stand in front of me, unsmiling.

The fire slowly subsided and the alarm bells in my head grew a little quieter. Then, my nerves began to send new signals to my brain, which seemed very much out of joint with my predicament. Absurdly, they triggered a happy feeling in me and deep satisfaction.

Unfortunately I no longer remember the aromas I perceived that day, and which flavor it was that took my heart by storm. But I can still recreate in my mind the joyful thrill that gripped me as a door to a new world was suddenly flung open and I stepped through it, for that was exactly how the moment felt to me. I had had a similar experience a short while ago in my father's library – when for the first time I pulled an entirely unknown book from the bookshelf and understood what the letters lined up there in front of me meant. It was the miracle of reading. And this, now, was the miracle of milk. When it finally happened, the devil took the white cap off his hair and became human – I think he even smiled for a brief second.

Mr. Ming, as the master cheese maker was called (in that area, everyone was called Gasser, Vogler or Ming), was not a man of many words – in fact, I am not sure he ever said anything to me. But whenever I turned up at his dairy over the next few days, he gave me a different piece to try – and a cup of milk or whey to go with it, which I poured down my childhood throat like precious nectar, in tiny little sips.

On returning to the city after three months in the mountains I was a different person – a milk-person like all my ancestors, with cheesy skin and thin blonde hair.

SALTED ANCHOVIES

Her clothes were much too thick for the midsummer weather. Especially as other young women lounged about the restaurant terraces on the port of La Cotinière with a beach towel draped around their hips, dressed in bikinis or light T-shirts. By contrast, her thin body was clad in heavy jeans and a brown-grey wool pullover. Yet she did not seem to be sweating, which might have been thanks to the careful movements with which she slid over to a table a little further away, in the shade of an 'Orangina' parasol and just a few meters from where I was sitting, cadavers of sucked-out crabs, oysters and whelks drifting through a sea of molten ice in front of me.

Without asking, the waiter placed a carafe with water, a glass of white wine and two plates on the table in front of the young woman. She pushed her thin blonde hair out of her face, sat up straight as a pole, then took half a baguette out of her bag with the uttermost of care, followed by a small tin of anchovies, and placed both on the white paper tablecloth as accurately as if she had been decorating the window of a jeweler's shop. She then proceeded to take a knife and, absorbed in calm concentration, cut the bread into exactly twelve slices – and each of these was, without a doubt, precisely 12 millimeters thick. She then placed the slices on the plates in front of her in flower shapes, before opening the tin containing the little fish, with a decisive, short jolt of her index finger – I could hear the gas escape from the can and smell the odor of the fermented anchovies: slightly bubbly, cheesy-salty, fishy-gingerbready. She pulled the metal strip off the tin completely, picking twelve filets out of the oil with her fingers and arranging them on the cuts of bread in a circle. She then dripped the remaining oil onto the bread – I tried to count the drops, but the Gros Plant du Pays Nantais had somewhat clouded my vision. I did however then notice all of the cats that had gathered around her table, trying to count them, but did not quite managing to, as the animals kept moving – but I am certain there were twelve of them.

The young woman looked at her bread-anchovy artwork for several minutes. Then she took the plates and placed them, without looking down, on the floor on both sides of the white plastic chair she was sitting on. The cats ran up quickly and lined up around the plates in such a way that their bodies formed two furry, silky-shiny flowers around the blonde girl's feet. Each took a fish between their teeth, pulled it into their muzzle with little jerking movements, and then licked the spicy oil off the top of the bread. As if by command, the cats then all disengaged from the flower formation at the same instant and disappeared in all directions.

The young woman put the plates back on the table – the anchovies had disappeared and the surfaces of the bread glistened with the animal's spittle, yet the slices lay on the plates in exactly the same position as before. Now she brought the glass of white wine to her lips for the first time and carefully took a sip. She closed her eyes, picked a slice of bread up from one of the plates and pushed it between her lips. I could hear her mouth draw the moisture from the surface with a small sucking noise, the crust burst between her teeth with a little crackle – and I thought I could feel a waft of salt drifting over to me from her; it was as though she wanted to tell me something with it. Having eaten the slice of bread she opened her eyes and suddenly turned her gaze towards me. It seemed to me her pupils were slightly elongated, her irises a watery light grey. Then she took another sip of wine, closed her eyes once more and brought another slice of bread to her mouth. When she then turned her gaze towards me once more, almost a little inquisitively, the color of her eyes seemed emerald green to me, the next time they looked golden-yellow, dark brown, icy blue, ochre, steel grey, sand colored, greyish-brown, mother of pearl, brown-red, honey-yellow and finally oyster-green.

I ordered another glass of Gros Plant from the waiter and hoped it would give me the courage to talk to the young woman. I quickly went to the bathroom for a minute to splash some cold water in my face and rinse out my mouth. When I returned to the terrace the young woman had disappeared and her table had been cleared. I walked over to the waiter, pointing to the 'Orangina' parasol: "La fille qui était assise là ..." – "Quelle fille" he asked, then drawing up his brows suggestively: "Ah, Monsieur cherche une fille!" I paid hastily. As I left the terrace I walked past her table. I thought I could make out some traces of oil on the otherwise spotless paper table cloth – but most notably, the table bore a small brass plate embossed with the number '12' in black writing. Of course I looked for the young woman at the port of La Cotinière – but to be honest I was a bit scared of actually finding her.

A few days later, back in Zurich, I tried to tempt the neighbor's cat with an anchovy sandwich. She sniffed at it curiously, then turned away bored and started to scratch herself behind the ears with her paws.

Schweineschnörli
als Sülzli
Gebacken

Schweinsohren

Milchpulver Mil

Milchhaut.

Milchglace

Mangold
ge eist

Mangoldblatt
in Gelatine o. Milch.
als Gemüse

No Title

Stefan Wiesner

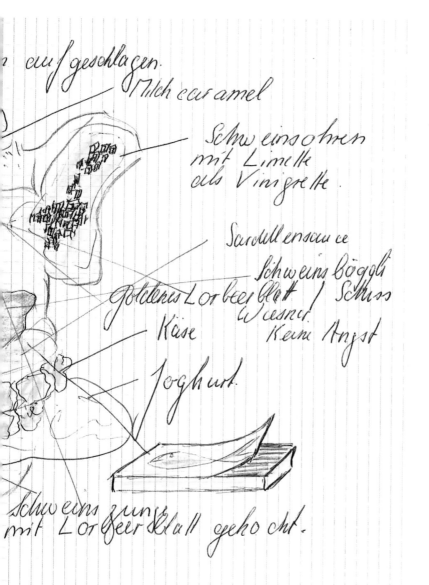

auf geschlagen.

Milch caramel

Schweinsohren
mit Limette
als Vinigrette.

Sardellensauce

Schweins Böggli

goldenes Lorbeerblatt / Schuss
Wiesner

Käse   Kein Angst

Joghurt.

Schweinszunge
mit Lorbeerblatt gekocht.

Tongue Cooked with Bay Leaves

1	pig's tongue
8	fresh bay leaves
1 liter	full fat milk

Bring the milk with the pig's tongue and bay leaves to boiling point and allow it to simmer for 20 minutes.

Pig's Cheeks with Anchovy Sauce

Pig's Cheeks

2	pig's cheeks
500 ml	red wine
	oil for frying

Wash well and trim the cheeks. Sear them in a little oil. Then place them in the red wine and bring to the boil. Allow to simmer for 20 minutes.

Anchovy Sauce

1	tin of anchovies (do not throw the tin away)
	cream or milk as you see fit
	salt, pepper, sugar

Put the anchovies in a mortar or small mixer. Gradually add some milk or cream as you see fit. Grind until you have a creamy consistency. Season. Use the anchovy tin to serve.

Pig's Snout

1	pig's head (halved)
	salt
4	bay leaves
	water

Wash the pigs's head well and if necessary remove remaining whiskers with a Bunsen burner.
Place the head in a sufficiently large pan. Add the seasoning and fill the pan with cold water until the head is 15 cm beneath the water

level. Now bring the water to boiling point and boil gently until the meat is tender (use a meat fork to test).
Drain. Reheat the broth and boil until reduced by half.
Season with salt.
Place the head in a baking tray and add the reduced broth.
Cool until it has jellified.

Pig's Brains

| 1 | whole pig's brain (fresh from the day's slaughter) |
| | water |

Remove the veins from the brain and then wash it. Blanch briefly in boiling water.
Then beat with a whisk.

Pig's Ears

| 2 | pig's ears |

Wash the pork ears and remove remaining whiskers with a Bunsen burner.
Boil for approx. 90 minutes until really tender and then cut into thin slices or strips. Then cool in the fridge for at least 2 hours. Fry in hot oil (180–200°C). Ideally the ears should pop like popcorn.
Dry on kitchen roll and season with a pinch of salt.

Pig's Tongue in a Lime Vinaigrette

Vinaigrette

100 ml	rape seed oil
20 ml	olive oil
40 ml	white Balsamic vinegar
1	lime
40 gr	onion
	Salt, pepper, sugar

Finely chop the onions. Grate the lime peel and squeeze out the juice. Combine the rape seed oil, olive oil, Balsamic vinegar, lime peel and juice in a bowl.

Stir well and season with salt, pepper and sugar.

Now peel the pig's tongue (ideally when still warm). Cut into approx. 5 mm wide slices, then into 5 mm strips, and finally into 5 mm cubes. Mix with the vinaigrette and add more seasoning.

CHARD

200 ml   milk
3 sheets gelatin
          Salt, pepper, 1 pinch of sugar

Pour the milk into a sufficiently large pan. Heat gently, but do not boil.
Soak the gelatin in cold water.
Separate the chard leaves carefully from the stalk but do not throw them away.
Season the milk, add the soaked gelatin and stir until completely dissolved.
Wash the chard leaves and dry well with kitchen roll. Using tweezers or pliers, now drag them carefully through the hot milk. If necessary, repeat the process. Plate up immediately.

Stalks

500 ml very cold water
400 gr ice or dry ice (100 gr) or even better liquid nitrogen
        (200–300 ml, no water)

Wash the chard stalks. At a slight angle cut them into very thin slices.
Blend the water and ice or dry ice.
Add the stalks and leave them there for 2 to 4 minutes, stirring occasionally.
Remove the stalks, drain briefly and serve. Season lightly with salt.
If using nitrogen: Add the stalks to the nitrogen for 2 to 3 seconds, then remove and serve.

FROZEN COW'S MILK

1 Liter cow's milk (3.5 %)
140 ml   full cream
22 gr   milk powder

40 gr   dextrose
215 gr   glucose
65 gr   granulated sugar

Put all the ingredients in a suitable pan and heat to 92 degrees, stirring continuously.

Cool in the fridge to avoid crystals forming when "shaving". Put in a Pacojet container and freeze. "Shave" into portions. Alternatively freeze in an ice machine for 8 to 15 minutes.

CARAMELIZED MILK

1 liter   UHT milk, 3.5 %
500 gr   sugar
6   barrique wood cubes à 2.5 × 2.5 cm
5 gr   Fleur de sel

Apart from the salt, put all the ingredients in a suitable pan.
Bring to the boil and reduce the milk until the consistency is thick.
Remove the wood cubes. Mix well to produce a homogeneous mass.
While still warm, add the salt.
If so desired put into preserving jars and sterilize in steam at 100 degrees for 10 minutes.

BAKED MILK SKIN

500 ml full-cream milk

Put the milk in a pan with as large a surface area as possible.
Slowly heat to approx. 70 to 80 degrees. Remove from the heat and allow to cool.
Wait until a skin forms. Using tweezers and a small brush carefully separate the skin from the milk and place it on a silicone mat. Repeat the process several times.
Heat the oven to 160 degrees and set the fan assistance to half power. Bake the skin for approx. 5 to 10 minutes.
Then allow to cool briefly until the skin is crispy.

Roasted Milk Powder

50 gr   milk powder

On a medium heat gently roast the milk powder in a coated Teflon pan. When roasted to the desired level put on a cold tray and allow to cool.

Yoghurt Espuma with a Hint of Whey Cheese

100 gr   natural yoghurt
40 gr   full cream
8 gr   sugar
3 gr   whey cheese
1 sheet gelatin

Soak the gelatin in cold water.
Put the yoghurt, full cream, sugar, and whey cheese in a bowl and on a warm bain-marie heat to approx. 45 degrees. Add the gelatin and stir until dissolved. Pass through a fine sieve. Put in an iSi bottle, attach a gas cartridge and cool for 2 hours. Dispense as required.

Pig's Head/Chard/Milk/Bay Leaf/
Lime/Anchovies

Marius Keller, dilettantin produktionsbüro

For two people

PIG'S CHEEK

2 loosened pig's cheeks, 1 bay leaf, one chili pepper, 1 clove of garlic, 1 sprig of thyme, 1 sprig of rosemary, 2 tablespoons of olive oil

Prepare the pig's cheeks and place in a vacuum pouch with all the herbs, seasoning and the olive oil, sealing the vacuum afterwards. Cook for 24 hours at 65 degrees using a sous-vide method.

PIG'S HEAD GRAVY

1 pig's head, 80 g each of diced celery, onion, apple, mushrooms, leek and carrots, 1 l red wine, 1 clove of garlic, 1 chili pepper, 20 g ginger, 2 sticks of lemongrass, 2 tbsp. tomato puree, 2 l veal stock, salt, pepper, 1 sprig of bay leaf, 1 tbsp. coriander seed, 1 tbsp. cumin seed, 50 ml Ketjap Manis, 20 ml Ponzu

Roast the pig's head in the oven at 230° C until golden brown. Brown the vegetables, ginger and garlic with a little rapeseed oil in the roasting pan and add tomato puree and seasonings. Deglaze with a little red wine and then reduce down further. Repeat this process three times. Add stock, Ketjap Manis and Ponzu. Add lemongrass, chili, bay leaf and salt. Allow to simmer carefully for approx. 3 hours. Strain the sauce and reduce down to desired consistency. Season with salt to taste.

PIG'S EAR STRAW

2 pig's ears, 1 bay leaf, 1 tbsp. olive oil, 1 tbsp. Ponzu

Vacuum-seal ears with oil and bay leaf and cook using sous-vide method for 72 hours at 65 degrees. Slice the tips of the ears into fine strips, fry until crisp and brown with the Ponzu sauce in a frying pan.

PIG'S EAR CHIPS

Cut the cartilage out of the pig's ear once it has been cooked sous-vide, salt the skin and crisp between parchment paper under a heavy pan on an induction plate.

CHARD KIMCHI

1 piece of chard, 60 g ginger, 1 chili pepper, 1 clove of garlic,
1 young leek, 1 piece of lemongrass, 2 anchovies, 20 g sugar,
20 g salt, 20 ml lactic acid 80 %, 120 ml water

Combine salt, sugar, lactic acid and water. Finely chop all other
ingredients and add to the mixture. Vacuum-seal with the washed
chard and allow to ferment for 72 hours.

ANCHOVY AND LIME MILK

200 ml milk, 8 anchovies, 2 pinches each of Iota Texturas and
Kappa Texturas, zest of half a lime

Heat milk, lime zest and anchovies and allow to steep for one hour.
Strain and combine with Iota and Kappa, heat to 80 degrees, place
in a mold and allow to cool.

Gratin of Green Tagliolini
with Braised Pig's Cheeks, Lime and Bay

Daniel de La Falaise

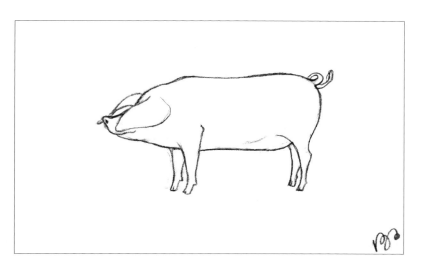

LIST OF INGREDIENTS:

Pig's head
Bay leaves
Lime
Milk
Anchovy
Chard

GRATIN OF GREEN TAGLIOLINI WITH BRAISED PIG'S CHEEKS, LIME AND BAY

The primary concern with ingredients relates to their provenance. Vegetables, fruit and herbs are best sourced from producers who farm by natural method, which is to say in live soil, irrigated with clean water. Agriculture that rejects artificial fertilizers and chemical pesticides and fungicides in favor of traditional practices that maintain and enhance ecological harmony offers far better flavor. In cookery, a deft hand in conveying vitality from field to plate is the objective.

So let us ponder awhile upon the ingredients listed above. What have we got and what can we do with it?

Chard is the new kale, soon to be eclipsed by ramps, today's hipster vegetable of choice. Shallow steamed with ginger, or rapidly blanched in boiling water, and then seasoned with fleur de sel, the tender shoots of chard are indeed delectable.

Anchovies packed in salt offer the best eating, and are preferable to those sold in oil or brine, where rancidity often lurks. Anchovies marked for salting are prize specimens; they are gutted and air dried to purge excess liquid, then packed in salt. To prepare them – they are whole and still wearing their heads – rinse them thoroughly under cold water. Then lift the fillets off the bone; they will surrender easily. Anchovy has an affinity for parsley and garlic. Think of anchovy as a secret weapon of umami.

Milk contains everything we need. My son is seven months old and he has more than doubled in weight since birth by eating nothing else. The key factor is the diet of the mother: spring pasture makes for fine sheep, goat and cow's milk. Milk from a single herd that grazes and ruminates as one is the ideal.

Limes enjoy a rousing aura with their tart juice and fragrant zest. With most citrus fruit, taste is to be found in the zest, and flavor in the freshly squeezed juice. Think of a clementine, an orange or a grapefruit. For limes the inverse is true.

Fresh bay leaves are an essential seasoning as their flavor is graciously ephemeral. Once dried they bridge from herb to spice – devolving to a bitter taste. Fragrant green turns to bitter gray once the chlorophyll of the leaves oxidizes when exposed to heat. So the key is an abundance of fresh bay leaves, branches of them, and ideally in flower. Replace bay regularly throughout the cooking of a dish, so as to harness optimal flavor.

The prize morsels of a pig's head are the cheeks and the tender eye sockets. You can of course use the whole head from ear to nose to make brawn, which you might serve sprightly seasoned with gherkins, parsley, raw onion and mustard. Such a salade de museau – snozzle salad – makes a rustic delicacy befitting a summer lunch. You can breadcrumb and fry the brains for breakfast. Or, as is the habit of my octogenarian neighbors, Roger and Huguette Vern, you can make blood sausage. Add to a cauldron and set upon a gentle flame to simmer, a pig's head wearing its tongue and ears with the lungs attached by the esophagus. This meat once cooked, picked and seasoned with the blood harvested from the animal's jugular at slaughter is then encased in short lengths of thoroughly cleansed lower intestine, before being carefully poached to make blood sausage. This all makes sense to the wise Verns who live the way they grew up: timelessly and autonomously. Each year they fatten a pig and come January kill it, taking the time to process every last morsel of the animal that has been their companion into larder staples for the year ahead.

Chances are that for most of us cauldrons are few and far between, so a use of a pig's head better tailored to modern life might lead us towards improvising a *dish* that tips its hat at an Italian classic: a gratin of green tagliolini with braised pig's cheeks, seasoned with lime and bay.

Dishes are one pot wonders with texture. Whereas a stew is liquid, a dish is unctuous. This is achieved with recourse to one of the *roux* based "mother sauces" of classic French cookery. The key to assembling a standout dish lies is conjuring fragrant broth-based veloutées. These are vastly more flavorsome and more nutritious than milk-based béchamel. Use lobster broth for fish pie, a dashi broth for universal umami, pork broth for a gratin of pig's cheeks, and so on.

We will need to add to our prescribed ingredient list: parsley, an onion, milled flour, mace, a little butter, egg yolks, cream and some grated parmesan. You can make the *tagliolini verde* yourself if you have spinach, eggs, flour and the elbow grease required – alternatively you will do well to purchase some ready made online from Cipriani.

Find a good butcher, the sort that might select his beasts alive and have them slaughtered to order. Ask him for a naturally farmed pig's head. Have him lift the cheeks and tender eye sockets from the head, and saw up the skull for you into fist sized bones with which you will make a broth.

Let the skull bones stand awhile in cold water to purge them of blood. Add them to a stockpot, cover with mineral water and bring this up to a gentle simmer, skimming away any impurities that rise to the water's surface. Then add bay leaves, a twist of lime zest (free of all pith), and parsley stalks. Patiently simmer the broth to taste. Strain it through muslin and set it aside.

Set a low oven and take a cocotte large enough to hold the meats. The plan is to braise the pig cheeks and eye sockets slowly in a shallow covering of broth so as to render them so tender that the meat will pull with the hand. Keep an eye on it as you go, adding a ladle of broth when and as necessary. Three hours at 150° C should suffice. Once cooked pull the meat into strips and reserve.

To make the skull broth velouté, think in terms of the following proportions: ten parts liquid, to one-part flour, one-part butter, plus herbs and spices. Bay and mace will be our herbs and spices in this instance, along with a seasoning of anchovy fillet and lime zest, all fused together with the help of a finely chopped onion.

Line a big pan with a thin coating of olive oil and a knob of butter; add anchovy, bay, and lime zest to infuse the fats. Then add a finely diced onion, to gently fry without coloring. Then all whilst maintaining a constant and moderate heat, steadily stir in the flour; amalgamating onion, seasonings and flour into one consistent mass. Raise the heat, and begin to add the broth; patiently and methodically whisking as you go. The objective is to progressively stretch the roux with the added liquid, *not* to have lumps of flour floating in broth. Once your velouté is successfully amalgamated, reduce the heat to very low indeed. Gently simmer it for a good half hour to cook out the flour, whisking often to make sure that no lumps form, nor anything stick to the pan's bottom. Change the bay leaves regularly, before they discolor and oxidize. Once the depth of flavor and desired unctuous consistency of your velouté is attained, strain it through a fine sieve and reserve. To finish the sauce, you will need to energetically incorporate egg yolks and whipping cream.

To assemble the dish:
Reheat the sauce, adding the double cream. Add the pulled meat, season with grated lime zest, and mace. Preheat the grill. Boil the tagliolini in abundant salted water for two minutes, then drain and add to the sauce. Sauté the pan with a flick of the wrist to combine the ingredients, rotating the top to the bottom and vice versa. Transfer to a gratin dish, grate a light covering of parmesan upon it and grill to just crisp.

Serve immediately accompanied by a chilled glass of unpasteurized milk.

Velouté Sauce

500 ml	broth
50 g	flour
50 g	butter
	The zest of a lime
	A branch of bay leaves
	A salted anchovy fillet
3	egg yolks

3 tablespoons of whipping cream
2 tablespoons of double cream

Pasta

Tagliolini verde (250g Cipriani)

Pig's Head

Skull sawn into fist sized bones for broth
Cheeks and eye sockets (to braise in a shallow covering of broth).

Garnish and Accompaniment

Shallow steamed tender shoots of chard (using a ladle of skull broth and a knob of ginger).
A chilled glass of fresh unpasteurized milk

Recipe Plan

Sonja Alhäuser

Fig. 1: Recipe plan pig's head, 2016, pencil, crayon, watercolor and acrylic on paper, 20 × 20 cm

Fig. 2: Chard pesto, 2016, pencil, crayon, watercolor and acrylic on paper, 20 × 20 cm

Fig. 3: Pig's Head I, 2016, pencil, crayon, watercolor and acrylic on paper, 20 × 20 cm

Fig. 4: Pig's head II, 2016, pencil, crayon, watercolor and acrylic on paper, 20 × 20 cm

Pig's Cheeks
with Crisped Ears, Chard and Bay Leaf

Sonja Frühsammer and Peter Frühsammer

Serves 4 people

Cheeks

600 g	pig's cheek
1	carrot
1	piece of celery
3	onions
1 tbsp.	tomato puree
0.2 l	white wine
	Rosemary, thyme
1–2	cloves of young garlic
	Veal stock

Clean the pig's cheek and gently brown in olive oil until it has an appealing color.

Dice carrots, celery and onions into walnut-sized cubes and add to the meat. As soon as the vegetables are also browned add the tomato puree, sauté again and then deglaze with white wine. Reduce the white wine down until it has almost all gone. Fill with veal stock – or water will also do – so that it is almost covered and stew in the oven until soft, stirring occasionally. Depending on the quality of the meat, this will take between 2 and 4 hours.

As soon as the cheeks are soft, remove them from the stock, pass the stock through a cloth strainer and taste – reducing further if need be.

Pig's Ears

2 pig's ears

Salt down the ears for 2 hours then rinse and allow to simmer carefully in lightly salted water until soft.

Then remove, dry, cut into fine strips, roll in corn flour and bake until crisp at 160°C.

Chard

1 l	Bärenmarke milk or similar with at least 3.8% fat
3	fresh bay leaves
3	shallots
2	limes
	Brown sugar
	Olive oil
1 to 2	chards

       Salt and pepper
1 to 2   top-quality anchovies, if preferred also sliced into the
          chard salad

Bring the Bärenmarke milk to the boil with the bay leaves and reduce down to half.

Separate the leaves from the stems for the chard, remove the skin from the stems – similarly to rhubarb – and slice into sticks.

Cut the leaves in julienne form and marinate like a salad with a dressing made from lime juice, salt, brown sugar and olive oil.

Dice the shallots into fine cubes and sauté in butter, add the chard stems and steam with the bay leaf milk just enough so that the chard is simultaneously reduced down as much as the bay leaf milk.

To serve:

Plate up the cheek with the sauce, placing the crisped ears on top. Add the chard, at least one top-quality anchovy, the salad and the remaining milk frothed up.

Dish(es) Using Pig's Head, Milk, Chard, Anchovies, Lime and Bay Leaves

Dieter Froelich

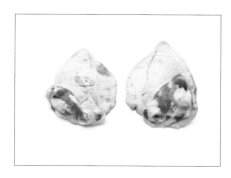

Stuffed Pig's Ear with Chard and Cheese Dumplings Cooked in Bay Leaf Stock with Anchovy Sauce

Preliminary Thoughts

An entire pig's head

Just as in days gone by when slaughterhouses were located outside of the city in peripheral areas in order to keep the slaughter of animals out of the consciousness of consumers, those parts of the animal that remind us that it was a living being have gradually disappeared from our plates. It is true that offal has recently enjoyed something of a renaissance in premium gastronomy, but it has virtually disappeared from our day-to-day culinary practice. At most, you might see an animal's head on a spit roast.

As before, the animal's head separated from its body is considered a trophy, a symbol of power. The very life itself seems to be contained within the head hence, more than any other dish, an entire head prepared for the table has an inherently symbolic character: It is reminiscent of archaic sacrificial rituals and of days when the oven was still an altar.

Aside from this circumstance and the difficulty of its procurement, an entire pig's or calf's head would be rather too much for a small family or indeed a single household. Nevertheless using all the parts of an animal for human consumption represents a suitable appreciation of the slaughtered animal. Incidentally, in contrast to the entire head, the individual parts of it can be prepared in broadly different ways. Ears, skin (mask), snout, tongue, cheek, brain, chopped meat and various bits of gristle and bone form the basic ingredients for countless different dishes (due to the considerations already mentioned, the eyes are disregarded).

From a culinary perspective, one might first think of various forms of aspic in relation to the parts of the head. The brain can be poached and thus transformed into croquettes, beignets, omelets or pâtés. The mask is perfect for a ballotine or for slicing into strips and cooking in rolls by way of a homage to Alfred Walterspiel, who introduced this "prized home dish" to premium gastronomy. The tongue can be prepared in a multitude of ways and, thanks to their cohesiveness, the cheeks are not only an indispensable element of raw sausages, but in the last few years have also become something of a trend in the culinary world – albeit generally from the more "fancy" veal. The list could go on at length, but now let's turn to the pig's ear.

STUFFED PIG'S EAR

1	pig's ear per person
	Pig's caul

FOR THE FILLING

4	pig tongues, raw or pickled
500 g	pig's cheek, raw
	Salt
	Pepper
	Vegetable broth or court bouillon
	Butter

The ears are first cleaned, any remaining bristles removed with the knife and the traces of the bristles singed off over an open flame. Then place the ears in a pan, cover with cold water and bring to the boil once. Remove with the skimmer, rinse in cold water and leave in cold water to cool. If required, slice the edges of the ear so they are straight and clean.

For each ear cut a cloth to size so the ear can be rolled up length-ways and bound up in the cloth so that it maintains its form during cooking. Put the rolled ears in a pan and allow to simmer covered with liquid for approximately three hours. The liquid used may be vegetable broth, a light court bouillon or even just saltwater with added vegetables and seasoning. At the end of the cooking time, take the rolled ears out of the broth, allow to cool and remove from the cloth. Then cover the ears with cloth and place in the fridge for approximately 3/4 hour.

Then prepare the filling:
Add the pig tongues to the cooking pot for the ears for approxi-mately one hour. To ensure they do not roll up during cooking, they are laid on top of one another with opposing ends touching (tip to base) and tied together. The cooked tongues are subsequently cooled until lukewarm and the skin removed. Cured tongues are not cooked.

The pig's cheeks are rolled through the finest disks of the meat grinder twice and combined with the finely cubed tongue, the egg, breadcrumbs, salt and pepper to create a forcemeat.

Take the ears from the fridge and fill with the forcemeat, press together firmly and cool once again. Then wrap each ear in a piece of pig's caul, which can then be held together with a toothpick on the underside of the ear. The little packages should then be browned all over in butter with a little liquid added, and finished off in the oven on a lower heat for approximately one hour. Baste with the liquid every now and again.

Alternatively you can do without the pig's caul and coat the filled ears with breadcrumbs, then baste them with liquid butter and finish them off in the oven. They will need to be basted regularly during this process.

STEAMED CHARD (COLD)

Chard
Olive oil
Salt

Remove the stalks and leaf clusters of the chard (and use elsewhere). Wash the leaves and dry well. Heat a little olive oil in a large pan, add the leaves, add salt and cover with the lid. Once the leaves wilt the lid can be removed for the rest of the cooking process. Use a spatula occasionally to push the chard together and be sure that nothing is burning. Ideally, there should be barely any liquid left with the cooked, wilted leaves. Once cooled they can be spread across a serving platter and drizzled with good-quality olive oil.

CHEESE DUMPLINGS COOKED IN BAY LEAF STOCK

12 liters of full-cream milk
or 1000 g Quark/cream cheese
2 eggs, 12 egg yolks
1 handful of flour
Salt
Bay leaf and laurel berries (dried)
Butter or lard

For the bay leaf stock, 4 medium-sized bay leaves are boiled in 5 liters of saltwater and allowed to steep until the desired level of taste intensity is achieved. Then the bay leaves are removed.

Full-cream milk must be used for the cheese dumplings. It is neither pasteurized nor homogenized and therefore still contains all the microbiological components and properties. Only milk of this quality can be "coagulated", i.e. allowed to become sour. This sour milk separates into whey and protein (casein). An alternative is heating the milk to 30–40°C and adding an acid (acid precipitation). The curdled milk is then pressed through a tight mesh until a non-greasy mass remains that you can knead.

Anyone wanting to avoid the coagulation process can press Quark or cream cheese instead.

The dry, almost crumbly mass (of approx. 400 g) is combined with 2 eggs and 12 yolks, a handful of flour, the zest of one lime and 6 ground laurel berry kernels to form a homogeneous mass.

Using two large tablespoons and occasionally immersing them in hot water, form the mass into dumplings and simmer these in the bay leaf stock. Here the water should not be allowed to boil fully; rather the surface of the water should ripple gently – it should "smile". In order to check the consistency and identify the cooking time, it is a good idea to prepare a test dumpling. A guideline for the cooking time is 10 minutes.

Once removed from the broth, drained and thus dried a little, the dumplings are browned in butter or lard.

This is also a way of reheating chilled dumplings prepared in advance.

ANCHOVY SAUCE

Anchovies preserved in oil
Butter
Flour

A decent quantity of oil-preserved anchovies are dried a little using kitchen towel and chopped up finely, then combined with room-temperature butter and passed through a fine sieve.

Using approximately the same (volume) quantities of butter and flour, create a pale roux, then deglaze with lukewarm water and allow the whole thing to cook through whilst stirring.

Shortly before serving add the anchovy butter to the cooled roux and heat the mixture, stirring continuously. A dash of lime juice adds the necessary acidity.

Pig's Head in Chard/Sautéed Chard Stems/ Chard Sponge/Bay Leaf Milk Froth/Candied Lime Zest/Anchovy and Lime Puree

Rebecca Clopath

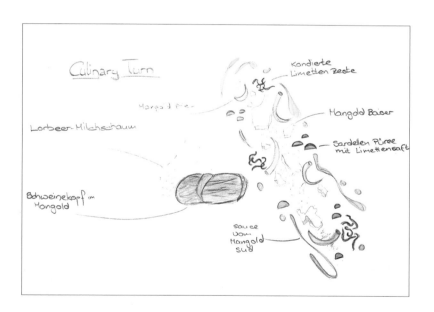

4 persons

PIG'S HEAD IN CHARD

300 g pig's head	by the piece. Cook until soft with 50g onion in lightly salted water, covered (min. 3h). Slice the head into 2 cm-wide strips. Reduce the stock. Put head and onion through the grinder (3.5 disk). Add
100 g whole spelt flour	and
5 g finely chopped or crushed garlic	into the mixture. Season.
9 chard leaves	Wash, remove the lower stem and set aside. Depending on the size of the leaf, cut part of it away and set aside. Distribute the filling onto the leaves and roll up so they are nicely full. Cook in a cream-bouillon broth half-covered with a lid.

SAUTEED CHARD STEMS

Remaining chard stems	Slice into fine strips and briefly toss in the broth before serving. Reduce the broth and serve.

CHARD SPONGE

Remaining pieces of chard leaf	Finely chop and dry in the oven at 120° C. Finely beat
30 g egg white	(with sugar if relevant) to form a snow-like mass (retain yolk). Gradually mix with the dried chard. Gradually add
30 g sugar.	Spread approximately 5 cm thick over a baking parchment. Bake for 10 min at 150° C, dry for 1 hour at 100° C. Depending on the thickness, the drying process may take longer. Crumble gently on the plate.

Bay Leaf Milk Froth

400 g milk
4 bay leaves (fresh)

Heat to 58° C. Add
to the milk and allow to steep for 10 minutes. Remove from the milk and froth until small bubbles form. This froth stays on the plate for longer.

Candied Lime Zest

Zest of 1 lime

Peel using a potato peeler and cut into fine strips.
Mix with

10 g sugar

and dry on baking parchment in a warm place.

Anchovy and Lime Puree

1 lime
40 g anchovies

Press juice and combine with

20 g egg yolk

Cook in a bain-marie for 35 minutes at 65° C.
Combine everything together. Season.
Puree finely in a mixer or use the PacoJet.

Discourse

Evolution – Culinary Culture – Cooking Technology

Thomas A. Vilgis

FIRE AND COOKING: THE FIRST EVOLUTIONARY MILESTONES

The history of humankind has always been, in addition to countless wars, a history of culture and scientific progress resulting in new technical possibilities. All people in all periods have had to eat in order to preserve the species. Food was and is a matter of survival.

Before the systematic use of fire, the food supply comprised raw foods such as raw vegetables, roots, berries, fruits, early vegetables, nuts, seeds, as well as birds' eggs and carrion as protein sources, carrion from animals killed by other predators.[1] Indeed, carrion, scavennging was despite aversion of great importance because meat and eggs, has supplied the early man with readily bioavailable nutrition down to the present: proteins and the amino acids they contain have always been essential for muscle development in humans.[2] Some early human species developed enzymes that facilitated alcohol consumption.[3] This expanded the food pallet, since this genetic modification also opened up another nutrition source: fermented, slightly rotten fruits and fermented vegetables. Another source of fermented food was the stomach contents of hunted or carrion animals. During gastrointestinal passage in ruminants, enzymes are present that can also break down cell materials such as cellulose into nutritionally valuable starch fragments and glucose. Pre-digested and hydrolysed proteins (split to fragments and essential aminoacids) also provided nutrients that were too valuable do without.

The human diet was thus clearly defined: Raw and fermented foods. Foods provided by nature that early humans only had to collect and perhaps

---

1 | See e. g. Kaplan, H. et al. (2000): A theory of human life history evolution: diet, intelligence, and longevity, in: *Evolutionary Anthropology: Issues, News, and Reviews*, 9(4), pp. 156–185.

2 | DeVault, T. L./Rhodes Jr, O. E./Shivik, J. A. (2003): Scavenging by vertebrates: behavioral, ecological, and evolutionary perspectives on an important energy transfer pathway in terrestrial ecosystems, in: *Oikos*, 102(2), pp. 225–234.

3 | Carrigan et al.: 2015.

clean off. Food was rare and finding it an essential strategy for "survival of the species". In order to eat and digest raw foods, humans had developed a different head shape, jaw muscles, greater intestinal length and intestinal flora over millions of years. Hard roots had to be chewed to obtain the nutrients they contained, it was only possible to break down and utilize the nutrient structures during longer gastrointestinal passages if ancient humans were equipped with an enzyme status and intestinal flora that were up to the task. A variety of germs, fungi and bacteria also contaminated all food, which was thus anything but "safe". Early humans had to rely on their taste buds. The species-adapted senses of humans and other animals provided the only way to test food for safety, edibility and nutritional value. Early humans obviously succeeded in all of this, since otherwise we would not be here today.

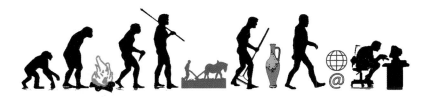

Fig. 1: Evolution (of cooking). From the first humans to hunters and gatherers to bloggers. The control of fire, development of agriculture and livestock farming, controlled fermentation and ultimately globalization and the "invention of the internet", were milestones in culinary culture.

A huge turning point came with the management and control of fire. For the first time in the nutrition of hominides, physico-chemical transformations were feasible. Foods were cooked, grilled and otherwise boiled. Their structure changed, foods were safe for the first time in the history of eating. Germs did not survive the cooking process. Therefore, the use of fire was the beginning of modern food technology and food processing. Control of fire was, in ethnological terms, the transition from "nature" to "culture".

New sources of food became available – what was not always edible raw could now be heated and consumed. Roots were made softer, inedible things edible, toxic substances sometimes toxin-free. Cooked food could be preserved somewhat longer, if only due to the resulting disinfection and reheated largely germ-free if the cooked food was not contaminated with fungal spores. At the same time, the food was also easier to digest. Meat and its proteins were denatured, hard plant cells burst to release micro-nutrients.[4] Macro and micro-nutrients were rendered more readily available; in physiological terms, less energy was required to break down

---

4 | Milton, K. (1999): A hypothesis to explain the role of meat-eating in human evolution, in: *Evolutionary Anthropology Issues News and Reviews* 8(1), pp. 11–21.

and digest the food. The energy balance for the (thermodynamically open) system "human being" improved further with the development of cooking techniques. Physiognomy and physiology showed adaptations.[5] The lower jaw receded somewhat, jaw muscles lost some strength, the intestines adapted to the new situation. The brain grew in response to the constantly increased energy supply due to the better yield.

FIRE, SMOKE AND EMBERS

Control of fire also includes making use of smoke. Smoking and drying foods around the edge of the fire developed rapidly as methods of preservation.[6] Even rapidly perishable goods such as hunted meat could be dried. The resulting dehydration and reduced water activity reduced germ proliferation. It soon became evident how smoking on impacted the shelf life of foodstuffs, in particular highly valuable meat. Meat, which had to be hunted first, was suddenly preservable for a longer period of time. Food intake, and survival, became significantly more secure.

A number of new preparation techniques developed centred around fire. This required development of equipment, skewers, containers, cooking utensils, etc.[7] Cooking by grilling, boiling, in earth ovens, on and with hot stones or steam are among the early techniques that differ but little from the supposedly modern methods in use today, aside from accurate temperature control. Even low-temperature cooking became possible at some point. A leather-lined earthen pit was filled with water and the food to be cooked was placed inside while hot stones from the fire gradually heated the water.[8] "Gentle cooking", as such procedures are now called, is thus thousands of years older than profession now known as nutritional consulting. These examples clearly demonstrate how fire was always bound up with technical progress: cooking utensils, be they made of clay, later metal, or alternatives such as leather, and early hunting tools, were often directly related to the cooking techniques used at the time.

5 | McCully, K. S. (2001): The significance of wheat in the Dakota territory, human evolution, civilization, and degenerative diseases, in: *Perspectives in biology and medicine*, 44(1), pp. 52–61.

6 | Atalay, S./Hastorf, C. A. (2006): Food, meals, and daily activities: Food habitus at Neolithic Çatalhöyük, in: *American Antiquity*, pp. 283–319.

7 | Gauvain, M. (2001): Cultural tools, social interaction and the development of thinking, in: *Human development*, 44(2–3), pp. 126–143.

8 | http://www.rheinland-saga.de/RLS-Steinzeit-LebensraumGoennersdorf.html, last accessed February 24, 2017.

EARLY COOKING AND FERMENTING: EVOLUTION OF THE FIVE BASIC TASTE QUALITIES

These consideratons imply also the function and meaning of the sense of taste.[9] The evolutionary process did not give humans this sense so that food critics sitting in starred restaurants could write their doggerel, but rather each of the five tastes – sweet, sour, salty, bitter and umami – is deeply rooted in the evolutionary development of humans.[10] The primary tastes reflect a profound relationship between the function of the cells comprising all biomaterials and the function of the physiology of biomaterials. Molecular cell function and taste have a common evolutionary denominator. Of course seasoning food with sweetness, salts or glutamate was not around early in the history of mankind, but the sense of taste did provide orientation, particularly in the case of the two extremes bitter and sweet, on which basis poisonous and edible are quickly differentiated. There has never been a food that is both sweet and poisonous (although imprecise and populistic sources have tried to characterize sugar in this way). Every food with a slightly salty taste, rock salt, a mixed crystal of the cations sodium, calcium, magnesium and the corresponding anions (mainly chloride), and many (vegetable) products from salted water, have always been good for the mineral balance in the diets of humans and other animals.

Taste quality	Cell function	Evolutionary function	Trigger
Sweet	Glucose, energy	Non-toxic	Glucose, fructose, glycosides
Sour	Regulating pH, Information transfer	Salivation, safe food (pH <5)	Protons
Salty	Switching function with multivalent ions	Physiological mineral balance	Sodium, calcium; magnesium
Bitter	Antioxidants, cell damage	Warning against poison	Phenols, polyphenols
Umami	Building blocks for muscle cells	Targeted protein intake	Glutamic acid, aspartic acid Nucleotides

Cooking and fermenting led us to perceive of the taste umami – tasty, savoury.[11] This taste is triggered by "glutamate", glutamic acid, and rein-

---

9 | See for different perspectives Le Magnen, J. (1985): *Hunger* (vol. 3), Cambridge and Hladik/Pasquet/Simmen: 2002.

10 | Mather: 2006.

11 | Kurihara: 2015.

forced by two nucleotides, the two phosphates inosine monophosphate and guanosine monophosphate, which are derived from cytometabolism. In fact, the amino acid glutamic acid is a very prevalent component of every protein. The umami taste is therefore geared to amino acids, i.e. essential amino acids, and thus guided humans to protein-rich foods. This was the only way our muscles and brain could develop as they have done. The development and character of this primary taste was crucial to human development.

It was quite natural that glutamic acid was selected as the main actuator in the umami sense: It is the most frequently occurring amino acid of all, is not essential, is in part enzymatically transformed in the metabolic process into another amino acid, glutamine, it is heat stable, does not undergo any Maillard reactions and is therefore always available, even in grilled meat, and last but not least does not react chemically to produce "harmful" products. Every time something is stewed or roasted, and every time bread is baked, the taste experience centres around glutamic acid, and thus umami. What was eaten during the evolution of Homo sapiens was controlled by umami and the other tastes. Umami, sweet, slightly salty and slightly acidic were the guarantors of human-oriented nutrition. These five tastes allowed humans to become what they are: an omnivorous species able to find food in different living situations and environments and under different climatic limitations. This is exactly what evolution theory teaches us.

COOKING AS A CULTURAL ACHIEVEMENT

Human culture begins with the control of fire and conscious exploitation of it. Fire is also the decisive key to what separates humans from other animals – a fact that is often forgotten. No other species on earth is capable of using fire consciously and with foresight, for example with the intention to cook food. Studies have shown repeatedly that certain species of apes use tools and prefer precooked food to raw food, but no other species has mastered fire. It may sound trivial from our current perspective, but fire from whatever source, be it flames or burning rods in nuclear power plants, is still the line that separates humans from other animals, nature from culture. These ideas led the ethnologist and cultural scientist Claude Lévi-Strauss to the concept of the culinary triangle on which he founded culinary structuralism.[12] They defined the aspects raw, cooked and rotten or fermented to describe the transitions between nature and culture on one axis, and from unchanged to changed on the other. Cooking is thus also assessed as a cultural achievement (a point denied relevance in many discussions).

---

12 | Lévi-Strauss/Weightman: 1994.

THE CULINARY TRIANGLE:
CULTURAL AND PHYSICAL STRUCTURALISM

Raw is thus defined as the original structure, for example the crisp apples just fallen from the tree, fresh carrots covered with soil, living animals or René Redzepi's seafood, still alive when served. Each further process, even washing the carrots, salad or apple is already, according to the definition in the cultural sciences, a "cultural act" leading away from the original "raw" state. If "the raw" is left to nature, without cultural interventions, it rots. Cultural measures, by "cooks", make it possible to control the rotting process, which is then known as fermentation. Cooking and fermenting are therefore to be honoured as basic cultural acts dedicated to the continuation of life.

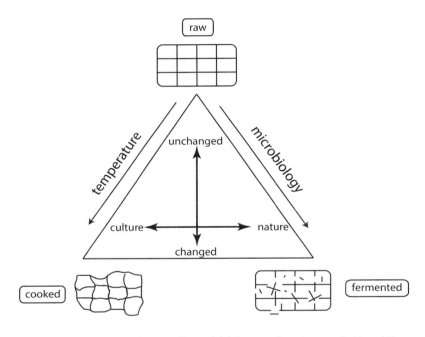

Fig. 2: The culinary triangle according to Lévi-Strauss (inner) expanded by adding the symbolism of the molecular processes (outer). The human transition from nature to culture was only possible through control of temperature and micro-organisms (Vilgis 2013b).

The abstract considerations on which the culinary triangle is based can be scientifically justified by taking into account the changes in molecular structures brought about by specific process techniques.[13] The techniques of fermenting and cooking involve different processes. Cooking is usually done by changing typical "thermodynamic" parameters such as temperature, pressure, or volume. At the fire, or on the stove or grill, it is always

---

13 | Vilgis: 2013a/2013b.

the temperature that is changed. The first changes are the modifications in protein structures, altering the texture of the food. The focus is on physical changes in the food items. Fermentation always involves the participation of micro-organisms, e. g. lactic acid bacteria, yeasts, etc. This initially facilitates enzymatic chemical reactions. The changes at the molecular level are of a different nature. Thus the natural science interpetation of the culinary triangle yields a strong link between cultural and natural sciences.[14]

In fact, down to this very day these cornerstones of food preparation have remained unchanged. Despite modern techniques and technological progress, the methods of preparation learned and defined in the early years of evolution, the basis of food consumption remains the triangle formed by the basic states raw, cooked and fermented. The molecular structure of foods stipulates these possibilities and allows for no others. So it is not surprising that all food transformations, whether through cooking, fermenting or methods that takes a different initial approach, can all be located within the culinary triangle. In the end, all that counts is the condition of the food, which can only be defined at the level of its molecular parameters.

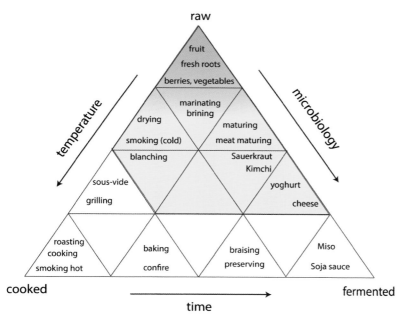

Fig. 3: The culinary triangle contains all of the preparation techniques so far developed by humans. A distinction between "old" techniques and "modern techniques" is not absolutely necessary from a "structuralist" and natural scientific point of view. Pseudo-raw (shaded area) reflects cultural acts such as washing or cleaning, whereby the molecular structures do not change significantly, but ethnologists categorize these acts also under "cooking" (Vilgis and Tzschirner 2014).

---

14 | Vilgis: 2013a.

Thus both old and new techniques are found within the culinary triangle. These molecular aspects, together with the knowledge of the molecular processes, result in many new perspectives. It is obvious, for example, that long cooking as in stewing or fondue will produce a molecular structure in the end that is thermodynamically similar to what is produced by complete fermenting, for example as in miso pastes or soya, fish, or oyster sauces: a predominantly "hydrolysed" status. Proteins and other food ingredients are disassembled for the most part. This can be tasted on the tongue: The state "fermented/hydrolysed" in the culinary triangle is covered for the most part by the primary taste umami. The shows once again how and why cooking and fermentation techniques have continued to evolve until today, be it in the first leavened recipes, lactic acid fermentation or Greco-Roman garum.[15]

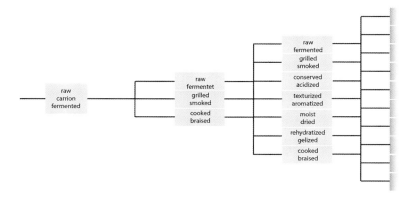

Fig. 4: New techniques do not alter the basic principles of cooking. They simply establish finer subdivisions in the physico-chemical parameters and facilitate a finer, more precise taste perception – as well as enhanced complexity of the dishes served (Vilgis 2013a).

Another aspect is of great importance: The culinary triangle does not reveal per se whether a cooking technology is "old" or "new". In fact, the old cultural techniques remain the foundations of modern cuisine. All that is "new" are the execution and technical possibilities. The diversity of nuances, textures and flavours is growing, and this variety allows us to create dishes with extreme complexities of taste. Nevertheless, the old techniques remain basically unchanged, since this basis is controlled by molecular processes. Even this aspect of the history of culinary culture is reflected in the scientific view of the culinary triangle.

15 | Corcoran, T. H. (1963): Roman fish sauces, in: *The Classical Journal*, 58(5), pp. 204-210.

All Roads Lead to Umami

These different cultural and processing techniques can be described clearly and understandably by the basic molecular changes (here the example of proteins) in the culinary triangle.

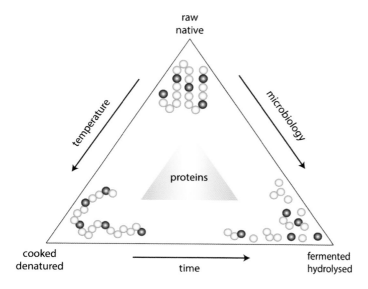

Fig. 5: The culinary triangle as a "triangle of states" for proteins during the cooking and fermentation process. The hydrolysed state is the result of the cooking process and of the fermentation. Long cooked foods thus have modified taste "umami" and please with "kokumi" as well as the fermented state.

In the primary raw state, the molecular components of food are present in their native form, proteins, chain molecules of individual amino acids (shown as balls) are "folded", and retain their original structure in most cases. The "raw" becomes the "cooked" by raising the temperature. The "thermal energy" unfolds the proteins, which lose their structural form, altering the texture of the food. When foods are fermented by the agency of micro-organisms that release enzymes, the proteins are gradually broken down into pieces, until individual peptides and amino acids are released, including glutamic acid (dark blue). This results in "umami", whereas some small fragments of two or three amino acids account for "kokumi" (mouth-filling sensation) if they are still carrying a glutamic acid. Fermented sauces, fish sauces, soy sauces (as well as Maggi-type seasonings) are therefore always umami, savoury and mouth-filling. Long cooking, as in gravy or sauce stocks results, after denaturing, in protein fragments and free glutamic acids, and therefore also in umami and kokumi. This is also the case in cooking stocks, broths, stews. Long cooking splits proteins, producing umami, savoury and mouth-filling sensations, as in fermented sauces and miso pastes. Different approaches, different cultures, one goal: the depth of good taste.

HERE AND NOW

Things changed when globalization led to a general dissemination of foodstuffs. Regional borders, seasonal limitations, harvest failures are problems of the past for the (Western) world. Above all the internet and social media such as Facebook allow for immediate dissemination of information in words and pictures for the first time in the history of mankind. The Spanish cuisine revolution triggered by Ferran Adrià (2014), the avant-garde cuisine, or the term "molecular cuisine" used by journalists showed this clearly: Videos and links have made it possible for anyone to call himself or herself a "molecular cook". The thickeners and gelling agents can be ordered using the same medium, with instructions in words, images and videos on the internet it was not surprising that even non-cooks mutated temporarily to "molecular cooks". The taste was mostly secondary, the effect was what counted. It has to be noticed: copying has never before been practised in such volume and so rapidly as in these times of Facebook, Instagram and blogs.

Cooking trends are also manipulated, pushed and spread via the web. The noise about this is louder and more fundamental than the realization will ever be: veganism, paleo-nutrition, detox, eternal health. What is forgotten in all these irrational hubbubs are the basic functions of food: nutrition, survival, enjoyment. Media such as television and the internet show prosperity and its dark shadow at the same time: abundance. In fact, abundance is a potent adversary of cooking culture. Everything is available all the time, mass convenience.

Harking back to the past makes logical sense, but it's also a specious game. Today, regionalism is celebrated as though it were the ultimate new trend. But we must not delude ourselves. These principles are ancient. This was the ultima ratio of bygone food culture, food history, born of need and deprivation. All one had to eat was what could be culled from the immediate natural environment within the narrow confines of the present. Fermenting and smoking were not practised primarily for the test, but rather to preserve foods as a basis for survival. Such preserved foods would help alleviate the always impending shortage of food. The media hype on all this is basically exaggerated. This becomes clear when we consider the hype on "dry-aging" and "nose-to-tail". These expressions sound new and chic for the moment, but what lies behind them is anything but new. These are also ancient methods, in particular "nose-to-tail" and "root-to-flower". In earlier times it was unthinkable to hunt an animal, then eat only the rack meat from the back. Everything edible had to be eaten, not necessarily for ethical reasons, but because there was always just enough to go around. Ethical aspects were first brought into play by the founders of religions and philosophies, not in the face of hard facts and technological progress. Hunger is the best cook. In times of need, food on the table certainly precedes morality. Humanity had to earn reversing these values – first morality and then food. Only a satiated society can afford this attitude, and it is not only overproduction that has got out of hand. If one shops among producers on the market square, instead of in the anonymous (organic) supermarkets, one learns a lot about the products and the relevant cooking techniques: the real farmer's wife (and not the one depicted on tinned food by marketing managers), can explain the principles of using entire vegetables, give long-forgotten tips and involve anyone interested in a culinary dialogue that is more valuable than 1000 clicks and Facebook comments.

THE ALIENATION AND DECULTURALIZATION OF FOOD

Rarely has the culinary world seen a greater alienation of culinary culture than in these fast-paced days. The "orgies" of the Roman Empire and the excesses of the Middle Ages may show a certain degree of decadence. The generations that have grown up in our time of affluence and overabundance, have never learned product-adjusted cooking techniques. It was easy to develop a sense of disgust for innards, tripe and pigsheads. These things need not be cooked and eaten at all if lying next to them are a selection of lean steaks ready for the pan at downright ridiculous prices: vacuum-packed, anonymous, the immediate animal origins just barely recognizable. Stoveside creative challenges are no longer necessary, new taste experiences are no longer possible.

On the other hand, a lot of technology is invested in vegetarian alternatives to derive quasi-meat from the "tofu animal". Vegan "sausages", vegi-meat and vegi-fish from plant and insect proteins as replacements for more natural sources? Such reconstructed foods are counter-evolutionary and perplexing: If we were to present in this book a recipe for a green, fresh salad made from meat we would be laughed at or driven off to the madhouse. On the other hand, markets and prizes for futuristic developments are showered on products comprising meat from plant protein, hydrocolloids, aromas and flavourings. A few years ago they called this kind of convenience products artificial analogue "cheese" made from cheap ingredients. If the first wise ones around the fire hundreds of thousands of years ago had foreseen such things, they just might have decided to put the fire out again.

Unfortunately, nowadays we keep forgetting how fundamentally important the development of culinary culture was, and still is. It was along our mastery and control of fire and micro-organisms that made possible the diverse and environmentally compatible achievements of humanity in technology, art and culture. It now seems absurd to buy "paleo-food" (or what people think nowadays is paleo-food) in the supermarket and carry it home in the boots of our high-powered motor vehicles? Novel invented terms such as "vegan paleo-smoothies" ignore the great cultural achievements of humankind completely.

Food in the Metabolic Era

Chus Martínez

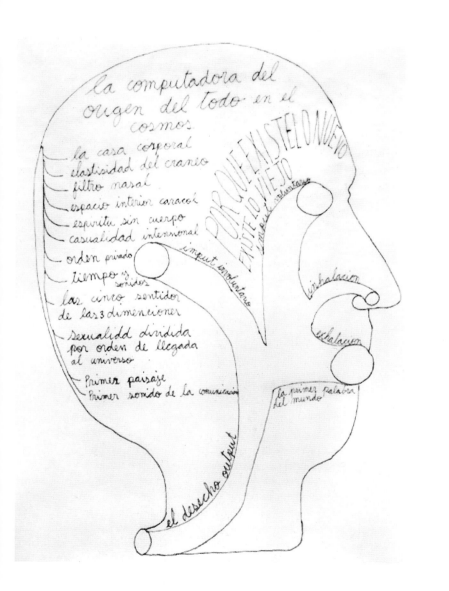

THE DEATH OF THE EXPERIMENT

I spent many of my summers at Fondazione Morra, in Naples, going through pictures, stage materials and films of *The Living Theatre*. Known for the organic integration of scenography and fashion into their text, dramaturgy and performance works, the company, founded in 1947 in New York by actress Judith Malina and artist Julian Beck, remained active until 1985. The film documents of these plays and performances reveal what made this group emblematic for over two decades. The footage, though not always in the best condition, is a unique document of an experimental practice based on radical transformations of social and gender values. These very speculative plays move away from scripts, relying on the possibility of integrating the spontaneous performances of both the actors and the audience. However, as much as their confidence in dramaturgy is compelling, one senses in their work the increasing impossibility of relying too much upon "experimentalism". Perhaps even more tellingly, all of these filmed performances and plays *look* "experimental". They assume the possibility of denying or accepting the basic assumptions which constitute our world experience. They test through feeling. Sitting there, watching for hours, I thought, this way of giving one's self up to experience has radically changed.

For me, these exercises of a body on stage, invoking freedom, peace and, above all, a will to make the body transmit these values via a vocabulary of gestures, recall the anti-psychiatric movement. I became aware of the social and political language of this movement thanks to the research and works of Dora Garcia and Luke Fowler. I decided to watch Fowler's films on R. D. Laing again. Of course, while watching the filmed plays of *The Living Theatre*, a million images from the 1960s counter-culture movements appeared in my mind, along with *The Age of Aquarius* by C.G Jung and the days of W. Reich's Orgone Chambers. However, these images appeared to me set in relation to the environment of crisis that has been growing around us over the past ten years. They had LSD and the anti-psychiatric movement and lived through the Great Depression, which remains the greatest financial crisis in history. How will our current crisis make us react and experience? What are the mind and body's answers to this feeling of living inside "well-defined limits"?

Of all the films the Scottish artist-filmmaker Luke Fowler made on the controversial figure R. D. Laing, *All Divided Selves* (2011) interested me most in the context of my current thoughts. The film looks back at the vacillating responses to Laing's radical views and the unforgiving responses to his late career shift from eminent psychiatrist to enterprising celebrity. Fowler's film is beautiful and dense, weaving archival material with his own filmic observations, and leaves us with the feeling that the days of experimentation, as well as those when the performance of experiments was a means of testing the boundaries between dissimilar groups and classes composing the social body, are over. The film elaborates upon Laing's transformation into a public persona, the radical approach he took to channeling his views towards increasingly broad audiences and the almost decadent way in which he transformed himself into a media star. In a scene towards the end of the film, Laing appears on screen, singing. The image is surprising. It looks as if he is delirious, or, then again, perhaps not.

In 1977 and 1978, Laing collaborated with the composers Ken Howard and Alan Blaikley, resulting in the album *Life before Death* (1978) with lyrics in the form of sonnets, many of them quite compellingly stupid, written by Laing. At the time, Howard and Blaikey were well known in the United Kingdom, the authors of many hits there during the 1960s and 1970s. One of the most famous tracks from the album goes:

It's all correct, and crisp, and keen and bright
A place of order, form, and right design.
A haven, in this world of dark, of light.
A Where to start a long and clean straight line.

It would be nice if all around we saw
The grace, decorum of the antique mind
Brought forward to the present as a law
Instead of our cacophonous and brutal bind.

It should not need to hearten me so much
To come across a little worth, among
The slush and drivel, dross and mulch
Which would be better formed of honest dung.

The game's not up. Some children still can sing.
Go tell the falling leaves it'll soon be spring.

There's light and love and joy and freshness yet,
There're those who have something to celebrate.
There can be times we hope we'll not forget.
A helping hand is not always too late.

Up really high there's still clear perfect blue.
Morning must dawn as long as there is night.
Without the old there's nothing to renew.
Occasionally, it almost feels alright.

Although I know that light needs dark to shine,
I don't expect to tell what atoms mean.
The universe is fine without being mine.
The flowers of countless valleys grow unseen.

What is above subsists on what's beneath.
The world is not entirely blasted heath.

The freedom that you seek is in the mean
Between opposing tensions in your soul.
Achieve the integration of the whole
And then you are, and not a might have been.

Remember that to live is to metabolize.
So don't forget en route to the sublime
To check on your mouth-anus transit time
Look at the ground as well as at the skies

You've heard it all before? That's fine.
Reiterated truths soon sound absurd.
To be blasé is not beatitude.
It's just your glutted tongue can't taste the wine.
One in a million hears the blatant word
Before it echoes into platitude.

What is more important than the lyrics is the mere fact that Laing performed and, crucially, the impulse that led him to sing. Why did Laing sing? In an article published in *The Observer* just a few days before the album's release, author Caryll Faraldi pointed to the fact that R. D. Laing was always interested in the voice (and in music) and that the record could be linked to a previous voice recording he made with Georges Cunelli, a voice expert, theorist and close friend of James Joyce. It was only natural that Laing was interested in the voice, for, as both a psychiatrist and a media personality, he was perfectly aware of how a presence and a voice produced an effect on listeners. Singing, however, is a different story. The voice that speaks is not quite identical to the voice that sings. Even the control one can exercise as a trained speaker can be lost in the singing voice since the latter requires a wholly different though equally thorough training in breath control and rhythm. The singing voice does not form spontaneously. Thus, Laing was revealing himself much more than when he spoke, both in his (lack of) technique and in his personality, since singing stressed that he was a performer aware of the stage and how the subjects from his counseling were transformed into an audience.

The surprise in seeing him singing in Fowler's *All Divided Selves*, however, lies in the discovery that, at the beginning of the 1980s, the days of "experiment" as understood by *The Living Theatre* and the idea of unmediated expression and self-expression, of experiencing the world as a "naked human", were coming to an end. This musical performance by a very well-known psychiatrist is not just an anecdote; it was a result of the radical transformation of expression into a more metabolic response. It was also the result of transforming information into a totally different substance, one that is more complex than knowledge since it is a form adopted by life that avoids contact with the naked body or the influence of LSD or any other substance. This singing is crucial because it does not proclaim or state; it addresses us from the inside. It is pure queerness as an accepted form and as an acknowledgment of the complex relationship between information, wisdom and culture. It revealed a need for a transformation that would go beyond action, that would live in us, transforming us first and then the world.

REMEMBER THAT TO LIVE IS TO METABOLIZE

During the 1920s and 1930s, a branch of scientific research appeared which focused on understanding human metabolism. The isolation of vitamins started in the second half of the 19th century and during the 1920s multiple experiments explained the role of vitamins A and D while further studies isolated vitamins C and K. Thus, interest in diet took on a new form and food was redefined in terms not only of accessibility, class and tradition, but also of health and self-control. Especially relevant in our context is the work and research of Catherine Kousmine (1904–1992), a Russian émigré who studied in Lausanne and developed a theory and practice for cancer treatment based on food or, more precisely, diet. Her first diet protocol, based on a 1949 case study describing the treatment and cure of a patient with intestinal cancer, was highly influenced by the research of another woman, Johanna Budwig (1908–2003). Throughout the 1940s Budwig, a German biochemist, studied fatty acids and their influence in curing cancer. Budwig published her first diet protocol in 1952, which expounded the virtues of consuming flaxseed oil, low-fat cheese and meals rich in fruits, vegetables, and fiber while avoiding sugar, animal fats, salad oil, meats, butter and especially margarine. Even if Kousmine was following up on the discoveries and the precepts of Budwig's diet, she was also a pioneer in a new understanding of the properties of raw food for our health. She put a special emphasis on the health value of cold-pressed oils. During WWII, oils were pressed under heats ranging from 160 to 200°C, allowing up to 70 percent of the fat from the grain to be extracted. This resulted in a dark, strong smelling liquid that required further processing and refining and, though this oil lasted forever, it was, as Kousmine put it, "dead". Cold-pressed oils, on the contrary, are alive, produced by simple physical processes like decanting and filtration, but are sensitive to light, become quickly rancid and require refrigeration once unsealed. Kousmine's texts are intensely eloquent in their explanations of how simple food had been transformed by industrial processes and how the loss of fatty acids, also known as vitamin F, plays a fundamental role in the weakening of our cell membranes' protection against external attacks, resulting in, for example, immunodeficiency disorders.

There is, of course, no proof that following diets, even those as rigorous as the Kousmine method, can cure cancer. I do not intend to present these methods as effective, but to note the parallel growth in understanding, at the start of the 20th century, of both drug use and diet. The common denominator is clear: an effect on our metabolic system.

Both interests, in drugs and in diets, are part of the exploration of the possibilities of enhancing our capabilities. The world of drugs centers on the brain, the possible chemical transformations that enable us to explore this organ and, therefore, the way we sense the world. Comparing the rise of interest in vitamins and raw food with drugs seems nonsensical at first sight. Food may indeed have an effect on our organism, but isn't it too slow, too long term a variable to provide a basis for proper comparison with drug use? Yet, after nearly 100 years, such thinking has allowed food to acquire the social and media relevance it has today. The revelation of the importance of food, not as gourmet cooking, but as a source of and structuring method for life, bears a strange but powerful relation with all sorts of experiments on "freeing the mind", with the psychiatric and anti-psychiatric movements of the last century, as well as with Modernism and the avant-garde and the idea of controlling the body, fueling it not too little and not too much to maintain productivity. The science of nourishment does not only aim to avoid an ill body, allow us to live longer and increase the productive years of humans. Food science goes beyond attempts to strengthen the body-as-machine towards attempts to generate a paradoxical state in which the human organism is not merely healthy enough to work more, but healthy enough to make us feel that we are in a state beyond labor. The body as resort. If drugs treat the mind as a skyrocket ready for takeoff, escaping the damaged body, the metabolic cult and super foods posit a body capable of making the mind stay.

POST-JUNKIE YEARS

This transformation in the scope of diet's influence on the human is part of a larger, radical shift in our understanding of the social and aesthetic conditions that determine our current relationship with the body and gender. It is defined by a tendency not only towards more freedom, but also towards increasing control, which in turn leads to shifts in the notions of gender that are central to art. Here gender is not understood as constituted by a dichotomy of the male and the female, but as an intelligent means of addressing the problem of the dichotomy of the inner from the outer. This is gender as a language we can adopt to grasp the possibilities of consciousness. This is gender as another name for art.

To imagine that great things can result solely from self-disciplinary mechanisms is difficult. Food is surrounded by confusion. It is difficult to remove cultural and geopolitical factors from the discussion and even more challenging to discuss food without invoking the names of star chefs and the exploration of the senses through food. The rise of the star chef has much to do with classical experiments in self-expression and an avant-garde or Modern understanding of a subject able to cross his/her boundaries through taste and express her/his relationship towards an inside and an outside in a radically new way completely determined, however, by the dramaturgy of the plating and the restaurant in the same manner that, with *The Living Theatre*, the stage determined the extent of the experiments. I am more interested in a different relationship to food, expressed by Catherine Kousmine's research, that studies the ingredients of a diet and considers diet as an act of absorbing nourishment that has nothing to do with aesthetic pleasure but, rather, with the strong intention to slowly affect the human system.

While a vast body of research exists on drugs and the many other means of exploring the limits of our mind in its relation to science, literature, music, and, later on, every other form of subculture, there is almost nothing written on how these early biochemical experiments relate to culture and art. The gendered aspect of this field must also be noted, for the history of research on food and diet as a means of altering life is peopled almost exclusively by women. Though there is as yet almost no existing artistic production in the form of raw food or vitamins, there is an unstudied aspect of art production based on the same principles as this new metabolic way of living.

Heroin and Calorie Counting

It was 1995 and I was in New York City. It was before the days of online newspaper reading, so I got myself a copy *El País* for the long train ride from Uptown down to Brooklyn. I read it nearly front to back, neglecting only the film section. The train ride continued, and was boring, so I decided eventually to read the film section as well. There, a critic used up an entire page smashing *Waterworld* (remember that one?). Though critics were nearly unanimous in their dislike of the film, this piece was masterfully humorous. The piece went on and on about the fact that the dystopia was set following an ecological disaster and that the bad guys were known as the Smokers. The Smokers! In a world of water where humans are almost fish: How did they manage to keep the tobacco dry?

Though the article was amusing, I could not completely accept the critic's argument since I come from a place where tobacco is preserved under water. Galicia, the region in Spain where I was born, has a particularly rough coastline. Piracy was common there for centuries and, during the dictatorship, the region was famous for the smuggling of goods over its border with Portugal. Economically underdeveloped in levels difficult to portray here, the virgin character of the region's water and land facilitated many farming initiatives. From the late 1970s into the 1980s we saw an increasing number of floating wood platforms drifting on the waters of the estuaries. These platforms, known as *bateas*, primarily served the farming of oysters and mussels, but were also used for smuggling tobacco. This is the origin of the name *Winston de batea* designating the tobacco illegally brought into the country that shared with the shellfish the cold, nourishing waters of the Atlantic. This same coast saw, some years later, tons of heroin and cocaine introduced into the country, producing both a total imbalance in the local economy and the genocide of a whole generation of drug users.

These were the same drugs that inundated both lower and upper class nightlife during the first years of democracy in Spain. For a whole decade, beginning from the age of 16, I co-existed with junkies in many ways. The village I am from and all the others like it were actively witnessing how drugs could shape life. On the opposite coast, the relatively tepid consumption by hipsters at the high schools co-existed with increasingly visible signs of a dependent population on the streets – the public spaces, clubs, bank lobbies and food markets where, every morning, junkies would beg to housewives who in turn prayed to God that their sons and daughters would be spared such a fate. Heroin was bridging the Atlantic Ocean and the Mediterranean Sea through this trade.

After moving to Barcelona, I went or, rather, was required as part of a school-sponsored prevention program, to attend many information sessions and to volunteer at one of the largest methadone clinics in Europe. Located in a neighborhood that no longer exists called Can Tunis, the area was a hellish island located behind the harbor, circumscribed on one side by a highway and on the other by the Montjuïc hill, both of which served to cut off this section from the greater urban fabric. I have never seen a place so desperate and isolated. The permanent population consisted of between 80 and 100 Sinti and Roma families who were accused of creating the biggest heroin market on the planet, even though they were the victims of extreme poverty and drug dependency. I started going there, scared to death, pretending to be a help to the organization while only managing to effectively cure myself of any desire to ever use such drugs. Indeed, my school's prevention program was highly effective. Methadone was presented at the clinic as the "solution", as a good substance that could replace the bad one and help one live a drug-free life. I was there every night for a year, over the course of which I discovered that methadone was an even worse drug than the one it was intended to replace. The whole operation was really a means of controlling the Sinti and Roma communities and their links to drug trafficking as well as a pretext for resettling these undesirables and expanding the harbor to its current size, effectively erasing Can Tunis.

Why I am recalling this episode? In my mind, the rise of the importance of food coincides with the drug war. I see these two phenomena linked in a dance that began in the Basque region with hopes of peace and at the Mediterranean coast as an attempt to absorb life and all its substances not from drugs, but from food. Food was required to overcome tradition and go through a complex, alchemical ritual of re-invention. All of a sudden, it became socially and historically necessary to translate and re-translate the most obvious ingredients, the most banal tastes.

FOOD AND THE POLITICAL ALGORITHM

Not long after my Can Tunis experiences came my first encounters with molecular cuisine. A friend took me to a seminar during which we were presented with an egg whose yolk had been replaced by café con leche. Actually, though my friend remembers this story, I am uncertain the memory is accurate. I am not even certain whether it was Ferran Adrià himself or a member of his team doing the "cooking" and presenting this new juggling act of taste and technology. Memory, not only that of the individual but that of the collective as well, always finds good reasons to eliminate objective information. The group attending this meeting, consisting mostly of architects, product and graphic designers, Web developers as well as two of the most important advertisement teams in the country, was truly shocked. However, this shock had nothing to do with food as a "dish" or culinary event. The cooking demonstration was received with as much enthusiasm, misunderstanding and resistance as when a new discipline of knowledge is introduced. This egg containing a café con leche was perhaps only described to us, but it is an incredibly powerful image. It produced among my fellow seminar attendees an endless series of jokes, repeated again and again, morphing the two original elements into things like a strawberry with a heart of anchovy and a thousand other combinatory variations. All society seemed, at this point, to be laughing at this extreme Pantagruelic game that the chefs were performing with food. Imagine that, the raw DNA of an animal product, the egg, was being replaced by a culturally made element, café con leche. Café con leche! Our breakfast staple had replaced the egg's "origin" point which, though still protected like the yolk before it, was transformed into a consolidated item ready to be swallowed whole without consideration, without thought. The ritual chain of small, familiar gestures, the unconscious steps taken from hand to mouth, had been, all at once, replaced by a single, determined act, as unified as taking a shot of liquor. The vast collective choreography of every Spaniard, every morning, across millions of counters, publicly performing the gestures of drinking their café con leche had, all of a sudden, been replaced by the precarious substance of an egg.

Such transformations had nothing to do with food and much to do with a metabolic revolution that emerged from under the flood of drugs that had submerged Spain as unexpectedly as a tsunami. The drugs were not merely there because of the convenience of Spain's geography and location, but also because of the intense appetite unconsciously created over many years of dictatorship now made manifest during these transitional years into democracy. Such appetites were the product of senses that had been restricted from performing their normal functions for too long and further oppressed by the fact that the old system was neither removed nor contested, but was merely being allowed to die away. The rise which occurred in drug use and, after its peak, in the importance of a new food played a fundamental role in creating the conditions in which a new self could be formed.

Like a metabolic reaction inside the social body, this new interest in food had a distinctly synthetic character. It could be linked with neither a long tradition of cuisine nor the bourgeoisie. On the contrary, it emerged, almost like an artistic movement, from an independent group. Molecular cuisine and its accompanying trends were somehow Kantian, focusing not on the food itself, but on invention and a kind of social training. This cuisine had as a goal, though of course impossible, to make us all eat through the mouth and sense through the nose in one special way. The very impossibility of this goal, that an entire culture would adopt an attitude towards eating which was deeply anti-culinary, made it into a radical proposal to challenge the habits of an entire nation. It suggested that a new historical period should not start with the same gestures and tastes of the previous regime. Food that is not food and recipes that are impossible to share are excellent antidotes to nostalgia. Almost overnight, a huge portion of the population was addressing food in a completely different manner and, thus, opening itself up to new possibilities in how and what it was consuming.

In my own strange memory, I see the fall in heroin use coincide, along with the rise of a new food, with the emergence of feet encased in the pneumatic forms of the first Camper and Camper-like shoes. In my mind, this is when the *Spaziergang* fever also began. The black rubber soles of Camper shoes that refused to stop at the limit of the foot's actual form, expanding pneumatically around it and abstracting the shape until it resembled a digitally enhanced paw, always fascinated me. These were friendly, democratic feet, without edges or borders, ready to traverse the asphalt plains of huge cities as readily as the dirt of the rustic Majorcan countryside from whence these shoes came. Their formed rubber shapes also recalled for me the dinghies so often used to transport bricks of cocaine, hashish and heroin along the cold beaches of the Atlantic coast. Yet, they were designed to convey a new era, never quite realized and now completely gone, in Mediterranean culture, populated by metropolitan neo-peasants who took to the markets and supermarkets to rehearse and proclaim their new values, wafting through the cities a balsamic-marinated social democracy. This unarticulated movement was so powerful and present, even if to this day it remains impossible to interpret its promise or the stakes of its speculative energy. It was clearly there, however, and I dislike it now as much as then, perhaps because I blame it, albeit unfairly, for mixing nostalgia with resentment and for encouraging a very specific form of unpreparedness. It was the diluted aftertaste of a movement, politically expressed with the worst kind of liberal defensiveness. It was the opposite of what the surrealist egg with its yolk of café con leche had wanted to announce. Something had gone rotten.

GENDER MOUSSE

Everything troubling about the image of the singing star therapist, as the mutated byproduct of the anti-psychiatric movement, can also be seen in what went wrong with molecular cuisine and its interpretations. And, as in the case of R. D. Laing, the first response may be to sing an ode to the incredible misunderstandings "food" created at the core of the social body at a very particular historical moment. Like the leaf on Siegfried's back, a point of vulnerability was created that was conquered by gourmet promises and comfortable, oversized rubber soles. Via the mouth of the middle class, a major transformation occurred that altered senses and modified tastes forever. I call it a tragedy because I am an optimist and see, as Laing saw, that it might be good to be singing this drama for a while. Most likely, though still unprepared to understand, we are soon to hear amazing news concerning a radical transformation of human sexuality. After the wave of drugs that promised both potency and resistance, but only exhausted the body to an unthinkable extent, exterminating its natural defenses and powers, food acted as an antidote. However, all elements of culture began to act very directly upon our sexuality. The construction of the body during the Camper era did not happen by chance, but was, rather, an already corporate-approved reinterpretation of a post-therapy hippie, now fully integrated into the productivity chain with a democratic body ready to present itself in a post-sexual state. The new food appeared at a crucial moment in the transformation of a body eternally oscillating between diets, drugs and anti-depressants, a transformation that is now moving us towards a completely different understanding of gender. Together, new food and fashion combined to produce forms of desire and anxiety that displaced sexual appetites. Corresponding with the rise of virtual realities and online pornography, a period defined by a kind of disinterestedness towards sexual interactions, especially heterosexual, took place which allowed for a new sexual revolution. It has not only given us gay marriage and rights, but also enabled a new imagination in which gender and its functions are also a matter of choice. Gender has become a key aspect in the liberation of the body from Modernity, labor and *Leistung* (productivity). The slow but steady deprioritization of body-with-body sexuality is a metabolic process within the social body that will create the organic space necessary for this new gender reality. This produces, of course, all sorts of anxieties, from eating disorders to extreme surgical operations. Food, with its incredible capacity for transferring to the mouth some of our genital sense, can most successfully compensate for these lacks and losses. Camper's inflated rubber paws, although as rudimentary and nostalgic as our current ideology, appeared to signal this transitional era. It will not last, however. Like the period of shedding old skin before the metamorphosis into a new creature, one whose form is as yet unknown to us, we are performing our old cultural-critical logic before acquiring a new one. We just need to sing it a little while longer.

Food as a Medium Between Art and Cuisine

Rirkrit Tiravanija's Gastronomic Installations

Felix Bröcker

Fig. 1

Fig. 2

In an early solo project at the Paula Allen Gallery in New York, conceptual artist Rirkrit Tiravanija served up the eponymous dish for *Untitled 1990 (Pad thai)*. For this purpose he used cooking and food as the medium and thus called into question generally accepted concepts of art. Not all the visitors actually realized the action was a form of art, with some assuming that it was simply a catering service.[1] The installation *DO WE DREAM UNDER THE SAME SKY*[2] at Art Basel 2015 also revolved around gastronomy and provided hundreds of guests with food every day of the art fair.

As a chef and graduate of the Curatorial Studies master program at the Städelschule and the Goethe University in Frankfurt, I am interested in the practices and discourses surrounding the interweaving of art and cuisine. In order to better understand Tiravanija's aesthetic practice, I took part in his *DWDUTSS* project at Art Basel 2015. As a conceptual artist, Tiravanija

---

1 | Grassi/Tiravanija: 2007, p. 5.

2 | Subsequently abbreviated to "*DWDUTSS*".

uses food quite naturally as a medium that conveys far more than just a flavor. The culinary execution of his dishes is less important here; if we assume cuisine aims at artisanal perfection, the food he serves is not of outstanding quality. Looking beyond this criterion, however, the specific artistic potential that cooking harbors in Tiravanija's aesthetic practice is something I aim to examine using this installation as a starting point.

In order to better define Tiravanija's art, the so-called *relational aesthetics* of Nicolas Bourriaud offer an important, widely-used methodology. However, Bourriaud uses the specified term exclusively with regard to the socializing dimension of a shared meal. What is meant here are the social bonds that develop between people who participate in a meal set up by Tiravanija. Nevertheless, with an eye on the use of food as a medium, gastronomic knowledge of the culture and traditions of the dishes Tiravanija serves is fundamental for the understanding of his work. The artist goes beyond social and satiating aspects in his use of food and through this medium articulates his own attitude, which is reflected in the examination of cultural identities in increasingly globalized contexts. A reference to gastronomy emerges beyond this in structural terms as well: With *DWDUTSS*, Tiravanija becomes an art-caterer, who distributes his now famous Thai curries as a "signature dish" each day to hundreds of visitors in Basel, adopting strategies of gastronomic entrepreneurs. The following sections begin with an examination of Tiravanija's installation in Basel with the aim of subsequently examining Nicolas Bourriaud's theory, which might explain at last partly the sense in which Tiravanija's culinary actions can be understood as manifestations of a relevant artistic way of working. In order to ultimately demonstrate what *Relational Aesthetics* are not able to achieve, I refer to some of Tiravanija's earlier works. These aim to make clear what I believe is an essential point, namely the importance of specifically gastronomic knowledge for the understanding of Tiravanija's works. Finally I trace Tiravanija's proximity to gastronomic enterprises, which becomes clear through the work *DWDUTSS*.

DO WE DREAM UNDER THE SAME SKY, ART BASEL 2015

What first strikes visitors to the exhibition site is the huge roof structure made of steel and bamboo, which covers an open kitchen and a few tables intended as a place for discussion. Here there is a clear association with bamboo as a Thai building material which, with its steel reinforcement, evokes certain impressions of *the land*. The site-specific installation is not a stand-alone piece, but rather points to another project with utopian potential: *The land* refers to a rice field (as conveyed by the Thai name) near Chiang Mai. The initiators Kamin Lerdchaiprasert and Rirkrit Tiravanija acquired a piece of land there, which is worked as a rice field by local farmers and at the same time is intended to serve as a place of retreat and a meeting point for artists and students. *The land* aims to facilitate a life independent of the western economic model. In simple huts built by artists, the site offers interested parties a place to stay aside from the art world.

Beneath the roof of the Basel installation are workstations where people cook, prepare and wash up, as well as several herb gardens. The small elements for the cooking were largely imported directly from Thailand and supplemented with gas and solar cookers. The entire area is designed to be barrier-free, and visitors can wander around beneath the roof structure. The roof is a striking design element, but at the same time it preserves the openness of the space. This way visitors are invited to discover what goes on here. Tiravanija himself is right at the heart of it, cooking and distributing free food. He is assisted in the kitchen by chef Antto Melasniemi, and by students who on a daily base help cooking on site, taking care of food supplies and organizing rounds of discussion. Tiravanija sees the project as an opportunity for exchange on topics such as sustainable nutrition. The exchange sometimes takes the form of a workshop in which participants develop something and share it with others. The artist is very clear that the food on offer is not to be seen as a gastronomic service, but rather as a hospitable gesture with the request that guests wash their crockery themselves after eating. The socializing power of food becomes immediately apparent – as soon as a dish is given out long queues form, firstly in front of the curry pots and subsequently in front of the washing basins. Most of the visitors are very willing to wash their plates themselves, and the long lines of people become a sculptural component of the installation.

In all of this, the food itself is a central element, not only for hungry passers-by, but specifically as a symbolic gesture to welcome visitors. As far as the dishes are concerned, the basic recipes for Pad Thai or Thai curries are varied according to the availability of products no longer suitable for sale, which are organized through food-sharing projects. Thus the action picks up on current trends of our food culture oriented particularly towards awareness of our food consumption. Alongside Thai curry there is also tea, which is prepared using the herbs from the beds, as well as *Nam Pla Eiskrem*, an ice cream made with Asian fish sauce.

DWDUTSS becomes a central meeting point thanks to food. What is extraordinary here is not so much the dishes, but rather the situation in which the many anonymous visitors meet and strike up conversations. With an eye to the traditional understanding of art, this performative, ephemeral cookery action breaks with preconceptions of art linked to the autonomous object and advances the ideas of the avant-garde movement of the 20th and 21st centuries, as well as the *Institutional Critique*. Yet aside from these influences, Tiravanija has also become known for cooking Thai dishes for visitors who gather in the social situation thus created. The leading theorist of this interpretation of his works is Nicolas Bourriaud, whose *Relational Aesthetics* established Tiravanija as a culinary artist.

The Possibilities and Limitations of the *Relational Aesthetics* as an Analytical Tool for Tiravanija's Art

In his theory of *Relational Aesthetics*, Bourriaud emphasizes the possibility of creating a social moment through food. In summary, Bourriaud proposes the following concept:

While the virtualization of everyday life has regressive effects on the development and the maintenance of "genuine" interpersonal relationships, the convivial nature of a shared meal in a museum or in other art institutions represents a socializing counterweight. The fact that the recipients become active participants and thus part of the artistic work themselves means that the developing contacts seem actually to be the result of the work. For Bourriaud, the fundamental aspect of relational art here lies in bringing people together in a social situation that is initiated and staged by the artist. How this gathering is achieved and under what circumstances people are brought together here plays a subordinate role for Bourriaud, which is why he is able to group together various artists under this aspect despite their works all being very different.[3] He thus highlights a new aspect of Tiravanija's work. The social power of a shared meal is a phenomenon that is culturally emblematic in the way it is anchored, but which has previously been little noted as an aesthetic practice. From the symposiums of the Greeks to the Last Supper and from business lunches to dining clubs and modern political banquets, meal-time gatherings are a powerful symbol of human togetherness.[4] Sociologists confirm the importance of shared meals at which, for example, we learn and practice skills within the family from an early age.[5] These days, the loss of this time spent together is much lamented.[6] In art and cuisine the focus lies on the traditions of food and the presentation of the dish on the plate, as well as the improvement of the taste, whereby the shared meal was previously granted scarce attention as a naturally given constant. It is only in more recent times that chefs have once again looked to various contexts of the eating situation and attempted to use this for a particular dining experience.[7] In parallel to this, Bourriaud sees Tiravanija's practice as a counter-proposal to the information society, which is increasingly isolating people. He offers the example of the automation of everyday services such as a morning alarm or a cash machine.[8] Hence the

---

3 | See Bourriaud's explanation: "Aesthetic theory consisting in judging artworks on the basis of the inter-human relations which they represent, produce or prompt." Bourriaud: 2002, p. 112. Alongside Rirkrit Tiravanija, Bourriaud also cites, among others, Liam Gillick, Pierre Huyghe, Felix Gonzales Torres, and Douglas Gordon.

4 | Därmann/Lemke: 2007.

5 | Simmel: 1957; Elias: 1969.

6 | Hauschild: 2014. The problem is also examined by family therapists: See Juul: 2015.

7 | Spence/Piqueras-Fiszman: 2014a.

8 | Bourriaud: 2002, p. 17.

creation of situations experienced together only gains aesthetic meaning because this togetherness is increasingly missing from our everyday lives.

In art-historical terms, Bourriaud's approach differs from earlier art theories which see a reference to a desirable but non-existent utopia in an artistic work. Bourriaud maintains: "It seems more pressing to invent possible relations with our neighbors in the present than to bet on happier tomorrows."[9] In line with this, artists now act differently: "[...] the role of artworks is no longer to form imaginary and utopian realities, but to actually be ways of living and models of action within the existing real [...]."[10] Bourriaud refers to the creation of this essential situation that results in exchange between strangers as "micro-utopias",[11] which take place in the here and now.

Bourriaud's perspective became a much-discussed art theory during the 1990s, specifically because he carved out a clearly tangible aspect from the apparently heterogeneous body of contemporary art and thus brought together a group of artists and made them explicable using one key term. Nevertheless Bourriaud runs the risk of reducing the artistic positions subsumed under the term of Relational Aesthetics to their relational aspect and thus diverting attention from other relevant contents.

DIY Utopia

From today's perspective it appears that Bourriaud recognized a trend in contemporary art relatively early on, which expanded to various aspects of life: Micro-utopias created both through and with a DIY aesthetic, as is the case with Tiravanija, can now be found fairly frequently.[12] The phenomenon of retreat into trusted, compartmentalized structures known as *cocooning* was identified by the media as a trend reversal, particularly following the attacks in New York in 2001: From a hedonistic society to homely contemplation, which is also seen as the return of Biedermeier.[13] Magazines offer instructions on how to make all sorts of homely items yourself. Whilst more

---

9 | Ibid., p. 45.

10 | Ibid., p. 13.

11 | Ibid., p. 70.

12 | See Friedrichs, J. (2015): Die Welt ist mir zu viel, in: *Zeit Magazin*, Jan. 8, available online at: http://www.zeit.de/zeit-magazin/2015/01/entschleunigung-biedermeier-handarbeit-stressabbau (accessed on Jan. 28, 2016) as well as Sievers, A.-C. (2015): Ich baue also bin ich, in: *Frankfurter Allgemeine Sonntagszeitung*, Aug. 9, available online at: http://www.faz.net/aktuell/stil/drinnen-draussen/warum-die-deutschen-im-do-it-yourself-fieber-sind-13740354-p3.html (accessed on Jan. 21, 2016).

13 | Christmann, H. (2001): Rückkehr des Biedermeier, in: *Frankfurter Allgemeine Zeitung*, Nov. 6, available online at: http://www.faz.net/aktuell/gesellschaft/gesellschaft-rueckkehr-des-biedermeier-138495.html (accessed on Jan. 21, 2016).

and more foods are being produced industrially, this trend is prevalent in the area of food production and preparation: Cooking, baking, gardening and brewing are all very popular activities among people aged 30 to 50. As described, Bourriaud interprets the focus on interpersonal relationships in art as a counter-reaction to the digital world without real contacts. Similar to this is the individual DIY principle against mass production and auto-mation. Paradoxically, exchange on this primarily takes place in virtual form. Images of food are staged specifically to balance out the lack of the multisensory experience through visual stimulation.[14]

The DIY aspect therefore functions as a claim of the self against anon-ymous large-scale production, as a gesture of freedom against the presets and adaptations to a thoroughly rationalized world. This is distantly remi-niscent of the approach proclaimed by Joseph Beuys in the sense of *social sculpture*, helping to shape society actively as an individual – although this now takes place, counter to Beuys' intention, largely apolitically.[15] Perhaps neither Bourriaud nor Tiravanija intended this, yet there are remarkable parallels to Bourriaud's hypothesis of micro-utopias. The fact that these take place in everyday life is only consistent given the connection between art and life as an aspect of many relational works. Yet if one assumes that Tiravanija's works are merely about eating together, then they would be "[...] unfathomably trivial and banal – in both a political and an aesthetic regard", as Juliane Rebentisch states.[16] The phenomenon described above makes it clear that actually artists are no longer needed as these sorts of micro-utopias are actually realized without their help.[17] Rebentisch offers a differentiated interpretation that addresses the specific dish served:

"[...] for him [Tiravanija], it was about making visible the factual particularity of a western art world establishing itself as universal by means of that which it

---

14 | See "Essen und Trinken auf Pinterest", *Pinterest* website, available online at: https://de.pinterest.com/categories/food_drink/ (accessed on Feb. 5, 2016).

15 | In keeping with Tiravanija's actions, shared meals also fall within the context of the trend of food festivals and markets, whereby the family unit is replaced by eating with friends. The theory that eating could replace the ubiquitous and much discussed phenomenon of art as a subject of discussion has also already been suggested, see Deresiewicz, W. (2012): A Matter of Taste?, in: *New York Times*, Oct. 26, available online at: http://nytimes.com/2012/10/28/opinion/sunday/how-food-replaced-art-as-high-culture.html?_r=0 (accessed on Feb. 5, 2016). On the topic of food festivals and markets, see also *Le Fooding* website, available online at: http://lefooding.com/ (accessed on Feb. 5, 2016) as well as the website of *Markthalle Neun*, available online at: https://markthalleneun.de/ (accessed on Feb. 5, 2016).

16 | Rebentisch: 2013, p. 68.

17 | An initial connection between gastrosophic and utopian ideas exists through Charles Courier, who helped to shape both concepts, on this see also Denker: 2015, p. 287.

excluded: What was served – hence also tellingly the title of the series of these actions – was Pad Thai."[18]

If one pursues this approach further, then one could formulate the idea that Tiravanija's actions can only be comprehended in their complexity if food is to be observed more precisely as a medium, since certain aspects are articulated through it that Bourriaud's theory cannot take into account as he leaves out culinary details for his argumentation.

GASTRONOMIC DECONSTRUCTION OF CULTURAL IMAGES OF THE SELF AND OTHERS

With an eye on cooking as a cultural practice and on the foods used and the dishes cooked, which come from a specific context, further interpretations are possible based on the notion of food as a medium. Alongside the significance of food as a medium in general, which appears in Tiravanija's work as a link to the historical and contemporary avant-garde, including *Fluxus* and *Institutional Critique*, and which was interpreted by Bourriaud as relational art, there is a second level that opens up through the use of the medium of food as a culturally defined symbol-bearer, which Tiravanija applies deliberately. In Bourriaud's terms a pizza can be used in precisely such a community-forming way as a burger or a kebab, yet in his exhibition Tiravanija deliberately served Pad Thai. Something that played no role at all in Bourriaud's argumentation is, in my opinion, key to Tiravanija's work.[19] Using examples of earlier works, in the following I will demonstrate how Tiravanija uses the specifically served dishes to convey messages that can only be appreciated through knowledge of gastronomy.

THE OWN IS THE ALIEN: PAD THAI AND THAI CURRY

Untitled 1990 (Pad thai) at the Paula Allen Gallery was Tiravanija's first solo exhibition in New York. Even in this initial cookery action, the type of dish was key to the understanding of the work; by no means was it merely about using food simply for its general socializing function. Tiravanija has Thai roots but was born in Argentina, initially studied in Canada and then came to the USA. The question of one's own identity is one that is very personal

---

18 | Rebentisch: 2013, p. 68.

19 | There was most likely no intention of examining food and cooking with the Relational Aesthetics, but Bourriaud seems to be thoroughly interested in this theme, as the exhibition *Cookbook* (Oct. 18, 2013 – Jan. 9, 2014) at the Palais des Beaux-Arts in Paris proves. He is represented in the exhibition catalogue for *Arts and Foods* with a text about cooking in art and cuisine (first published in the catalogue for *Cookbook*). See: Bourriaud: 2015, pp. 860–71.

and is part of his artistic practice.[20] The irritation of a traditional under-standing of art through food culminates in the fact that the dish served is Pad Thai, i.e. here the alien element is not only that we are not looking at an object as a work of art, but we are also eating a foreign dish – the food itself is alien. Tiravanija is an outsider in the American art system, and this is reflected in the dish: "[...] Thai food wasn't something that everyone had experienced. It was still something on the edge, something exotic perhaps; it definitely challenged your normal sense of food."[21]

The fact that Tiravanija serves Pad Thai as a reference to his own heritage may be a banal observation and not necessarily evidence of the use of the dish as a medium. A closer look at this "typical" Thai dish also com-plicates the correlation between the dish served and personal identity. Tira-vanija is Thai in terms of his nationality, but as far as his cultural identity is concerned, he has close links with other cultures.[22] This complexity in determining an identity is reflected in the Thai "national dish", Pad Thai: The dish originally came from China and was only proclaimed the national dish in 1940 by Prime Minister Phibunsongkhram or indeed Field Marshal Plaek Phibunsongkhram – Phibun for short – in order to strengthen the identity and establish a western orientation in the young Thai state, which was founded in 1939 and was previously known as Siam.[23] The dish is prepared using a special rice noodle, the use of which was supposed to support local farmers.[24] Historians Eric Hobsbawm and Terence Ranger talk about this as "invented traditions" which, as the example of Pad Thai shows, are used deliberately in order to strengthen the feeling of national belonging.[25] Hence national dishes function as idealized, identity-forming self-images.[26] To prepare the dish, Tiravanija used a *West Bend* brand electric wok. In this way he references a work by Martha Rosler, which focuses on the relationship between the USA and China and involves a wok by this brand in the video work *The East is Red, The West is Bending* (1977).[27]

---

20 | Grassi/Tiravanija: 2007, p. 4.

21 | Interview with Tiravanija: Birnbaum: 2015, p. 163.

22 | For the exhibition *Traffic* in 1996 in Bordeaux Tiravanija exhibited his passports and visa. See Krause-Wahl: 2006, p. 156. He is continually concerned with travel and travel regulations, see Obrist: 2010, p. 32 as well as Kellein: 2010, p. 11.

23 | Greeley: 2009, p. 78–82.

24 | Ibid.

25 | Hobsbawm: 2012, p. 1.

26 | Barlösius: 1999, p. 154. The fact that this ideal can also topple is demon-strated by defamations of citizens of individual nations as *spaghetti-eaters*, *frog-eaters* or *krauts*.

27 | See "Martha Rosler The East is Red, The West is Bending 1977", *Moma* website, available online at: http://www.moma.org/collection/works/159791?lo cale=pt (accessed on Jan. 28, 2016) as well as Kellein: 2010, p. 14. With the work *Semiotics of the kitchen* (1975), Rosler had previously examined feminist

Going beyond the dish's particular history, Tiravanija also added subtle variations to a very typical Thai curry and thus deliberately examined its function as a cultural symbol. In the *303 Gallery* he served two different versions of the dish for *Untitled 1992 (free)*: an "authentic" version with imported ingredients as well as a New York version with ingredients from the USA and less spice,[28] whereby there is a focus on the assimilation and integration of other cultures as well as the approach to what is one's own and what is foreign. The two abovementioned dishes, which he later replaced with foods primarily associated with local contexts, make it clear that for Tiravanija, food as a medium has never had merely a socializing function even from the beginning, but rather raises questions of identity and belonging in increasingly globalized contexts.

BEYOND CURRY

Taking the early works as a basis, for the Venice Biennale 1993 Tiravanija ultimately tackled the identity of an entire nation. His installation *Untitled (1271)* consisted of cooking pots in a canoe, which point to Native Americans, and at the same time is reminiscent of the floating markets in Thailand. In the installation, visitors were able to prepare noodle soup for themselves. The *Cup O Noodels* provided for this work are a ready-made product from Japanese firm Nissin, but they are produced in the USA.[29] The number 1271 in the title points to the year in which Marco Polo is thought to have imported noodles from China to Italy. The reference to the myth of the noodle importation also links Asian and western traditions, in this case even the local story of Venetian Marco Polo and the Italian pasta tradition with the cultural history of China. Identity is once again interpreted as a complex construct which can be highlighted using food as a medium. As in many of Tiravanija's other works, global lines of connection play an important role. Alongside this historic interpretation, the instant dish is also relevant on a sociological level. As a one-person dish it is symbolic of a time-saving single meal and is in contrast to the large curry pots from which the artist otherwise distributes food in order to encourage strangers to gather for a family meal. The fact that the visitors can consume the product alone, just as this single-serving ready meal implies, and can thus remain isolated in spite of participating in the artwork, makes it clear that his installation does not force interpersonal exchange, but rather deliberately allows it to occur. The addressed circulation of goods, but also of people through tourism and in a more elementary way through migration,

---

perspectives using the sphere of the kitchen. The connotation of cooking as a female activity contrasts with the dominance of male actors as chefs in art and gastronomy that becomes clear in this work.

28 | Krause-Wahl: 2006, p. 142.

29 | Obrist: 2010, p. 12.

which ultimately determines one's own identity, remained important for the works that followed too.

As part of the preparation for the group exhibition *Backstage* (1993) at Hamburg's Kunstverein, in his work *Untitled 1993 (flädle-suppe)* Tiravanija served a typical German soup, or more precisely a Swabian specialty that is no less alien to a resident of Hamburg than a Thai curry. Here the soup was prepared by a foreigner resident in Germany as a symbol of his willingness to integrate. As part of the installation there was also a screening of the film *Drachenfutter*, which is set in Hamburg and in which one character says: "You have to cook Flädlesuppe if you want to be German."[30] In the film an asylum-seeking Chinese waiter befriends a Pakistani who is a chef in a Chinese restaurant and together they follow their dream of opening their own restaurant.

In keeping with the exhibition title *Backstage*, Tiravanija's soup was cooked and served for participants in the loading area before the opening, so the visitors saw only the remains of this action, which form an exhibit. The fact that Tiravanija prepared the soup using ready-made products here is more than just a gastronomic detail. Preparing Flädlesuppe using a ready-mix for pancakes and stock powder, plus the addition of a little cayenne pepper, clearly contradicts the traditional recipe and probably also the general expectations of the soup's taste.[31] The perceptions of integration that are supposed to be manifested through the cooking of a typically German soup, which is nevertheless perceived as such only by the Swabian part of Germany, were thus broken ironically multiple times over. With this location-specific installation, Tiravanija addressed the perception of foreign identities on several levels: He evaded the expectation both that he will give out free food and also that he always serves only "exotic" dishes.

The artist followed a similar strategy around ten years later: For *Untitled 2003 (social pudding)* at the *Zeitgenössische Galerie Leipzig*, Tiravanija teamed up with the Danish art group *Superflex* to serve pudding. This was produced from the ready-made pack that is very recognizable in Germany, which was designed specially for this exhibition based on the products of a large German manufacturer.[32] Even today the great-grandson of the company's founder Arend Oetker is still the Chairman of the Board for the exhibition venue's foundation. Here Tiravanija was once again reacting to the circumstances in situ. The coconut and orange flavor prepared for the exhibition nevertheless pointed once again to his own heritage: Orange

30 | Drachenfutter, Jan Schütte, D 1987. See Probst, C. (2010): Globale Koch-Kunst in Bielefeld, *Deutschlandfunk.de*, Nov. 11, available online at: http://www.deutschlandfunk.de/globale-koch-kunst-in-bielefeld.691.de.html?dram:article_id=54398 (accessed on Feb. 5, 2016).

31 | See Trippi: 1998, as well as Kellein: 2010, p. 12.

32 | *Superflex* website "Social Pudding,", available online at: http://superflex.net/tools/social_pudding//4#g (accessed on Jan. 23, 2016).

as the color of Buddhism is a recurring color in his works, whilst coconut milk is a basic ingredient of his Thai curries.[33]

The works mentioned here demonstrate that Tiravanija's gastronomic installations cannot be reduced down to the mere serving of Thai specialties. Using food as a medium, he returns time and again to various aspects: Social, topographic, cultural and historic. In addition, he addresses the role of the chef, the prepared dish and the ingredients used in the process. Thus it becomes clear that using food as a medium he explores the circumstances encountered and integrates these into the work. What is unique about Tiravanija's works is that, as a conceptual artist, he also integrates gastronomic knowledge into his works and likewise gives artisanal qualities a certain meaning. So how does this relate to the work developed in 2015, *DO WE DREAM UNDER THE SAME SKY?*

FROM MEDIUM TO BRAND

In comparison to earlier works, with *DWDUTSS* it appears that gastronomic knowledge actually comes to the fore somewhat less. Against the background of Tiravanija's formerly intensive examination of food as a medium, only a superficial indication of earlier works is inherent in the Thai-inspired food given out as part of this work. In Basel Tiravanija presents himself as a well-known artist-chef, whose curry dishes are long since established as a brand within the art world. Instead of using food as a medium through gastronomic knowledge, the artist takes the role of a gastronomic service provider. Alongside the architecture of steel and bamboo, Thai curry becomes an exoticized representation of *the land*.

With an eye on Tiravanija's earlier works, the philosopher Harald Lemke identifies: "Tiravanija's intercultural 'gastrosophy' circumvents the problem of a conceptual traditionalism and ethnocentrism, which naturalize and exoticize the cultures to an immutable identity by deliberately highlighting the real artificial nature of the food-cultural identity."[34] For *DWDUTSS* however, other parameters that contradict these observations nevertheless appear central. After all, the attempt to create a Thai ambiance follows the logic of tourist exhibition stands that are supposed to bring the flair of a travel destination to life. Here *DWDUTSS* shows parallels to the Milan Expo 2015, which took place at the same time and for which various countries presented their typical dishes under the motto *Feeding*

---

33 | Krause-Wahl: 2006, p. 168.

34 | Lemke: 2007, p. 96. A description of the work in the Grand Palais likewise defends Tiravanija's work *Soup/No Soup* against the accusation of exoticizing: "En outre, bien que Tiravanija privilégie les recettes thaï dans ses repas, il évite les associations simplificatrices de l'exotisme, soulignant plutôt les dimensions intangibles et interpersonnelles de l'expérience partagée." See: *Grand Palais* website "Rirkrit Tiravanija, Soup/No Soup", available online at: http://www.grandpalais.fr/fr/evenement/rirkrit-tiravanija-soupno-soup (accessed on Jan. 30, 2016).

the Planet, Energy for life (May 1 to October 10, 2015). This is problematic not only because it serves certain clichéd preconceptions. The practice is in contrast to Tiravanija's earlier way of working, which always called existing preconceptions into question and highlighted over-simplification. It is true that food continues to serve Tiravanija as a medium that is bound up with the question of identity, yet this is not a central theme nor critically examined here, rather only banal associations are prompted. Food becomes an enhancement of the installation for *Greetings from Thailand*, but to Bourriaud's mind it at least serves as a medium for bringing people together in a specific place and social situation.

This gathering in front of the art exhibition has event potential. As far as Diedrich Diederichsen is concerned certainly: "[...] Participation is the new spectacle",[35] even if the exhibition, with its high sales and visitor numbers, is perhaps the greater spectacle. As a primarily economically defined venue it offers a framework that unavoidably twists Tiravanija's practice entirely. Even visitors who are familiar with neither the artist nor his work and who have a traditional understanding of the museum as an institution are far less confused by eating and cooking in front of an art exhibition than in the middle of a museum or a gallery. Having a meal here is not seen as a surprising intervention, but rather as a service offering. The installation thus shifts more clearly towards gastronomy than Tiravanija's previous works. In previous works detailed gastronomic knowledge made food a medium, whilst now it is much more structural references to gastronomy that come to the fore.

THE ARTIST AS A CHEF[36]

Contrary to expectations, here the overlaps between art and gastronomy do not lie primarily in the fulfilment of culinary desires on the part of the guests, as the concept of *service art* coined by Christian Janecke would imply, but specifically in the negation of these desires.[37] As a gastronomic installation *DWDUTSS* aims to evade the service nature of regular exhibition gastronomies, but at the same time highlights astonishing similarities with the restaurants of top chefs. These venues are now seen as places that not only serve good food, but also aim to offer a comprehensive experience. As such autonomous places for experience, like Tiravanija's installation they detach themselves from conventional service gastronomy. This effort towards autonomy includes serving a tasting menu as the highest expres-

---

35 | Diedrich Diederichsen quotes from Rebentisch: 2013, p. 64.

36 | See Krause-Wahl: 2006. p. 166 and Beil: 2002, p. 219. Whilst Beil calls Joseph Beuys a chef, Krause-Wahl highlights Tiravanija's leadership qualities in comparison to managers. Here I connect these two perspectives.

37 | See Janecke: 2011 and his "Partizipationsfolklore" ["Participation Folklore"], *Faust Kultur* website, April 2015, available online at: http://faustkultur.de/2236-0-Maschen-der-Kunst-Partizipationsfolklore.html (accessed on Jan. 23, 2016).

sion of culinary art. This is generally offered as the only possible option, so there are no à la carte dishes. The guest has to embrace a menu created by the chef. This is for pragmatic reasons on the one hand, because the dishes served are complex and are easier to create with a standard menu. On the other hand, the chef as the author of the menu is given the opportunity to steer the culinary experience entirely. These kinds of restaurants are sometimes booked out months in advance, and part of the overall experience is only getting a reservation with a bit of luck. This scarcity enhances the restaurant's attractiveness.

DWDUTSS also avoids a varied culinary offering. Here guests eat whatever is placed on the table. Food is cooked and then distributed for as long as it remains. Due to the high demand and limited quantities, in Basel too there is likewise a scarcity of the coveted food. What is more, the visitors can continually follow the cooking process and look over the shoulders of the chefs at their workstations as they prepare the food. An open kitchen or visits to the kitchen are another element of many top restaurants, which give the curious guests insights into the site of production.[38] The herb beds of *DWDUTSS* also suggest local production and the direct link to *the land* points towards close contact with the producers of foodstuffs,[39] similarly to premium restaurants that cultivate their own vegetable gardens.[40] Something that is a fundamental element of the concept in top restaurants is at least visually proclaimed by means of design considerations in fashionable locales, where pots of basil on tables, a visible service station and relatively stereotypical elements of interior design such as ceramic tiles or wooden bars are enough to convey craftsmanship and authentic food in a systematically thought out and relatively mechanically functioning establishment.

Similarly to the strong presence of the head chef in his own restaurant, always appreciated by guests, for *DWDUTSS* Tiravanija plays a greater role at the center of his own work than he otherwise would. Generally his presence in the gallery or museum space has been seen as non-essential for the relevance of his works, argues art historian Jacqueline Burckhardt: "The personal presence of the artist does not play a role in the experience of his art."[41] At the art fair, however, his presence takes on a different significance: Here Tiravanija is in demand as a star of art and cuisine, as the following press report suggests: "The food was ready. And, having tried it, I can say this: brave the lines and try Rirkrit's curry. If you're lucky, maybe

38 | Adrià/Soler/Adrià: 2008, p. 341.

39 | The artist as a farmer was a theme as early as 2013, see: Art Basel: Art Basel Conversations: The Artist as Farmer, available online at: https://www.youtube.com/watch?v=YxUQK31oWVk (accessed on Oct. 20, 2015).

40 | In the cookbooks of famous kitchens the producers used are not only mentioned but also illustrated and presented in detail. See: Redzepi: 2010, pp. 346; Keller: 1999, pages 28, 122, 194, and 248.

41 | Burckhardt: 1998, p. 230.

he'll ladle it into your bowl himself."[42] Through his presence, the artist as caterer to the art world attracts an audience that is "programmed" to artistic authorship.

THE AESTHETICS OF FOOD

The gradual approach to gastronomic undertakings, which was slowly taking shape back in 2001 at the Venice Biennale, where Tiravanija teamed up with artists Tobias Rehberger and Olafur Eliasson to run a temporary restaurant, reached one of its high points at Art Basel 2015. The road towards a restaurant of his own did not seem far away and indeed the artist opened his first restaurant in summer 2015. Tiravanija's gallery-owner Gavin Brown sees this as a logical step: "It's the first time he's had a commercial kitchen, so it's a departure in that sense, [...]. It's a natural progression, in a way. It's about entering into the same place but from a different direction."[43]

Chefs, for their part, are discovering the potential of using food as an art medium. Chef Ferran Adrià's invitation to documenta in 2007 established just such an understanding of cooking in art. Adrià sees cooking as a language: "Cooking is a language through which all the following properties may be expressed: harmony, creativity, happiness, beauty, poetry, complexity, magic, humor, provocation and culture."[44]

In both cases the artisanal activity, conceptual thinking and aesthetic medium all complement one another. Chefs and artists who use food as a medium thus operate together in an area of congruency between art and cuisine. The analysis of this practice requires both gastronomic and art-historical knowledge in order to grasp the works in their various aspects. Hence food as a medium can be understood both in art and in cuisine as no longer solely of a culinary function and significance, but rather must be confronted with various other contexts in order to tap into the significance it holds beyond purely aesthetic parameters.

An aesthetic of food that combines the aesthetic and art-historical approaches with gastronomic knowledge represents a fruitful expansion of a purely culinary perception for the post-Adrià generation of chefs, such as Massimo Bottura, René Redzepi or Andoni Aduriz. These chefs tackle cultural aspects as much as changing taste patterns, even if initially, in contrast to fine artists, they are focused on products, their processing and their presentation.

---

42 | Freeman, N. (2015): Curry on the Messeplatz: Rirkrit Tiravanija on his much-hyped installation in Basel, June 15, available online at: http://www.artnews.com/2015/06/15/curry-on-the-messeplatz-rirkrit-tiravanija-on-his-much-hyped-installation-in-basel/ (accessed on Feb. 5, 2016).

43 | Herriman: 2015.

44 | Buergel: 2009, p. 10.

This is less about the question of whether and under what circum-stances cooking is an art form, and rather about being able to appropriately place cooking as an aesthetic practice. Chefs ever more frequently cross the threshold between art and cuisine and are thus active within the area of congruency with artists like Tiravanija. With an eye on Adrià and Tira-vanija, who both use food as a medium, Adorno's statement that "[...] the emancipation of art from cuisine or pornography is irrevocable" is proven to be a misjudgment.[45]

---

45 | Adorno: 1997, p. 15.

For a Good Time

dilettantin produktionsbüro: Transitory Spaces
of Art Production, Presentation and Distribution

Paola Bonino

The compound name *dilettantin produktionsbüro* [dilettante production bureau] embodies the multi-layered artistic procedures and questions posed by the eponymous artistic collective and the development its practice has undergone over the years. "Dilettante", a word originated during the Italian Renaissance and then translated almost unchanged into other languages, originally designated the artist as a well-respected researcher who wants to affirm the autonomy of art in opposition to artisans who depend on outside commissions and from whom he wants to distance himself.[1] A little later, with the birth of academies, the difference between dilettante and professionals (trained artists) arose and the word came to indicate someone "who does something because he or she loves it. The actions are driven by passion, not by skill or craftsmanship."[2] Goethe and Schiller coined the binary value system around the concepts of the virtuoso and the dilettante, with the latter becoming the outsider of academic and artistic virtues. Dilettante thus places us in the realm of leisure and free time, of an activity not undertaken for income or profit and not recognized by any institutions, laws or contemporaries: everybody can be, at any time and in any field, a dilettante, it is his or her own decision!

Unlike this, "produktionsbüro" brings to mind a well-structured office, where professionals meet and take decisions, manage things, receive clients who recognize and trust them thanks to their certified education, to their fame in professional circles, and, last but not least, to the presence of the office itself. The bureau – borrowed from French "bureau", which becomes "Büro" in German – has been conceived for material and/or immaterial productivity, which must generate some profit. It also recalls the studio/atelier of many international renowned contemporary artists, whose role has become the one of the manager and entrepreneur, hiring a

1 | See Perniola, M. (2015): *L'arte espansa*, Turin.
2 | Anneli Käsmayr quoted by Elke Bippus in Käsmayr: 2012, p. 33.

number of assistants and collaborators, all deeply involved in the artwork's production process.

Acting along the fluid borders between art and everyday life, trying to catch the sleeping moment when the one dissolves into the other, the *dilettantin produktionsbüro* collective nimbly moves between amateurism, professionality in art and gastronomy, the production of art objects and art as consumer service, making the ambivalences and contradictions among these realms its field of investigation.

Although one could easily recognize the artist and musician Anneli Käsmayr as the heart and soul of the group, she has always rejected any claim to main authorship or leadership. *dilettantin produktionsbüro* is, in fact, an elastic group, which expands the ranks of its participants depending on the project; each artwork is thus the outcome of a collective working process, involving also collaborations with other artists, designers, and subjects external to the collective.

Starting from this premise, I shall examine two projects by the collective: the artist-run restaurant *dreijahre dining room project* (2007–2010) and the dinner experience *Eating the Forest* (2015). I shall then conclude with some thoughts on possible, future developments. Some historical references, considered of interest in relation to *dilettantin produktionsbüro*'s practice and to the present publication, will be made. This is obviously not intended as an extensive overview of the artistic procedures which, starting from the early 20th-century avant-garde, have focused on food, hospitality and ephemeral situations of conviviality.

ART AND BUSINESS – *DREIJAHRE DINING ROOM PROJECT*, BREMEN 2007–2010

"A. Käsmayr: So what makes a restaurant into art for you?
R. Block: I don't know, but I think it all starts with a claim. It must first be declared a work of art by the person operating it. Then you need a public, some people who are willing to share this concept. Naturally, some guests might feel disturbed by the idea and ignore being part of a work of art."[3]

While still in a master class at the University of the Arts in Bremen and after some projects which engaged in the production, presentation and shared consumption of food as artistic activity,[4] *dilettantin produktionsbüro*

---

3 | René Block, Anna Bromley, Anneli Käsmayr in conversation in Käsmayr: 2012, p. 117.

4 | See, for example, dilettantin menu, which marks the very beginning of *dilettantin produktionsbüro* dinner settings when still in the Art Academy. The project was a response to people questioning if a dinner could be an art work at all and was developed following the idea of a social sculpture, pinpointing specific marks in *dilettantin produktionsbüro*'s artistic attitude, e. g. white linen napkins that were printed on with statements such as: "Aesthetic experience as context dependent

opened a restaurant in the year 2007 – involving management consultants and business partners – right in the middle of Bremen's Viertel district, the most popular, hipster and alternative area of the town. As the name of the project seems to suggest, its duration was strictly fixed to a period of three years ("drei Jahre" in German).

"Before we had done a café project for several weeks and a hotel installation for three days, which were perceived very clearly as artworks. There was no question whether they were art or not. It was in a certain sense not satisfying since we were more interested in the question when art becomes art. So, extending this kind of timeframe, even three months is still a typical exhibition length. But three years are something severely different. Three years are not easily consumed as art. They are much more radical in that sense and since we were looking for this boundary where the thing might actually tip, it felt right."[5]

Due to the pre-fixed timespan of the project, the necessary condition for its existence was to make the business successful, enabling the work to reach its completion. And the business ran quite well, dishing up a genuine regional cuisine, with fresh and seasonal ingredients. *dilettantin produktionsbüro* was responsible for managing the venture and the cuisine, as well as for the design of the place, aimed at creating a welcoming and relaxing atmosphere, encouraging people not just to have a meal, but to spend time chatting, reading, exchanging opinions and experiences. The staff was made up in part by students from the Bremen University of the Arts, on hire as regular waitresses.[6]

Not too openly advertised as an art project, the restaurant attracted a heterogeneous clientele: artists, people from theater and creative fields as well as grandmothers on Sundays, families, lovers, business people and the young crowd at nights. The artists took advantage of this situation, observing from a protected position how such an artistic operation was perceived by the guests/users of the work, who were aware or unaware of what lay behind the normal restaurant. Although probably not evident for the guests, distracted by the usual activities of the place, the conventional relationship between artist and observer was overturned and the procedures of art production and distribution affected.

As noted by Boris Groys, the traditional understanding of creative work wants it to take place beyond public control and, usually, beyond the con-

---

embodied experience. Directing life onto art and directing art onto life. The inevitable disaster of not understanding. To see what has not been shown." The dinners were held in different spaces – a gallery, a restaurant, an industrial space, a private home – and were aimed to explore how the perception of the events was influenced by the space itself, the setting, the people and the intention.

5 | Anneli Käsmayr in conversation with the author, February 2016.

6 | For a detailed description of the restaurant and its activity see Käsmayr: 2012, in particular, the texts by Elke Bippus, Michael Glasmeier, Rolf Thiele and the conversation between René Block, Anna Bromley and Anneli Käsmayr.

scious control of the artist himself; creative work happens in a separate phase of seclusion, in secret, marking a desynchronization of the time of work from the time when the result is revealed.[7] In the case of *dreijahre*, any secrets are denied: Here, art production, presentation and distribution coincide; the artwork is not only produced in the public eye, but the spectator/guest also takes an active part in this process, and in the profit it generates. *dilettantin produktionsbüro* successfully established a self-sustaining structure that skipped any need for its institutional recognition as a work of art and was independent of the art market; it made a profit without delivering anything finished and ready to be sold, and rather solely through the process of the artwork production.[8]

This brings us to a key issue. If the artwork is a business, but the business is not aimed at virtuous growth, and instead aligned to a pre-fixed end and was stopped the very moment it took off (after three years), can we still consider the project *dreijahre* a real business? The role of the artist as entrepreneur is denied in the very moment when it is affirmed. On the edge between professionalism and amateurism, *dilettantin produktionsbüro* decided to follow neither the rational rules of the enterprise, nor those of the art system:

"Thus *dreijahre* radically treads that narrow line between everyday life and art, since it no longer looks anything like art and is only opened up to the potential space within art as a result of the artist's own assertions. It is not merely pretending to be a restaurant, it IS a restaurant. Nor is it otherwise described as art, as it would be in the larger context of an art exhibition or based upon a museum setting, for example. It therefore completely sidesteps the obvious criteria according to which one could distinct identify it as art."[9]

dreijahre situates itself in a long tradition of artist-run restaurants and cafés which, starting from the avant-gardes of the early 20th century (for instance, the Futurist "Taverna del Santo Palato" [Restaurant of the Holy Palate]) shared the common goal of seeking to shorten the distance between art and life, doing it through the most basic human need: nutrition.

Specifically in the revolutionary climate of the late 1960s and the 1970s, various artists experimented with restaurant projects as attempts to escape from the formal, commercial and institutional structures of the art

---

7 | Groys, B. (2013): Art workers: Between Utopia and the Archive, in: *e-flux journal* #45, May 2013, http://www.e-flux.com/journal/art-workers-between-utopia-and-the-archive/ (last accessed March 15, 2016).

8 | "The art market and the industry as we perceive it is very brutal and in a way oppressive and exploitative, the more we were confronted with how it works, who gets paid or not paid, the more frustrated we became with our choice to do this as our profession. It seemed so fake and pathogenic." Anneli Käsmayr in conversation with the author, February 2016.

9 | Anneli Käsmayr quoted by Elke Bippus in Käsmayr: 2012, p. 35.

world, doing it in good company, encouraged by food and drinks, in spaces designed and authorized by the artists themselves.[10]

For the purposes of this essay, and by virtue of the pseudo-business components they involved, I shall focus on projects by conceptual artists Allen Ruppersberg and Gordon Matta-Clark.[11] In 1969, Allen Ruppersberg installed a temporary restaurant called Al's Café in downtown Los Angeles, which opened once a week for three months. The interior resembled an all-American coffee shop with hyper-familiar decor. Alongside coffee and beer, clients could order conceptual dishes from the menu; they were based on those one would buy from a coffee shop and cost the same. "Bubble gums and raisins", "Double decker", "Pally Melt – Patty Page Photo (or Reasonable Facsimile) Covered with Toasted Marshmallows" were all assemblage artworks, nominally edible, available for convenient prices. This allowed the artist to achieve a double by-pass, both of the institution (as the place that legitimated the art work) and the market (as the platform for its distribution). But the café was not just an environment installation artwork, it also functioned as a gathering place, and was intended to fill the lack of opportunities to hang out for L.A.'s art community at that time, in opposition to the liveliness of New York and the East Coast. Ruppersberg ran it by himself, doing everything behind the counter (as cook, service manager, bottle washer) and hired waitresses to serve at the tables.

As the name of the place spread, the number of customers grew immensely, forcing the artist to do extra work to get all the necessities for the preparation of the dinners and luckily allowing him to make some money. According to Ruppersberg, "the idea was to set up a situation where anybody was welcome",[12] without great concern for who the clients were or whether they grasped the project as an artwork and the activities inside as performances. Suspicious about the activities goings-on at Al's Café, located in a slightly seedy area of the town, the police started to investigate the place and finally closed it down; the artist and the staff were arrested officially for having served beer without a license.

In 1971, Ruppersberg extended the concept behind Al's Café to a further project: Al's Grand Hotel, a two-story house in Hollywood, which he converted into a fully-functioning hotel for a period of six weeks. Before its opening, Ruppersberg sent out a brochure advertising the hotel's uniquely decorated and named rooms, such as the Jesus Room and the Bridal Suite, inviting guests to reserve them for rates of 15–30 dollars a night.

---

10 | See Introduction in Smith: 2013.

11 | A key reference for both artists is the work of Daniel Spoerri. Before opening his well-known Eat Art Gallery (1970), Spoerri turned the Allan Stone Gallery in New York into a three days restaurant (1964) and his room at the Chelsea Hotel into an exhibition (1965). Once back to Europe, he started the Restaurant Spoerri, a serious culinary establishment and a convivial artwork, in which hosts and guests experimented together with the blurring boundaries between art and life.

12 | Allen Ruppersberg interviewed by Constance Lewallen at the Kadist Art Foundation, San Francisco, September 21, 2011, in Smith: 2013, p. 120.

Fig. 1: Allen Ruppersberg, Al's Grand Hotel, 1971

Fig. 2: Allen Ruppersberg, Al's Grand Hotel, 1971

Fig. 3: Gordon Matta-Clark, Food

Fig. 4: Gordon Matta-Clark, Food

Fig. 5: Rirkrit Tiravanija, Untitled 1994 (angst essen Seele auf)

"It will be, like Al's Café, in all respects a full operational hotel, including a bar, a comfortable, relaxing lobby, music, continental breakfast, daily maid service, souvenirs and adjusted rooms for your sleeping comforts [...] The rooms will be open for inspection until midnight, however, everyone is welcome to come, have a drink, and enjoy the luxurious atmosphere whether or not you stay the night."[13]

While both projects – Al's Café and Al's Hotel – claimed they were inclusive and open to anyone who felt comfortable and enjoyed the time spent there, they ironically suggest that "perhaps art is a service industry like any other"[14] and that the artist, who tries to act independently of the institutions and the market in fact can be judged by the same criteria in terms of public acceptance and satisfaction.

During the same years, in New York, on the opposite coast of the USA, young artist Gordon Matta-Clark, fascinated by the alchemical proprieties of food-related processes, was creating, through the selection, preparation and cooking of food, some major artworks, anticipating his famous building cuts and splitting.[15] In early 1971, Matta-Clark thus involved a number of fellow artists in starting the restaurant FOOD, which opened in SoHo thanks to an investment by dancer Caroline Goodden. In order to fully understand the significance of the project, one should consider it in the context of the creative early-1970s SoHo and as part of a cooperative community network which included, alongside FOOD, Avalanche magazine, the performance and exhibition space 112 Green Street and the artists' collaborative Anarchitecture Group. FOOD was less than a business and more than a restaurant, it was an art piece, the place where Gordon Matta-Clark organized special Sunday night guest artist dinners, where artists were invited to design and cook a meal, where performances, food theater and fashion shows were staged (featuring, for instance, edible clothes by fashion designer Robert Kushner) and films shot, alongside many other things which happened on a daily basis. It created also a sort of welfare state for artists, who could earn quick and unproblematic money waiting tables.

"I wanted to show off my/our cooking to 'the world'. I wanted to have a place to eat with food that I liked that was open when I needed it to be, and I wanted to create

---

13 | http://blogs.getty.edu/pacificstandardtime/explore-the-era/archives/i46/ (last access March 15, 2016).

14 | Smith: 2013, p. 118.

15 | "Consider a complete set of nutrient (culinary) operations – [excess delights though simplicity is more convincing].

Selection (the ingredients in their natural forms are separated from the landscape).
Preparation (each substance is cut, soaked, mixed in short undergoes a variety of imaginative alterations).
Cooking (here the flame, time and the elements are one's palette – moisture versus dryness, charring, sautéing, all the degrees of exposure to heat)."
Text from Matta-Clark notebook (1969) quoted in Morris, C. (ed.) (1999): *FOOD: An exhibition by White Columns*, New York/Münster, p. 23.

a work place for artists that had no restrictions on how many hours a day or days a week the artist worked so that they could be free to suddenly drop out as needed to produce their show and still have a job when they're through."[16]

The business part was dismissed in the name of art experimentation and an attempt to support artists; Matta-Clark started to lose interest in the project during fall 1972 and, after some years during which Goodden managed the restaurant with some collaborators, it was finally sold.

"Though we consumed food, *Food* consumed us. It was a free enterprise which gave food away much too freely. *Food* (me) was much more concerned with how it looked than how economically it ran and it (Gordon) was much more concerned about how charming, stimulating and friendly it was than how much customers and workers followed the rules."[17]

While redesigning the space before the opening of the restaurant, Matta-Clark used his cutting process in a pragmatic way, underlying how for him, as well for his peers, operations with food, architecture, art, fashion and other media were all related in a common attempt to occupy, transform, envelope, consume, digest new spaces and to deconstruct existing structure, anything they were. FOOD and its parallel projects stressed the rules and boundaries of the art system, effecting radical changes in the *way* and the *where* art is conceived, created and presented.

The conceptual operations by Ruppersberg and Matta-Clark have formed a strong reference point for a group of artists who, starting from the 1990s, placed immaterial work, conceptual think-tanks, information, encounters and the critique of institutions at the center of their practices. Although many of them created situations of exchange and conviviality involving edible material,[18] I have decided to focus here on *Untitled 1994*

---

16 | Caroline Goodden in *Gordon Matta-Clark*, exh. cat. IVAM Centro Julio Gonzalez, Valencia, 1992, p. 370.

17 | From a Letter from Caroline Goodden to Corinne Diserens, September 5, 1992, published in Morris, C. (ed.) (1999): *FOOD: An exhibition by White Columns*, New York/Münster, p. 47.

18 | There are ample names and occurrences to cite, here just a few, mainly taken by Nicolas Bourriaud's Relational Aesthetics: Angela Bulloch set up a café where, as a certain number of visitors sat down, the seats broadcast a piece of music by Kraftwerk (CCC Tours, 1993); Bulloch, together with fellow artist Liam Gillick, offered whiskey to help participants of the performance *An Old Song and A New Drink* to enter a state of trance while the song Ten Commandments of a Man Given to a Woman by Prince Buster played over the sound system (Café Beaubourg, Paris, 1993); Georgina Starr performed lonely and paranoid meal for one, distributing topic-related texts (Restaurant exhibition, La Bocca, Paris, 1993); Philippe Parreno decided to organize a party "occupying two hours of time, rather than square meters of space" (Le Consortium, Dijon, 1995); Rirkrit Tiravanija set up a relaxation area for artists, equipped with a table football game and a full fridge

(angst essen Seele auf), a bar that Rirkrit Tiravanija opened at Friesenwall in Cologne in 1994. Rainer Werner Fassbinder's movie *Angst essen Seele auf* [Fear eats the Soul] was broadcast on a television set inside the bar, where, as a reference to the film, just beer and Coke were served. The artist refused to reinforce the event by adding his presence, spending basically all nights outside, watching people coming and going and occasionally pulling beers from the fridge or rewinding tapes, remaining simultaneously "involved and disengaged."

"Anyone arriving to 'watch' or 'view' was immediately absorbed, and became complicit in a social/cultural interchange that offered new models for passing the time and asked new questions about facile separations between art and everything else. Those who passed by were neither included nor excluded. They became partial participants and had no choice but to overhear precise discussions. 'The big other' of Lacan was exposed and something real revealed."[19]

The hidden authorship creates an ambiguous situation, which remains suspended, without a precise scope, definition, temporality and location (art or life?). Eluding strategies of control and unwritten rules of fruition, the artist occupied a fractured time and space, in which the unpredictability of what came next enabled the possibility of new and parallel scenarios to happen.

To return to the *dreijahre* project, one can observe a hybrid attitude towards authorship and artists' statements: As noted above, *dilettantin produktionsbüro* acted literally under the eyes of its guests, without loudly claiming the restaurant was an art project (i.e. there were no signs above the entrance door, just a couple of lines on the back of the menu, indicating that the restaurant was an art project for the duration of three years). This created an unclear situation in which the guests of the restaurant (the users of the work) unconsciously contributed to the production and development of the project, while allowing the artist collective to observe its audience and question its own practices. This structure was able to work quite well as long as the traditional protocol of the restaurant was respected.

However, on the last night of *dreijahre*, coming unexpectedly for many of the guests,[20] something happened which reversed the rules and the routine of the place. A pompous banquet in the form of a still life was served on the tables in the dining room, but no staff was around. Art was suddenly revealing itself through one of its most traditional forms. At first confused and even annoyed, some guests left the place complaining loudly about the lack of service. After a while, though, people started to

---

(Exhibition Surfaces de reparation, Dijon, 1994). He is also well-known for cooking and distributing Thai Soup inside art galleries and institutions.

19 | Liam Gillick: Outsiding. Rikrit Tiravanija's Places, in: Gillick, L. (2006:) *Proxemics. Selected Writings (1988-2006)*, Zürich/Dijon, p. 269.

20 | *dilettantin produktionsbüro* anticipated on purpose the closing date of *dreijahre* little before the forecast 1095 days. This emphasizes the idea of *dreijahre* as a vanishing place.

Fig. 6: Finissage dreijahre dining room project, 2010

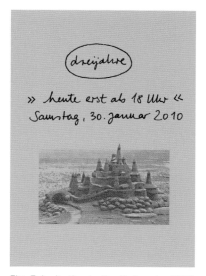

Fig. 7: Invitation to the Finissage, 2010

help themselves and take advantage of the buffet, without looking for many explanations. As night came, a huge party unfolded. The senses were stimulated, an interaction between body and mind was triggered, the tortuous question of the intellect: "So where is the art here"?[21] and "Is this art? Or

---

21 | Käsmayr: 2012, p. 117.

life? Or something in between?" finally dissolved in the enjoyment of food, music and good company.

A Dinner Experience – *Eating the Forest*, Milan 2015

Five years have since passed and during that time much of the work by *dilettantin produktionsbüro* has been dedicated towards creating special temporary atmospheres and conceptual dinners or hospitality settings that respond to a specific context and invitation. Leaving the business aspect to one side for a while, the central question became: "What does it do good for you?" in terms of material nourishment and immaterial fulfilment.[22] The focus has been on taste and sensory stimulation, exploring how people's behavior, discourses and decision-making processes are affected by the shared enjoyment of food, good company and relaxation. In order to create the appropriate atmosphere, the projects often entail a number of disciplines and are developed in cooperation with professionals from different fields.[23]

Eating the Forest was a conceptual dinner experience in which I participated together with an exclusive round of seven other invited guests, all women from the art world, in October 2015 at the archive of DOCVA Fabbrica del Vapore in Milan. It was the first in a series of dinners, which, at the moment I write this, are going to happen in various spaces around Europe and the United States.

"The series *Eating the Forest* is about the creation of an atmosphere for one night, it is more of a pompous magical painting that you can sit in, breathe in and perceive with all of your senses."[24]

For the event in Milan, Karin Laansoo, Director of the Estonian Contemporary Art Development Center in New York, invited *dilettantin produktions-*

---

22 | The project *SLOE* (2014) marks the beginning of the series *Tu dir Gutes [do thee good]*. For a public art exhibition in Paderborn, *dilettantin produktionsbüro* created a food truck that moved around the town, offering a heterogeneous audience nourishing food: green juices, tea mixes, herbal spice lemonades and energy cookies made with the recipe of naturalist St. Hildegard von Bingen. As usual in their work, the food served to invite people to stay and engage, have a moment of slowing down or a good conversation, between art and everyday life. http://www.dilettantin.com/sloe-do-thee-good/ (last accessed March 15, 2016).
23 | See, for example, the performances *Swinging Plasticine* (Errant Bodies, Berlin, 2011) and *Swinging Plasticine Shifted Two* (Note On, Berlin, 2012), in collaboration with artist Michael Fesca. Both performances featured Plasticine dishes by Fesca and the live cooking of food conceived for the occasion by *dilettantin produktionsbüro*. http://www.dilettantin.com/en-swinging-plasticine/; http://www.dilettantin.com/en-swinging-plasticine-shifted-two/ (last accessed March 15, 2016).
24 | Anneli Käsmayr in conversation with the author, February 2016.

büro to conceive a performative dinner space, inspired by the Estonian Forest, featuring the work of artists Kris Lemsalu and Adeline de Monseignat, whom she had worked with before. During the development of the project, fashion designer Julia Heuer and the wood designers Malin Workshop also came on board. *dilettantin produktionsbüro* then created a setting that included an eating experience to allow a different approach to the artworks; for the occasion, the extraordinariness that is art was translated into a very daily use, and the ordinary act of eating was raised to the status of aesthetic experience.

Fig. 8: Eating the Forest, 2015, DOCVA, Milan

Fig. 9: Eating the Forest, 2015, DOCVA, Milan

As guests entered the DOCVA archive, lit up with candles for the occasion, they were welcomed by a long table, decked out solely with artworks: the table-cloth designed by Julia Heuer, the sock cups by Kris Lemsalu, the various plates (wooden trees and utensils by Malin Workshop, glass bowls by Adeline de Monseignat, underwear plates by Kris Lemsalu), the food itself.

Each course (seven in total), accompanied by a specific drink and served on a dedicated artwork/plate, was introduced by *dilettantin produktionsbüro*, who shortly presented the concept and the ingredients of what was about to be eaten, strictly by hand as no cutlery was provided. Dishes such as Cream Cheese & Young Radishes, Mackerel, lactic acid & cabbage, Mushrooms, moss & leaves broth, Cod, kama, lichen savory cabbage, Moose, sea buck-thorn & chervil tuber, Apple, beetroot, sour cream & spruces followed one another. The artists worked to one side, cooking on an open kitchenette, where guests could walk around, have a glimpse and ask questions. Once between courses, participants were asked to stand up, wash their hands and approach the kitchen station, where a sensual mix of hyssop anise foam with caviar, fennel and bread crumbs was served right on the back of their hands, to be eaten at once, like a spicy kiss.

Involved in a 360-degree experience, eating the flavors of the Estonian forest with their hands and chatting with the other guests, it was hard to clearly define what was happening: Was it a networking night for women in the art field? An exclusive, highbrow event to promote Estonian culture and to present new creations by the participating artists (we were excep-tionally allowed to drink and eat *from* and *on* artworks, which were simul-taneously part of an installation and, on request, on sale)? Did any borders exist between the dinner, the performance and the art piece? Which role did we have, that of viewers, witnesses, guests or parts of the production of the work?

Framed just by its duration – the time of a dinner – and by the shared act of eating, the night left the same feeling of excitement and fulfillment of a successful party, when one has deeply enjoyed the hours spent in a par-allel, ephemeral dimension, which vanishes the moment you walk out the door. The act of eating by hand and the use of ingredients such as berries, leaves, dried moss, roots revoked ancestral memories, turning the experi-ence into something primordial and extremely physical.

In this context, the fact that one of the artists, Kris Lemsalu, who made the sock cups and the underwear dishes, joined the dinner via Skype from an artist residency in Japan, seems to me if not problematic then at least open to question. We saw her, projected on the wall, performing and dressed up as a Japanese doll, but she could not see us; the communica-tion ran via Skype chat, with her not knowing the identity of the person writing. Although her "absent presence" enabled an extension of the din-ner's spatial and temporal framework, it appeared slightly detached from the context of a site- and time-specific project, where all the focus is on the interaction between bodies (and minds) sensually stimulated.

Starting from this episode, I would like now to broaden the current analysis to a further level: In what is today a hyper-stimulated, multidimensional and over-connected reality, where everything is intended to nullify distance and dematerialize interactions, what is the significance of artistic practices such as that of *dilettantin produktionsbüro*, focused on the surrounding environment, participations and the pleasure of being together?

DANCING BODIES – ON THE POSSIBILITY OF OPENING A CLUB

An interesting element of the *dreijahre* project, which I did not mention before, was the hidden club hosted in the basement of the restaurant. Without any precise program and opening time, guests who wanted to party could discover it simply by following the music or drawn by their companions. It was an important extension of the restaurant, a separate dimension dedicated to night life, which enabled a further level of involvement, triggered by music, some drinks, dance.

Fig. 10: The Secret Club in the Basement of dreijahre, 2008

Fantasizing about future, (im)possible projects, Anneli Käsmayr told me about her idea of starting a two-function place, half club and half restaurant. Through a multidisciplinary approach to the work, involving architecture, design, the choice of the staff and decisions regarding the music, food and beverages, *dilettantin produktionsbüro* would create a unique environment with a bar in the center and, on one side, the restaurant, where tiny little morsels and beverages would be served, on the other side, the club with music and dance. As opposed to traditional discos, the place is envisaged to open at 9 p.m., with the main music act before midnight, slightly changing the accepted time for clubbing and introducing a taste of night life in the everyday routine of the guests. For its focus on the ideas of both amusement and collaboration, the project takes full account of Carsten Höller's 24-weeks *Double Club*, opened in London between 2008 and 2009 as a cross-pollination between Congolese and western culture.

"If you go to a club to get drunk, to have a blast, you go to be another person. [...] It is frustrating to be confined in one personality. It would be great to have the two at the same time, half of you drunk and half of you sober. But I think that's the best part of it, you can calculate the duality."[25]

Fig. 11: Carsten Höller, The Double Club

Framed by a limited time-span, the *Double Club* was a place where, through separation and juxtaposition, different realities were simultaneously produced. Each space (the restaurant, the bar and the club) was divided into equally-sized western and Congolese parts on a decorative and functional level, and guests could choose between Congolese or western cuisine, or to merge the two, doing the same with drinks, music and aesthetics. The DJ played on a circular rotating dance floor which slowly revolved at about one turn per hour. He alternated between western and Congolese music, depending on the side of the club he was playing.

25 | Carsten Höller in James Collard, "From Conrad to the heart of disco", in: The Times, November 18, 2008, published in Obrist, H. U./Höller, C. (2011): *The Double Club. A Carsten Höller Project by Fondazione Prada*, Milan.

In response to what is now a hyper-complex reality, where the individual has to deal with a number of stimuli at the same time, the approach Höller proposed challenges the presumption of a centric vision on the world, revealing the possibility of a diverse, double – or even multiple – perspective on the self, the other and the surroundings. It was a double (or multiple) club also in the sense that it related art with design, fashion, music and food, involving collaboration on many levels and enabling each participant to contribute with its specific skill to the final result. Lastly, the project rooted on amusement and fun: "So understandable, but so strange, so parasitic, and at the same time so important, so much of a guide in terms of taking decisions",[26] recognizing these as key elements in our life and in art.

A similar investigation of the potential of viewer's physical and emotional involvement, activation of senses, fun and self-enjoyment is central to *dilettantin produktionsbüro*'s artistic projects, be it a restaurant, a conceptual dinner or something in-between a bar and a club. Although present in the arts down through the centuries in various forms and degrees, these categories have historically been devalued or considered irrelevant to high culture; due to their ephemeral nature, as well their time- and site-specificity, they have been hard to accommodate within art institutions and they have been unfit for the art market.[27]

This is the reason why these categories have been taken fully into account by those artists who tried to dismantle the accepted structures of the art world, exploring possible alternatives or establishing their own. As one can glean from the even cursory historical references presented in this essay, much has already been done in this field, and questions about the significance of current artistic practices dealing with food, drink, hospitality and forms of entertainment can be put.

We are currently witnessing a multi-directional development. On one hand, there is an attempt to (re)introduce these artistic practices inside the institutions, with a view to their musealization and presentation in the context of traditional exhibitions. The institutions also tend to make use of these strategies to develop towards more flexible, welcoming and public-friendly structures, in opposition to the traditional understanding of museums as boring and authoritarian places dedicated to an exclusive circle of academics. There is an attempt to create pleasant visitor experiences, by attractive public programs and a number of events which merge culture, entertainment, food (e.g. initiative as lunches, happy hours and special Sundays at museum). On the other hand, an approach like that of Carsten Höller envisaged cross-disciplinary projects, viewer's experience and amusement as a road out beyond the traditional exhibition format, considering the latter insufficient for the schizophrenic world of the 21st century.[28]

---

26 | Ibid.

27 | See Introduction in Smith: 2013.

28 | See Carsten Höller in conversation with Hans Ulrich Obrist in Obrist, H. U./ Höller, C. (2011): *The Double Club. A Carsten Höller Project by Fondazione Prada*, Milan.

Certainly, life is now developing towards transitory and parallel experiences – be them real, virtual or a mix of the two. Bombarded daily by an incredible flood of stimuli and information, we continuously enter and exit from a number of simultaneous situations, and often we have to deal with two or three of them at the same time (i.e. we chat on WhatsApp while in a meeting and having a Skype call). I therefore consider the 360°-surroundings created by many artists today such as Höller and *dilettantin produktionsbüro* and in which sensory experience is key to be an attempt to create art capable of including this hyper-stimulation, directing it towards fulfilment rather than fragmentation. An attempt to enter and arrest the flow, creating the condition to be present for a while in a specific time and place. A stimulus to turn life, as art, into an aesthetic experience – in the Greek meaning of the term: *aisthetikos* "sensitive, perceptive" and *aisthanesthai* as in "to perceive (by the senses or by the mind), to feel".

Babette's Culinary Turn

An Essay

Jörg Wiesel

This exposition suggests rewatching "Babette's Feast" by Gabriel Axel with a view to the questions addressed by this book.

In the first episode of the Netflix series "Chef's Table" by David Gelb, the Italian chef Massimo Bottura presented his risotto recipe as a "social gesture" – and not just in light of the Modena earthquake, which has posed a major threat to the existence of many regional producers. Bottura places a strong emphasis on supporting local businesses by incorporating their characteristic products into the menus at his restaurant "Osteria Francescana" in Modena. For the TV production, he once more encapsulated the principle of the so-called Nova Regio cuisine, which has drawn a great deal of attention to local rural culture and environment through referencing regional and seasonal products. David Gelb's decision to show the three-Michelin-starred chef ambling around local markets, chatting to regional producers and shopping locally was therefore absolutely logical. And Bottura was happy to play along, assertively expounding his political ambition for ecological and economic sustainability in the context of culinary and gastronomical responsibility. The lavishly produced documentary highlights the unique nature of Bottura's cooking, developed first in the chef's mind, then in his kitchen. Traditional cinematographic audiovisual strategies place the visit to a restaurant in the same category as a trip to the opera, theatre or attending a concert, as guests can often look forward to an evening conceived, rehearsed and perfectly prepared over the course of weeks, an experience with a unique aura. A visit to sophisticated gourmet restaurants can take longer than a musical drama written by Richard Wagner: often up to six hours. In order to assert this cultural and aesthetic equivalence in the documentary format, David Gelb engages the artistic and aesthetic methods of those genres, towards which gourmet cooking is now moving and with which it is orchestrated: verismo (in the sense of a staged authentication), mostly symphonic music, theatrical editing (slow motion).[1]

---

1 | David Gelb's father was appointed General Manager of the New York Metropolitan Opera in 2006.

Elisabeth Raether addressed this aspect back in 2015 in a dossier on Kevin Fehling for German weekly newspaper Die Zeit: "Haute cuisine follows trends and fashions, and this is something it really does share with high culture, with music for example, or painting."[2] Until the end of the 20th century, top-level cuisine spared no pains to discover a new product, a new fruit, a forgotten "tuber one had to get their hands on",[3] in order to create a marked difference and perform a gesture of distinction in comparison to everyday cooking through the presentation of an innovative product. In the context of Nova Regio cuisine, it is no longer the exclusivity of a (foreign) product that is central, but "the work that has gone into a dish",[4] which involves the often international audience in a culinary and regional experience. David Gelb's digital streaming format stages precisely this work and the knowledge of ingredients, cooking techniques and local agriculture: as a grand operatic production with the kitchen as its stage.

Gerhard Neumann has firmly established the "cultural topic food" in the debates held in literary and cultural studies circles. Drawing on Roland Barthes' semiology, Neumann expounds critical analyses of filmed and literary portrayals of eating and food.[5] When looking at the cinematographic dramaturgy of eating and cooking, he focuses on the Danish film "Babette's Feast" (1987) by Gabriel Axel time and again. Karen Blixen located the narrative of her eponymous novella in the solitude of Norwegian village life, where the provost of a Lutheran sect watches sternly over his two daughters. In Axel's version of the story it is the rugged landscape of Jutland upon which the former head chef of the "Café Anglais" irrupts with her culinary expertise, having escaped the political upheavals of the Paris Commune of 1871. In order to reconcile the feuding village community, the sisters Martine and Philippa plan a dinner, to be held on the occasion of their father's 100th birthday. Babette, who has won 10,000 francs in the lottery, wants to cook a special menu for the event. In the end it turns out that it is one of the menus she used to serve to her guests in Paris: Turtle soup, Blinis Demidoff with black caviar, cailles en sarcophage with foie gras and truffle sauce, cheese from the Auvergne, Baba au Rhum with freshly candied fruit salad and a fruit platter with pineapple, figs, dates and white and blue grapes are served by a boy named Erik. Babette remains invisible to the dinner party at the sisters' house as she operates offstage, in the kitchen. The only character able to read, decipher and appreciate the successive dishes is the General, who had eaten at "Café Anglais". The General had fallen in love with one of the sisters, but she had declined his advances. He tells his story of the Parisian head chef as the mood at the table begins to relax, old conflicts are set aside and the dinner guests finally reconcile in memory of the provost and his sermons.

---

2 | Elisabeth Raether, Lucas Wahl (photos) (2015): "Die Poesie der Gurke", in: *Die Zeit*, November 12, no. 46, pp. 17–19, here p. 18 (trans.).

3 | Ibid.

4 | Ibid.

5 | Cf. Barthes: 1961; Neumann: 1993a/1993b; Ott: 2011.

I am at this point interested in illuminating a further aspect that under-
lines the cinematographic dramatization of cooking and eating in a specific
way. Jan Cocotte-Pedersen, head of the restaurant "La Cocotte" in Copenhagen's Hotel Richmond from 1976 to 1990, cooked the menu for the film
according to the description in Blixen's novella. Or, more precisely, Gabriel
Axel integrated the starred chef, very well known in Denmark, into his film
in a documentary fashion. The actors in the film eat a menu whose ingredients and preparation comply with classic French cuisine. Cocotte-Pedersen
served Blinis Demidoff with black caviar, the cailles en sarcophage filled
with foie gras and truffles, candied fruits for dessert, tropical fruits with
the cheese platter – and to accompany the food, Amontillado, Veuve Cliquot
and Bordeaux. Axel's cinematographic delivery takes great pains to present
all of the food and ingredients for the feast as having been imported from
France: Babette places an order with her nephew, a ship's cook. Live quails,
a hissing turtle, caviar and champagne confound the village community.
Unable to read the signs of Babette's lavish culinary art, the Jutlanders are
quick to interpret the arrivals as potentially being the media of a "witch's
kitchen". Yet in the context of its illegibility in the Scandinavian surroundings, the menu presented by Babette and Cocotte-Pedersen is further
encoded on the narrative level of both the novella and the film: In Paris – as
the General relates – he savored it in the presence of Colonel Galliffet. We
learn that Galliffet, who was later promoted to general, was responsible for
the violent killing of Babette's family and her subsequent flight from her
home country. Babette cooked for the man who in both Blixen and Axel's
versions of the story stands for death and violence and who drove a culinary
discourse into political exile in Scandinavia, where it is neither read nor
tasted in a spiritual or gustatory sense. In the film's final sequence Babette
resolutely explains to the sisters that she does not want to return to Paris –
and not just because she used up her entire lottery winnings to pay for the
banquet. She reveals that she "no longer has anyone" in Paris and that the
time when she was able to make her guests at Café Anglais "happy" with
her culinary art is over. In answer to the comment that she would now be
"poor for the rest of her life," Babette exclaims: "An artist can never be
poor." Philippa responds by saying that Babette will enjoy an afterlife in
heavenly paradise, where she will be "the artist God the Almighty created
you to be." The expensive feast thus marks both the culmination and the
end point of French cuisine in Danish exile. However, in certain sequences
Gabriel Axel's film stages Babette's culinary expertise in an almost incidental way, in that her attention is drawn to local products and – this is
at the heart of my argument – regionally anchored cooking techniques.
Axel does not follow these few scenes up in a "culinary" sense, does not
manage to integrate them successfully into his cinematographic narrative
and its dramatic composition. For it is the "culinary turn" Babette accom-
plishes over the course of her forced migration in the asperity of Jutland
that turns out to be the culinary transfiguration of the film's central character. Indeed, even before preparing the final feast, Babette has already
left her culinary provenience behind and prepared regional food, just dif-

ferently and better than the locals. In the film's opening sequence Axel already frames the sisters in a particular way, by showing them walking past dried fish hung on wooden poles outdoors. Martine and Philippa cook for the poor and sick in the village, bringing them soup and other dishes every day. While Axel certainly has an eye for the culinary sparsity of this food, he must at the time – in 1987 – have had no idea as to the unintended aesthetic connotations both soup and tableware would gain in our day, now employed by high-end Nordic cooking in contextualizing its regional roots: The crockery and soup look as though they had been designed and pre-pared by René Redzepi. Upon Babette's arrival in the village, Martine and Philippa show her how to soak dried fish and bread, then how to cut the fish and produce a bread soup fortified with just a very small amount of beer, which Babette then serves the poor. But Babette refines these foods and gives them a new emphasis in terms of taste – and while the film does not reveal how she does this, it does focus on the evidently displeased face of a sick man eating a soup prepared by the sisters when Babette is not there. After the sisters have explained their cuisine to Babette, she and the pair eat the bread soup in different rooms. Babette does not particularly like the soup. In what I regard as a central scene we then see her looking out of the window, watching a farmer walk through the dunes with a sheep; her gaze follows him intently and she then rushes to visit the village shop. I would go as far as calling this most important sequence of the film in terms of my line of argument the main character's "culinary turn." Stéphane Audran as Babette now goes on to discover the unique culinary character of the region which gave her exile. The sheep, which the farmer leads through the landscape and allows to feed, rings in a process of agro-culinary re-defini-tion in Babette. This is accompanied by an economic optimization of the sisters' household: "It's rather astonishing: Since Babette has been here we have been spending far less money." In the village shop Babette smells two onions before buying them, she haggles over the price for fresh fish and another time smells a plant (a herb), then picks and cooks it. Axel stages her acceptance of her exile and its agricultural character as an emblem of Nordic cooking against the backdrop of a magnificently framed sunset. In her "Nordic Food Lab" Babette experiments, bringing together different regional microorganisms; in the cultural history of cooking she can be located between Nouvelle Cuisine and Nova Regio cooking. And it is the village's poor and sick who notice this culinary turn, not the sisters and their guests at the banquet. Babette's final French feast for the quarreling community in the film overshadows a chef's reinvention of herself, who departs from Jan Cocotte-Pedersen's style of cooking to the same degree as she moves towards Nova Regio cuisine.

A Taste of Home

Sandra Knecht

"The men's cooking club is centered around a hobby that provides an opportunity to make ever new discoveries. Hobby chefs like to spread joy through their cooking; they have fun practicing their hobby and setting their tables beautifully. A hobby chef is a gourmet, but most importantly also someone who cultivates the art of hospitality."[1]

What does cooking have to do with identity and home? And how can this be investigated? In our era of endless cultural diversity cookery and food are the smallest common denominator. They concern everyone and

---

1 | From: Swiss hobby chefs SCKM, http://www.sckm.ch/de/00_VEREINSTEIL/01_ werwirsind/wirstellenunsvor.php, last visited February 20, 2017.

run through all strata of society like orbiters. What is the essence of food and taste? There is no vertical social hierarchy when it comes to these questions. The essence of taste, which links everything and everyone, runs horizontally. There is no surrogate for it. Diversity is not just defined through what can be individually useful or pleasant, but pertains to the appreciation of existence per se, to the appreciation of other existences, of their unique properties. Biodiversity also means preserving the pluralism of existence in itself and not fostering or curtailing it according to functional criteria.

One's place of origin as a notion and source of identity formation is now obsolete. Home is no longer a given fact. Home, the German *Heimat*, as a place must be constantly re-negotiated because it is subject to constant change. This constant change, retrospection and re-negotiation are essential cultural elements.

In the 19th century numerous Swiss communities that found themselves in financial straits tried to get rid of their poor by paying for their passage to America in return for them relinquishing their citizenship.

Home is a human construct; it is not based on natural laws. Home is also a memory, burnt into our subconscious memory and pervaded by tastes, smells and sounds.

The "Älplermagronen" are today regarded to be a traditional Swiss dish of the Sennen – the Alpine herders and dairymen. Yet pasta only came to the central Alps in 1872, during the construction of the Gotthardtunnel. At that time the Italian construction workers brought the pasta they ate at home with them. Soon this food became a staple in Alpine cooking, where eggs were added. Potaoes were used to make the dish go further and it was seasoned using onions. Cream and cheese were produced locally, and together with the pasta and the potatoes they made up a very filling dish.

"Mir Senne hei's lustig, mir Senne hei's guet
Hei Chäs und hei Anke, das git üs guets Bluet."
(We Sennen have a merry time, we Sennen have it good,
We have cheese and butter, which gives us good blood).

ÄLPLERMAGRONEN

Place waxy potatoes in simmering broth, add Magronen [macaroni] 5 mins later. Use an amount of water that will be entirely absorbed by the potatoes and pasta as the Magronen are al dente. Then add cream, roughly grate cheese (Gruyère, Alpine cheese, Emmental, etc.) on top, then mix in until cheese is melted. Season to taste with nutmeg and black pepper. Flour the onion rings, then fry in hot butter until crisp. Scatter across the Magronen and serve immediately. Serve with slices of cooked pears or apples.

"Lioba, lio-o-ba ..."

When these few syllables are intoned in the right place and at the right time, then all "truely Swiss men and women" will feel as one people of sisters and brothers.

This pastoralist song of praise was first documented in the 16th century. It originally announced the time for milking, returning to the stable or the Désalpe in many rural areas.

It is said to have even driven some Swiss mercenary soldiers to desertion – that is how strongly it stirred in them the "delirium melancholicum", the Maladie Suisse, in short: the longing for their home. The name "Maladie Suisse" is thus derived from Swiss soldiers stationed abroad and suffering from homesickness.[2]

RANZ DES VACHES, KUHREIHEN, LIOBA

Refrain

Hüopa, hüopa, chämet mer na!	Hop, hop follow me!
Chämet doch allu,	but come all,
wyssu, schwarzu,	white, black,
rothu, tschäggetu,	red, piebald,
jung u altu,	young and old,
unter de Icha	under the oak trees
wull n' üöch mälche,	I want to milk you,
unter der Oscha	under the ash
tuen i chäse	I will make cheese
Hüopa, hüopa, chämet mer na!	Hop, hop, follow me!
Die mit de Schölle	Those with the bells
vorna ha sölle!	Shall walk in front!
Chalber u Ründer	calves and bulls
A bitz bas hünder.	In the back
Hüopa, hüopa, chämet mer na!	hop hop follow me!

"We have long since swallowed some of the snakes that you are now hiding in the back yard, and they will jump out from our mouths whenever we need them. Yes, we had to swallow them. In order to survive. In order to signal you our submission. In order to know you better. In order to operate your weapons with ease. In order to express ourselves fully."[3]

---

2 | http://www.lebendigetraditionen.ch/traditionen/00100/index.html, last visited February 15, 2017.

3 | http://www.maiz.at/sites/default/files/anthropophagischer_protagonismus. pdf, last visited February 15, 2017.

When people eat what I have cooked they partially turn into what I am. But the products I use to create my dishes also become a part of them. The energy we absorb through our food makes us what we are. This is why we must exercise due diligence in choosing the foodstuffs we work with. In order to ensure accountability in this respect, it is important that our producers and suppliers are trustworthy.

The Tunisian greengrocer Mohamed Bouazizi set himself on fire on December 17, 2010 in protest of the arbitrary force exercised by the public authorities. His death triggered colossal upheaval in the Arab world.

"El Soor"

"In front of the wall/In front of those who were building it/In front of those who were erecting it/Stood a poor man/Peeing/Onto the wall, and onto those who were building and raising it."

"I was completely taken aback by the revolution in Egypt. When the first calls to protest were circulated on Facebook we actually made fun of them. And a few days later, everyone was suddenly on the streets. We were all very nervous and thought "My God, is this really happening here?" It was magical. I believe that we discovered feelings in us that we hadn't known existed, for example how much you love your country."[4]

SYRIAN FLATBREAD (CHUBS)

Ingredients

500 g	Rye flour
42 g	Yeast
500 g	Wheat flour
1 Tsp	Salt

Mix both types of flour in a bowl. Make a hole in the center and crumble the yeast into it. Add 6 deciliters of water to the yeast. Scatter the salt onto the flour sides. Dissolve the yeast in the water starting from the middle, then allow to rise for 10 minutes before kneading the ingredients to form a smooth dough. Dust lightly with flour and allow to rise for about 15 minutes. Place the dough on the floured work surface, knead and shape to form a thick roll. Cut this into 10 pieces of equal size. Shape the pieces of dough into balls and allow to rise, covered, for 10 minutes. Press the dough balls down to form round flatbreads of approximately 20 cm in diameter.

---

4 | Youssra El Hawary, from: https://de.qantara.de/inhalt/interview-mit-der-saen gerin-youssra-el-hawary-mit-dem-akkordeon-gegen-mauern, last visited February 15, 2017.

Cover a baking tray with baking parchment and place the flatbreads on top. Bake in an oven pre-heated to 250 degrees for 10–12 minutes.[5]

In order to stop the rhizome-forming plant from spreading across the garden uncontrollably, a rhizome-barrier must be installed around the place where it is to be planted. Polyethylene plastic sheeting may be used as a rhizome barrier; this should be 70 cm wide and 2 mm thick. The sheeting must be flexible enough to create the desired shape for the patch. The rhizome barrier is dug approximately 65 cm deep, with 5 cm protruding above ground. This upper edge is important in order for the gardener to see the rhizomes trying to grow across the barrier and be able to remove them. The foil has to be sealed with a fastening ledge so that the plant may find no gaps.

"Forget provocation and revolution. Rise up."
MARLENE STREERUWITZ

---

5 | From the blog of the Swiss hobby chefs (see note 1).

Perception

Foreign Food and Table Arts

Bernhard Waldenfels

In contrast to image, sound and even dance, food and drink are not part of the repertoire of traditional sensory learning and do not belong to the core themes of the construction of meaning. At best, they are part of the infrastructure of meaning and reason. In order to convince oneself of the trivial role played by food and drink in traditional philosophy, a glance at the comprehensive German philosophical lexicon *Historisches Wörterbuch der Philosophie* will suffice: It lists Esse commune and Essentialism, hubris and humor, Mahayana and maieutics, but nothing of 'essen' (food/to eat), 'Hunger' (hunger) or 'Mahl' (meal). Taste is discussed at length, but merely as a springboard for the more recent theories on aesthetics, and hunger is portrayed as a primary need that we share with other anthropoids. The question as to what may be the reason for tradition being so sparse in this respect is rather more difficult to answer. One might be tempted to proceed by simply rectifying this omission by seeking recourse to the ample findings in the sphere of cultural history, as has been done in similar cases. Yet this would leave the question as to the specific place of eating and drinking within empirical knowledge and their significance for thought itself unanswered. A philosophy that explicitly understands itself as one of experience, as phenomenology does, then finds itself shouldered with a task of which neither cultural studies nor cultural philosophy can relieve it.

1. TRADITIONAL FOOD AND DRINK MENUS

Three reasons for the lack of consideration philosophy shows for food and drink immediately become clear. They are in part obstructive and in part prohibitive, meaning that the appropriate thresholds for the discussion of the issue are not actually crossed. However, obstacles often possess an ambiguous character, as they force us to speak of that which has been pushed aside or diminished. Seduction by the phenomena further contributes to surprising finds being made time and again – even where common wisdom would never have expected it.

A first obstacle takes the form of the aspect of *vital necessity*. Food and drink are part of those basic requirements without which a living organism cannot survive. They therefore belong to the realm of *sine qua non* similarly to the physiological mechanisms of the body that allow us to sit, walk and speak – rather than falling within the scope of what is good in itself and worth striving for.[1] The production and preparation of foodstuffs therefore join the ranks of the elementary activities serving to satisfy our other equally elementary needs. In Plato's polis, which emerges from a universal need, as well as from the need for help,[2] the role of the farmer as someone supplying vital food products occupies the most important place among the professions. It is difficult, however, to clearly demarcate the sphere of what is vital, as wishes, including desires for food and drink, surpass the essential by searching out the pleasant rather than the purely wholesome. Man is prone, from the very beginning, to give room to the *superfluous, excessive, luxurious*. And the "healthy city" is therefore infested by outgrowths of a "bloated city". Yet Plato did not glorify simple primitivism. Glaucon, one of Socrates' partners in conversation, called the frugal primeval state a "city of pigs", which merely require feeding.[3] In actual fact, transgressing the confines of pure necessity not only gives rise to a need for cooks, cleaners, nurses and doctors, but without it there would also be no poets, sound artists, dancers or actors – and certainly no philosophers either; for wonder is not particularly preserving of life, but rather tends to interfere with it. Side dishes and desserts[4] then become culinary emblems of a culture not satisfied by essentials alone. In his *Metaphysics* (I, 1–2), Aristotle later made a clear distinction between those arts geared towards human subsistence and knowledge sought for its own sake. Even Marx still linked his order of the realm of necessity and the realm of freedom to this notion.[5] Yet this cultural exaltation does not stop food and drink from belonging to the sphere of the animalistic; it is only humanized by way of rational governance. This holds true to an increased degree for the

---

1 | Cf. on this distinction initially *Phaidon* 98b-99b. As is so often the case, discovery and concealment are closely linked here, too.

2 | Cf. the founding history in Book II of *Politeia*: 369b-373d.

3 | This is already a retrospective reading, as just a few lines on, the pig is described as a useless creature, which in contrast to the ox cannot be used as a draft animal and therefore has no place in the primeval city. Kant observed that Rousseau did not intend for people to *return* to the natural state, but instead only to *look back* on it (*Anthropology*, VI, 681) – and similar things can probably be said of Plato.

4 | Side dishes, plural ὄψα: anything eaten together with bread – such as meat or fish – literally translated as 'that which has been cooked' (from the Greek ἕψειν, see also ὀψοποιία: the 'culinary arts'). Dessert, plural τραγήματα: consisting of nuts, almonds, sweet pastries and suchlike.

5 | The questionable nature of this two-step model, in which overabundance follows shortage and which sustains the prevalent notional contrast between the civilized and the primitive, is addressed in the chapter "Zwischen Not und Überfluß. Metaökonomische Überlegungen zum Marxismus", in: *Der Stachel des Fremden* (1990).

guardians in Plato's city, who undergo sensory deprivation from childhood onwards in order to stop them from being encumbered – a state described as similar to that of being weighed down by lead balls (used by anglers to sink their bait) – by a taste for elaborate foods or an inclination towards other luxuries or extravagancies (*Politeia* 519a-b). They are later prescribed a frugal, field-gray diet devoid of both flavorsome seasonings (ἡδύσματα) and culinary artistry, let alone the excesses of intoxication, which would lead to the guardian needing a handler himself (*Politeia* 403c-404e). In contrast to the culinary arts as a practice centered on illusion "aiming at the pleasant and ignoring the best" (*Gorgias* 465a), medicine ensures moderation and that sensible conduct of life is not being eroded by gluttony and alcoholism. Thus in his *Anthropology*, Kant still differentiated between opulence *(luxury)* as excess with taste, and debauchery (luxuries) as excess without taste (VI, 578). The sense of taste is sublimated to aesthetic taste. When it comes to the common "feeding", Kant stuck to basic dietary principles, allowing intentions and habits to make up for a declining appetite (VI, 383–385, trans.).

A second obstacle to the appropriate estimation of food and drink can be found in the central theme of *self-preservation*.[6] A plant withers and an animal starves when deprived of the necessary sustenance. In his writings on psychology, founded in physiology, Aristotle posited the *nutritive capacity* (θρεπτικόν) as the first, fundamental psychic capacity, one that even plants possess in the shape of a vegetative soul (*De anima* II, 3–4).[7] This ability not only ensures nourishment, allowing an individual life form to grow and keep itself alive, but also the creation of kindred beings that sustain the species. Hunger and love therefore together form life's primal urges.[8] Aristotle thus left no doubt about the fact that self-preservation requires the help of others. Parents, and mothers in particular, are the origin of the child's existence, nourishment[9] and education. Yet this remains *extended self-preservation*. "For parents love their children as part of themselves (ὡς ἑαυτῶν τι ὄντα); children love their parents as the source of their being (ὡς ἀπ᾽ ἐκείνων τι ὄντα)", and through their detachment, children become like "another self (οἷον ἕτεροι αὐτοί)" for their parents (*Nic. Ethics* VIII, 12, 2). Children are therefore natural friends, in a way, in contrast to chosen friends, who are also termed "other selves" (cf. ibid., IX, 9).

---

6 | The Greek word σωτηρία, deriving from σῶς: 'whole, healthy' (lat. *sanus*), is less reactive than the Latin word *conservatio*, referencing a preservation of that which already exists.

7 | Aristotle uses the term nourishment (τροφή) very widely; he even says of water that it is food for fire (*De Anima* II, 4, 416a27).

8 | Cf. on this W. Theiler's commentary on Aristotle, *Über die Seele* (writings, vol. 13), p. 114. The teleological conception of life, whether as ζωή or as βίος, leaves no space for "naked life".

9 | The Greek verb τρέφειν: originally meaning to make "solid" or "fat", also means "to nourish", "to rear" and "to educate" in the most basic sense.

This cosmically anchored self-preservation loses its communicative backbone in modern times, when individual self-preservation *(conservatio sui)* represents the highest interest for each person (Hobbes, *De homine* 11, 6). In Kant's thoughts on the *Conjectural Beginning of Human History* it is the natural instinct, via smell and taste, that allows us to perceive some things as food while prohibiting us from ingesting others: The "instinct for sustenance through which nature preserves each individual" is complemented by the "instinct for sex, through which it ensures the preservation of each species" (VI, 87, 89, trans.). The assistance others provide becomes a refuge in itself: We need each other.

This leaves us with our third factor, namely *culinary delights*. Here, eating and drinking goes beyond the intake of essential sustenance. A particular social bond is formed between those who come together at the table to eat. Even the citizens of Plato's primal city will "sit down to feast with their children on couches of myrtle and bryony, and they will have wine to drink too, and pray to the gods with garlands on their heads, and enjoy each other's company" (*Politeia* 372b-c, trans. Lee). The simple bucolic feasts in the countryside are surpassed by urban banquets. In Plato's *Symposium*, these reach the unexpected apex of providing an arena for communal philosophizing, with drinking however now marginalized by speeches – if we are to disregard the drunken escapades of Alcibiades ensuing from these events. Summits of this kind stand out from the mundane table manners we practice on a daily basis, which remain in danger of fizzling out into mere habit. Addressing the rarity of true friendship, Aristotle observed mutual intimacy only being achieved after the proverbial salt has been eaten together (*Nic. Ethics* VIII, 4, 1156b 27 f.). Conversely, he found it hard to get much out of the social life provided by cult communities and associations, with gatherings of this kind serving pleasure and relaxation purposes only, as in the case of the harvest festival. Gatherings rooted in the moment are subordinate to the life of the political community, as the latter "aims not at present advantage but at what is advantageous for life as a whole" (ibid., VIII, 9,5, 271). It is obviously difficult to view the communal consumption of food and drink as the expression of a general goal. This would indeed require that the abovementioned sacrificial rites carry weight in their own right and mean more than external rites that acquire their ethical cohesion from elsewhere, for example from the agreement as to what is good and bad, just and unjust (see *Statesman* I, 2). Kant in turn traced "sociability" to the realm of the senses. Taste hereby fares better than smell, because when eating and drinking everyone can choose his or her own dishes or bottles without causing annoyance to their fellow diners, as for example the smoker would (*Anthropology*, VI, 452, trans.). That Kant himself was not averse to culinary delights is well known.[10] Yet the conviviality that unfurls around the dinner table is not per se brought about by the

---

10 | I am referring to a study by Iris Därmann: "Kants Kritik der Tischgesellschaft und sein Konzept der Hospitalität", in: ibid.: 2009, pp. 98–114.

meal taken together. Physical satisfaction merely provides the "vehicle" for the social pleasure that combines virtue with wellbeing, without the latter being able to replace to former (VI, 618). Virtues expected at the table are social virtues that lend grace to goodness itself, but they are nevertheless little more than *accessories* (parerga) of virtue (cf. *Met. of Morals*, Doctrine of Virtue, § 48). Or in other words, table manners cannot be generalized; they may be cultivated but never moralized.

2. INFERIORITY OF FOOD AND DRINK

Our initial breakdown of the problem cannot obscure the fact that there are a multitude of nuances between the thinking of Plato and Aristotle, between Descartes, Hobbes and Kant, and it shows that in reading classical texts we face secondary themes that run counter to the main ideas time and again. Yet without doubt there is a theme that amounts to disregard for food and drink. In the sense of Aristotle, eating and drinking has to do with *man as living being*, in Kantian terms with *man's animal nature*,[11] in a Cartesian sense even with *man's mechanical nature*. Some examples follow to illustrate this.

Gods do not eat and drink. Shedding light on his mytho-theological predecessors' blunders, Aristotle revealed as utterly incomprehensible the presumption that all the creatures that had never tasted nectar and ambrosia were mortal. "If the gods take nectar and ambrosia for the sake of pleasure, their doing so does not explain their being; and if the gods do so for the sake of their very being, how could beings who need nourishment be eternal?" (*Met.* III, 4, 1000a 15–18). Eating and drinking have no place in metaphysics, in the realm of eternal wisdom and final goals.

With Descartes is it not God, but the thinking self that rejects food and drink. In his answers to Gassendi, the philosopher is adamant that nourishing oneself must be exclusively attributed to the body, just like feeling and walking – and not to the soul as the place of thought (AT VII, 351). He saw the sentence "I eat and drink" as nonsensical in the strictest sense, except when used in everyday language, in which soul and body are comingled without inwardly belonging together. *The cogito does not eat and drink,* or in more modern terms: *Consciousness (the brain) does not eat and drink.*

---

11 | Cf. Kant, *Metaphysics of Morals*, A 112. Man is more beastly than any creature when he indulges in purely physical pleasures. In book IX of the *Politeia* Plato vividly describes the life of those who wallow in "feastings": "with eyes ever bent upon the earth and heads bowed down over their tables they feast like cattle grazing and copulating, ever greedy for more of these delights ..." (586 a-b, trans. Shorey, online available at: http://www.perseus.tufts.edu/hopper/text?doc=Perseus%3Atext%3A1999.01.0168%3Abook%3D9%3Asection%3D586b [accessed on Jan. 10, 2017]).

In Kant's philosophy, Descartes' onto-theological rift morphs into a double human existence. *I do not eat and drink as a rational being, I do so as a creature of the senses.* The way in which we eat and drink therefore becomes subject to the law of rationality. The cultivation of food and drink itself constitutes a moral demand that leads to man's animalistic nature conforming to humanity. Yet eating and drinking remains something secondary and lowly as compared to conduct informed by moral precepts. The classification of taste and smell as being among the base senses, which affect us rather than teaching us something, is in keeping with this view. As a whole, the senses belong to "perception by the organs stemming from the many external gateways with which nature has provided the animal in order to differentiate between objects" (*Anthropology*, VI, 447, trans.).

The hierarchy of the emotive faculties and the corresponding senses entails that the ennoblement of food and drink gains a mythological, symbolic or merely metaphorical complexion.[12] With the crickets chirping in the mid-day heat, Socrates told his students the story of the people who were so enraptured by the songs of the muses that they forgot to eat and drink up to the point of being on the verge of dying – in return they were transformed into the species of the cicada, a kind that needs no nourishment from the moment it is born and may promptly burst into song needing neither food (ἄσιτον) nor drink (ἄποτον) (*Phaedrus* 259b-c). But also the mythical concept of the food and drink of the gods returns in philosophy in the shape of the divine nourishment of reason, a blessing the soul receives having repeatedly seen the truth (*Phaedrus* 247d). Augustinian theology turned this into the divine nourishment the believer is granted in the *frui Deo*, in rejoicing in God.[13] The biblical "hunger and thirst for righteousness" can then only be metaphorically interpreted as a transferal of the vehemence of physical needs onto a mental or spiritual desire.[14] Within the bounds of pure reason, Kant saw the Christian sacrificial meal as little more than a moral memento. Communion, which may take place "through the formality of a common partaking at the same table", then constitutes a mere means towards vitalizing the moral disposition of brotherly love, and this despite its being carried out in order to

---

12 | I here comprehend the metaphor in the sense of a transfer of meaning that makes mental aspects accessible by way of the senses, and invisible ones by way of what is visible. The possibility of a vivid metaphor amounting to more than a 'mere metaphor' in the sense suggested by Paul Ricœur is not precluded by this.

13 | The enjoyment of and pleasure in God returns in manifold figures of speech in Pietism and in the sentimental era. Cf. on this and on a Kantian criticism of this the article "Genuß" by Gerhard Biller and Reinhard Meyer in: *Historisches Wörterbuch der Philosophie*, vol. 3 (1974).

14 | Cf. in contrast to this the greater proximity to the physical in Pascal: "We do not weary of eating and sleeping every day, for hunger and sleepiness recur. Without that we should weary of them. So, without the hunger for spiritual things, we weary of them. Hunger after righteousness, the eighth beautitude." (*Pensées*, 264, trans. W. F. Trotter)

keep the memory of the act of foundation alive (*Religion within the Limits of Reason Alone*, IV, 876). The cosmo-theological reflections of Hölderlin's verses now seem far removed: "Bread is fruit of the earth, yet it is blessed by the sunlight, / And from the thundering god issues the joy of the wine." Even everyday expressions such as "hungry for love", "thirsty for knowledge", "biting mockery" or "swallowing one's anger" take on a merely metaphorical character when eating and drinking is relegated to the realm of crude physicality. In this sense food and drink would merely serve as an outward vehicle helping us to understand an inner life that is difficult to access. The sexual coloring of alimentary expressions such as "loving someone to pieces" (to be devoured), which Freud calls attention to,[15] could then be dismissed as nothing more than the confusion of basic instinctual spheres.

3. Food and Drink Incarnate

The disregard for food and drink changes when we see the consumption of it as a bodily and inter-bodily occurrence that produces its own orders and which is overdetermined in the same way the contents of dreams, physical symptoms and traumatic events are. Only eating and drinking that is in itself more than mere eating and drinking becomes part of the order of things, of the formation of the self and the origin of the self from the other.

A phenomenology of eating and drinking, of which we have so far established only an outline, will know better than to equate eating and drinking with processes of nourishment intake, digestion and excretion. It will further abstain from reducing food and drink to aliments that can be assessed according to their nutritional value, and from confusing them with foodstuffs bought and sold on the market. Calories are measured values just like weight and temperature; they belong to the mathematical matrix of alimentary experience and can only be experienced indirectly. In terms of a phenomenology of food and drink, the question arises as to how physiological, economical, socio-cultural and religious factors interact in lived experience. Nietzsche's provocative recourse to physiology may serve as a stimulus, but does not spare us from working through the phenomena.

The complexity of alimentary experience can be seen even in the classical texts taken as our starting point. Plato for example makes it clear from the very beginning that eating and drinking are not processes that simply conform to causal laws, but that instead the soul of the hungry or thirsty person has "an *impulse* to what he desires" and in each case this is an impulse towards a "particular kind" of nourishment, such as for example a hot or cold drink (*Politeia* 437b-438b). With each of our desires we look

---

15 | Cf. "Aus der Geschichte einer infantilen Neurose" (GW XII, 141); phenomena of disturbance, such as anorexia or an addiction to sweets, are here connected to the early phase of a cannibalistic or oral sexual organization. More on this in Därmann: 2005, pp. 227-234.

for something that we ourselves do not possess as a quality.[16] Furthermore, one aspect of eating and drinking is that our sense of taste understands – as rudimentary as this knowledge may be – how to differentiate
between palatable and unpalatable. Even Aristotle described the striving
for something going hand in hand with the perception *of something*, with the
perception of food, beginning with touch, playing an irreplaceable role in
our quest for nourishment (*De anima* II, 3, 414b 1–10). Current physiology
here speaks more precisely of "taste buds" scattered inside the mouth and
throat area that respond to basic qualities such as bitter and sweet, sour
and salty. Plato further emphasized that a primordial memory is inherent
in desire. The person experiencing thirst desires the opposite of what he is
experiencing in that moment, namely, a "fulfillment" in the future, to end
the current "depletion". But how is the soul to know of the "fulfillment"
if not via memory, by retaining an earlier state of fullness?[17] After all, the
fact that our desire for food and drink is driven by our imagination is one
of the self-evident truths assumed by an anthropology of the senses. If
this was not the case, there would be no common phantasies surrounding
food and drink like that of the Land of Cockaigne. Kleist provided a lively
demonstration of the extent to which perception and appetites hereby
interlock. His "Brandy Guzzler" hears in the ringing of the Berlin church
bells a cascade of commands ordering him to drink, beginning with the
solemn "Bitter orange! Bitter orange! Bitter orange!" before shifting to the
pressing "Caraway! Caraway! Caraway!" and finally to the breathless rush
of "Anisette! Anisette! Anisette!", which sounds somewhat akin to a death
knell.

We see, then, how the multifaceted character of food and drink is
shaped by intentionality, perception, memory, imagination and desire.
But is that enough? What happens to the rest, that which actually constitutes the act of consuming food and drink rather than merely anticipating
or circumscribing it? Eating and drinking are evidently not confined to
intentional action aimed at a specific object or to actions following specific
rules. The blades of phenomenological or analytical philosophy go blunt
when directly applied to alimentary phenomena. If satiety is considered
nothing but the satisfaction of alimentary intentions or the adherence to
alimentary rules accompanied by the corresponding physical and mental
processes, then eating and drinking dissolve into *disjecta membra* – that
which we want, that which we must do and that which happens without
our involvement. As in similar cases, we would then be faced with a cognitive or cultural superstructure housing a set of social rules and founded
on a natural basis. The formation of hierarchies, which we have encoun-

16 | It is remarkable that the simple formula of "being intent on something" (εἶναι
τινός, 438a-b), which contains the seed for the later theory of intention, is developed gastro-nomically from food and drink.

17 | Cf. *Philebus* 35a-c. In this later dialog we find traces of the theory of anam-
nesis, which from the start was constituted in terms of affect and eroticism rather
than in a purely cognitive sense (cf. *Phaedo* 73d).

tered time and again, would endure. Neither would they disappear even if we were to invert the conditions according the motto: "First comes a full stomach, then comes ethics".

Hierarchizing and dualistic tendencies may be suspended if we are to assume both a corporeal eating and drinking as well as a physical manifestation of hunger, such as becomes grimly personified in Knut Hamsun's famous novel – here reaching its most extreme incarnation in the "happy folly of hunger" (2009, p. 125, trans.). In Husserl's words, the body functions as a "point of interconnection", where intellect and nature, or culture and nature, but also the self and the other are in a constant process of merging. In her extensive and provocative study combining ethnology, psychoanalysis and phenomenology, Iris Därmann also sees the body as playing a special role – namely in the form of an *incorporation*, operating on the threshold between the self and the other and giving the oral aspect a special significance.[18] The following experiment, which has the above-mentioned work to thank for manifold stimuli, is much narrower in scope. It assumes an *otherness of one's own body*, which finds a *pars pro toto* of sorts in foreign foods. The individual themes of otherness are suited to the correction of the traditional bottlenecks we have encountered, as well as to the reinforcement of contrary themes, of which there is no shortage in the great tradition either.

4. THEMES OF OTHERNESS

To begin with, let us consider the aspect of vital necessity. Simply citing elementary needs and the means necessary for sustaining life proves questionable when we reflect on the mechanisms of taste and pleasure. *Taste* contains an excess that directly breaks the cycle of appetite and satiation, of emptiness and fulfillment as well as that of memory and effect. The taste of food and drink exhausts itself in its nutritional value just as little as does love in reproduction. If Aristotle generally views lust as something that *joins* our striving for a goal,[19] then this likely holds true for the taste of food and drink, too. In relation to eros, Aristotle occasionally spoke in a Platonic manner of a *surplus* or *excess* (ὑπερβολή).[20] When it comes

---

18 | Cf. Därmann: 2005, in particular the discussion of Marcel Mauss and Sigmund Freud in chapters 2 and 3.

19 | Cf. *Nic. Ethics* X, 4, 1174b 31–33: "Pleasure completes the activity not as the corresponding permanent state does, by its immanence, but as an end which supervenes as the bloom of youth does on those in the flower of their age." However, surplus itself is here still conceived in a teleological sense as an epiteleology of sorts.

20 | Cf. *Nic. Ethics* VIII, 7, 1158a 12; this section looks at the love of an individual. In a *Problemata Physica* originating from the Aristotelian school and concerned with sexual intercourse, a distinction is made between necessary desires such as for food and drink and the desire for sex, the latter being said to stem from

to food and drink we repeatedly find reference made to ingredients that have more to do with opulence and superabundance than with necessity. More specific is the previously mentioned aspect of *flavor*. The Greek term ἥδυσμα literally refers to that which makes food palatable, of which only a small dose is needed (cf. *Nik. Ethics* IX, 10, 1170b 29). It also appears in the Aristotelian theory of nutrition, which forms the basis of his psycho-physiology. In hunger, desire is here said to be geared towards the dry and warm, in thirst towards the wet and cold.[21] The contribution provided to the perception of nourishment by the senses is said to be incidental, as nourishment itself has neither color, sound, nor smell. There is one exception to this, namely, taste – or, to be more precise: the nourishing fluid (gr. χυμός, deriving from χεῖν: "pouring"), perceived via the nutritive faculty of touch. It is noted here regarding the flavor observed via the sensation of taste: It is, as it were, a kind of seasoning of the nourishing substances mentioned (*De anima* II, 3, 414b 13 f.). Salt also belongs to the sphere of flavoring, and in Latin the word *sal* also means wit. In an exclamation such as "You are the salt of the earth" it takes on a missionary dimension, while we encounter it in a more mundane sense in the previously cited salt-eating as a mark of friendship. But why salt, in particular? Salt, which does not fill us up, but which, as well as providing us with mineral substances, lends our food a savory, delicious flavor, has more to do with the event of *eating* together than with *what is being eaten*, that which each person is consuming and digesting. The differentiation between the tale and what is being told here finds its culinary echo. In the same way as speaking always surpasses the words that are spoken, we find a sensual excess manifested in taste that can never be entirely transposed into nutritional terms, despite contributing to our diet. Each and every dish and each and every drink contain traces of nectar and ambrosia, in much the same way as every meal reflects the luster of a feast, even if our everyday eating and drinking is much sparser than the fancy dinners described by Proust in the opulent tones of the Flemish Masters. When it comes to drinking, we must consider the bouquet of wine, something that has to be tasted rather than merely drunk. Culinary and drinking cultures draw on this type of surplus, which is as old as mankind. The multitude of cultures allows for considerable variations, expressed for example in African societies using pot ash instead of salt or Inuit peoples making do with drinking sea water

an excess (of fluids); and one was said not to be ashamed of the former, but certainly of the latter (online available at: http://classics.mit.edu/Aristotle/nicoma chaen.8.viii.html [accessed on Jan. 10, 2017]). As this section and many others show, something ambiguous clings to hyperbole, let alone excess, reprehensible as a failure to achieve virtuous moderation (*Nic. Ethics* II) or as having too many friends (IX, 10, 1170b 23).

21 | This theory of the elements has also left its marks on the cosmology of the sexes (cf. the discourse on sexual intercourse mentioned previously). The connection between the spheres of nourishment and sex, which can only be clarified in genetic terms with great difficulty, is indicated by such physiological speculations.

and consuming algae. Spices belong to an odd section of the culinary arts. As André Leroi-Gourhan remarked in relation to this sphere, "The combination of thyme with salt and nutmeg cannot be translated into movement, not even into words."[22] What is crucial, however, is that this formation of taste is part of the physical foundations of our culture. This is true even for so-called "primitive" culture and arts. "A compilation of fragrances, a gastronomic meal may well be described as an art work", wherever these may appear.[23] The degeneration of culinary culture, as indicated by the increasing consumption of fast food, is a sign of cultural demise – or, in fact, of poverty. Those dying of hunger or thirst lose their sense of taste. Conversely, what is seen as a culture's crude beginnings may well become part of that culture's projections if it lacks confidence and hopes to escape this by modeling itself after the very antithesis of its origins.

Enjoyment is related to taste. Enjoying relates to something exceeding an immediate "tucking in" and even exceeding purposeful pursuit; it requires a certain delay within which the food may exercise its forces of attraction and repulsion. Fasting rites, which we find in all cultures, should not primarily be viewed as a scorning of food, but rather as an enhancing of the latter by making use of a special kind of *alimentary epoché*. The memory of desire, which Plato brought into play, opens up perspectives into the future as well as into the past. Yet savoring something involves neither remembrance nor expectation, but rather taking pleasure in what arises in the moment. Pleasurable savoring is not an intentional activity carried out in order to affect anything past, future or present. Related to savoring is *sustaining-oneself-by* ..., or *subsisting on* ..., which surpasses all imagination and production, all meaning and desire.[24] That which we nourish ourselves with becomes part of us. Yet Kant's approach was too simplistic when he defined the higher senses as being characterized by "superficial" perception and the lower senses by "most intimate ingestion" (*Anthropology*, VI, 451, trans.) and when he located enjoyment within a subjective interiority along with feeling. The common subjectivization of that which resists objectivization – and thereby also a general verifiability – disregards the distance from whence that object came, which now touches us inwardly. The bodily seat of feelings, which shall be discussed in the next chapter, finds its completion in the bodily seat of enjoyment or pleasure. What we savor remains 'other' to us as something we draw *on*, without consuming it in its entirety or possessing it. Common categories in the theory of goods fall short if they presuppose something that nourishes us to be an entity

---

22 | Cf. *Hand und Wort* (1984), p. 364; the paleontologist author examines gustatory perception, olfactory sense, gastronomy and cuisine from a cultural-theoretical perspective.

23 | Cf. Franz Boas, "Primitive Kunst" (engl. 1927), cited after Prussat/Till: 2001, p. 86; among others, the ethnologist author refers to Alois Riegl's formal aesthetics.

24 | Cf. on this the extraordinary passages Emmanuel Levinas devotes to enjoyment in chapter II of *Totalität und Unendlichkeit*, which also look at the enjoyment of food.

we acquire by producing, consuming, conserving and capitalizing on it. Even the interpretation of desire we find in Plato in relation to hunger and thirst, namely as a shift between depletion and fulfillment (*Philebus* 35a), only manages to uncover a minute aspect of the matter. Enjoyment does not involve something flowing in and out like in a leaky barrel that is forever filled and emptied (*Gorgias* 493b). Rather, the person enjoying and the source of enjoyment undergo a change in the pleasurable act. Aristotle encountered this very problem in considering the question as to whether a creature is nourished by like or unlike. He decided that the answer lay somewhere in the middle. By digesting food, unlike is turned into like through a process of equalization, or assimilation (*De anima* II, 3). Yet metamorphosis, or to put it in modern words, metabolism, means more than just filling. At the same time, the question arises as to whether assimilation does not always contain moments of an *otherness that cannot be assimilated*, as contradictory aspects are incorporated, and something is made edible that may not be readily eaten. In this sense all foods are prepared, not just cooked comestibles but raw ones, too. The distinction between raw and cooked, on which Claude Lévi-Strauss based his theory of food culture, does not refer to a divide, but rather a threshold value that varies in culinary terms depending on a combination of natural and cultural circumstances. And so every dish we consume contains a "small piece of nature", an inedible piece of nature that belies its origins, be this a few drops of saltwater on the shell of an oyster or a gnarly piece of vine shoot complete with yellowed leaf on a bunch of grapes (Proust, *Recherche*, II, p. 416). Yet what we ingest to nourish ourselves resembles the air we breathe in and out, which we may hold, but cannot store at our convenience. We cannot stock up on enjoyment. Entelechy, which Aristotle brings into play whenever something living is concerned, reaches its limits here, as do our modern conceptions of the construction of meaning and compliance with rules. Culinary normality is achieved through normalization; it is not an instant given, and like all normality it remains contestable.

A phenomenology of food and drink must further incorporate the theme of *giving*. It is common knowledge that considerable efforts were required to make this topic acceptable for philosophical debate.[25] What this means in our context is that eating and drinking must be regarded – in a similar way to speaking and acting – as an occurrence that *ab ovo* has to do with the other and with others. Yet this by itself will not suffice. The otherness of an offering we obtain from another place is lost when giving is integrated into a reciprocal relationship of give and take and channeled into the paths of an exchange of equivalents. We find producers in the Platonic proto-polis that not only produce food but also employ tradespeople to offer their sur-

---

25 | The accomplishments of authors such as Mauss, Levinas, Lacan, Derrida and their successors must be called to mind here, including the most recent analysis by Marcel Hénaff: *Der Preis der Wahrheit* (2009). I have myself attempted to provide a way of approaching this topic, which does have an – albeit underestimated – backstory in the ancient world, from the angle of giving an answer in my *Antwortregister*.

pluses for sale on the markets. The division of labor in the production and circulation of goods implies that all those involved will communicate to each other what they have cultivated (*Politeia* 371b), by using money as a symbolic medium of exchange. It is only the day laborers, hackneys, wage workers or however else one might translate the Greek word μισθωτός who give something of themselves, namely, the use of their strength and energy (371e). A community thus forms in which justice consists in everyone doing their part and receiving in exchange the equivalent in goods corresponding to how much they have given, and giving as much as they have received. Giving (διδόναι) is then turned into par-giving (μεταδιδόναι), taking (λαμβάνειν) into partaking (μεταλαμβάνειν), all of which is founded on a multi-layered system. In idealized terms food and drink are therefore shared food and shared drink. Peace is threatened, however, by each individual's insatiable wanting-more (πλεονεξία). A munificent nature that gives without taking only appears in the backdrop against which the myth is set. In the naïve era of Cronus, which Plato portrays in the *Statesman*, agriculture did not yet exist and humans gathered fruits that "sprang up of their own accord for men"[26] from the earth and the creatures did not eat one another (271e-272a). Ovid described the Golden Age in similar terms: Humans were "content with given food, and none compelling [it to grow]", whilst "rivers flowed milk and nectar, and the trees, the very oak trees, then gave honey of themselves". The age of Zeus brought an end to this childlike dream: "The food which had formerly offered itself freely had failed them", so humans needed to make use of the "gifts of the gods", such as fire and the arts, in order to fend for themselves (*Statesman* 274c-d).

The question remains, however, whether this turn from helplessness to self-help, from being preserved by another to self-preservation, does not belong to the myths of civilization itself. This installation as myth would consist in the recasting of a personal and collective *case history* that always takes place *too early* as nothing more than an *ancient history*, which merely begins *earlier on* and can be left behind incrementally. This is of course a reframing; for what characterizes the gift – for better or worse – is the aspect of anticipating obligingness that can never be entirely caught up with. This holds true for the early life of the infant, the *nourrisson*, who not only subsists on something but at the same time on someone, his mother – who in turn gives (or does not give) a part of herself with the food. This primal gift falls into line with a succession of other gifts.[27] Yet beyond it there is a gesture of giving that runs through an entire life and that aims

---

26 | Literally 'gave up', 'handed upwards' (gr. ἀναδιδόναι). This vertical giving belongs to a different dimension than horizontal giving and taking. The fact that in mythical language the earth has a gender connotation as mother earth is in keeping with this.

27 | Iris Därmann's paper must be mentioned here again for not only having contributed valuable insights into Freud's analysis on early childhood sexual development, but even more radical observations on Laplanche's general theory on the libidinous character of food.

at something beyond what is given itself. Under the right circumstances I can provide myself with gifts, but I cannot receive the gesture of giving – which I accept in the same way I would accept a promise – from myself. If this were any different, a gift could be acknowledged like a payment, and thanks would be no more than an empty phrase to lubricate the social gearing mechanisms. The excess of giving is also reflected in table manners, such as for example in Japan, where it is customary for diners to pour each other's drinks. This does however require paying special attention to each other and in this way one is present with one's table companions as though skillfully playing a musical composition together. In this sense a meal that someone eats would always be partially someone else's, just as according to Michail Bachtin every word we speak is "half someone else's word", answering to the other's words and carrying them on – even if we were talking with ourselves.

The last theme of otherness to be addressed here concerns the meal, in particular its property of being a *banquet*, a meal served for guests. Of course, this theme opens up utterly vast perspectives, so a few aperçus must suffice here. A meal is not a simple succession or cluster of individual acts, but rather an event taking place here and now as well as in repetition. In this sense we have *meal times* such as, for example, the classical Roman succession of *ieientaculum, prandium* and *cena*, and *places of eating and drinking* such as dining rooms or halls and taverns. Further, we have courses, utensils for eating and drinking, recipes, instructions for eating and drinking and much more besides. A meal always references others, just as self-talk is held with others and with oneself as another. It takes place in a shared world.

Beyond all this, a certain unfamiliarity remains inherent in every group of diners. This begins with *table etiquette* in the broader sense. Like all other arrangements and orders, these rules were invented or established by agents that for the most part remain anonymous – as is generally the case with clothing, housing and language. The individual eats and drinks *how one* eats and drinks, and this *How*, as well as the *One*, may take on more or less diffuse or homogenous patterns, as is generally the case. A *third aspect* is always at play that makes something like companionship at a table possible. This third element may in special cases be represented by a third person, such as, for example, in the formality of the ancient symposiarch, the *magister bibendi*, who tasted the wine, distributed and mixed it, or in the shape of a Georgian tamada, a traditional table master (now also admissible in female form), who ensures, by prompting the guests to deliver dinner speeches and reciting toasts, that the dinner party does not break apart, the social interaction does not become too vapid and the celebration does not turn into a drinking binge.

Yet the order of the third party is also countered by the unfamiliarity of the other. A table etiquette that is the way it has become over time but that could also have turned out differently cannot help but appear exclusive and selective. This not only means that not everyone is included, but that no-one is entirely included in their singularity. Foreignness or otherness begins at the table, as every child who has been taught to behave in a curious fashion while eating knows. Like all systems, table etiquette ranges between the extremes of compulsion and arbitrariness; it is more or less open. But beyond that there is the space for absentees. The custom found in many places of reserving a seat for the deceased makes this void perceptible. Yet guests who could possibly come are also absent. No dinner company is complete; there are always surplus diners, even if one is to stick to the rule of thumb, as Kant did, that the number of diners should not fall below the number of graces or exceed the number of the nine muses (*Anthropology*, VI, 617). *Hospitality*, which imbues every meal with the features of a banquet and every dish with the features of foreign food, then does not constitute a special case, but an enduring vexation that cannot be entirely solved through the *right to hospitality*, either. Kant recalled the Arab, "whom the foreigner, had he managed to obtain from the former a refreshment (a drink of water) in his tent, could also trust with his safety", as well as "the Russian empress receiving *salt* and *bread* from the deputies meeting her from Moscow, and knowing that having consumed these foods she would be safe from ambush as she was then secured by the right to hospitality" (VI, 619). On what is this security founded? And what about those dying of hunger and thirst, who have long since been more than mere marginal figures? If we are to seriously consider just how close otherness and hostility are and how quickly the gift of food can turn into poison and receiving into taking away, then we will be careful not to dismiss table manners as mere customs.

Plating Food

On the Pictorial Arrangement of Cuisine on the Plate

Nicolaj van der Meulen

Referring to a plate as a picture is not necessarily par for the course. It makes sense though, if one assumes that the food arranged on the plate has a display function, or if it represents something, and refers to something more than just itself. What is intended with what I eat, and how is it prepared? What memories and associations does the dish trigger at the moment it is presented? Given the way it was produced, fermented, and put together, in what historical, cultural or transcultural context is it embedded? Whether fast food, slow food, fusion or Haute cuisine: In the way it is chosen and arranged, the food on the plate reveals a certain understanding of culture. It makes statements about aspects such as authenticity and historicity, globalization and regionality, about enjoyment, sustainability and health. It is possible that the representation of food refers to a certain cultural concept or to a particular social discourse, as the plate now makes visible as food what was previously a commodity. The commodities are released from their production and manufacturing context. The picture on the plate, no matter how naturally it is arranged, is no longer nature, agriculture, or sustenance, but food to be enjoyed, presented to me on a plate to be sampled. The plate, astonishingly consistent in terms of its basic design for at least 4,000–5,000 years now, is at the beginning of a cultivation process, which allocates me a portion of the community's (tribe's) limited supply of sustenance. Even today, the food arranged "for me" makes for the magnetic attraction of the plate's appearance. It is frequently given to me by somebody. It is a "gift". The shoulder of the plate forms the framework marking the difference between nature/sustenance and culture/food, so as thereby to make one aware of a quite specific cultural concept. The base of the plate, no matter how shallow, raises the arranged food from the table and at this particular moment makes it an event for me.

Over the past 20 years, visual and pictorial studies have addressed in detail the philosophical, religious, iconic, epistemic and anthropological dimensions of pictures and their impact. The philosophical, creative, political, social, and communicative characteristics of pictures and their significance for creative or architectural drafts was also discussed. To date, however, there has been no long-term discourse on the iconic characteristics of food and how it is arranged on plates.

"Plating" describes both the preparation and presentation of food on a plate. The primary intention of plating is a visual or sensual attraction, though as a cultural concept it entails far more. If plating is characterized as a certain form of picture, the fact that the look of the plate is highly unstable presents a particular difficulty and is also linked to other sensual experiences such as the sense of touch and smell. If I taste what is on the plate it would appear to be no longer a picture, if I just see it, it appears not to correspond to its actual intention. Although some cooks make drawings when creating their recipes, artistic or creative practices do not appear to be explicitly used in the arranging of food on plates. Top-flight chefs' artificial plate arrangements in particular combine aesthetic, cultural, culinary and scientific knowledge, which is expressed in the plate's look. The arrangements on the plate have to stand a visual but also a taste test. They have to be meaningful not just at the very first moment but during the entire process of consuming the food.

MYTHOLOGICAL SPECULATION AND ANTHROPOLOGICAL FICTION

Several years ago Richard Wrangham highlighted the evolutionary significance of cooking meat over a fire, and in doing so triggered a broad discussion of the relationship between cooking and the history of mankind. Cooking, in particular of meat but also of root bulbs, created nutrition with a greater energy value and requiring less physical effort. In terms of energy, the reduced strain on the digestive tract could be used to build up the brain, he stated. As such, the rapid increase in the size of Homo erectus and its predecessors approx. 1.6 million years ago went hand in hand with the controlled use of fire for cooking. Put in simpler terms: Cooking, especially of meat over an open fire, first lays the foundations for the evolutionary conditions for the development of the human brain. Fire, cooking, eating are the fundamentals of human incarnation.[1]

Although from an anthropological point of view it was argued that the systematic use of fire for cooking is at most 200,000 to 800,000 years old, and as such far younger than the decisive evolutionary stages in the development of the human brain,[2] and that the close pairing of meat and fire defined early man's menu too rigidly, "Catching Fire" had a wide social impact.[3] Michael Pollan followed on from this and associated a return to

1 | Wrangham: 2009.

2 | Gibbons: 2007.

3 | Organ, C./Nunn, C. L. et al. (2012): Phylogenetic rate shifts in feeding time during the evolution of Homo, in: *PNAS*, 108/35, http://www.pnas.org/content/108/35/14555.full?sid=95c4876b-9870-4259-888f-24a6179be4fc, last accessed Jan. 31, 2017; McBroom, P. (1999): Meat-eating was essential for human

older cooking techniques with fostering a greater awareness of the "real" significance of them.[4] As a result among other things old cooking techniques, such as cooking on open fires and gained in popularity again.[5] As "nose to tail", "root to leaf" or "local food" a new take on nutrition became popular that not only set itself off from its predecessors (molecular cuisine, nouvelle cuisine), but in an era of digitized, globalized and critical living conditions held out the prospect of, to adapt the phrase by Theodor W. Adorno, a "right life in the wrong one".

From the point of view of the "Culinary Turn", Wrangham's theory about the birth of mankind from the spirit of cooking is interesting in that it reveals that not only are there indications of crucial processes in the development of mankind in specific concepts of cooking and eating, but they were also driven by them. In terms of cultural history "Catching Fire" can also be seen as a rereading of the myth of Prometheus. As is well known, according to Hesiod ("Works and Days", Book II) and in later versions, Zeus refused mankind fire and proclaimed: "They shall have their meat! But I refuse them fire! They will have to eat their meat raw". Thereupon, Prometheus brought fire (back) to the people secretly in the form of a fennel stalk (narthex).[6] Unlike the myth, which are things that "never happened, but always are"[7], Wrangham makes the plot a fact in the history of mankind. Just as the myth has the character of necessity, and states why things had to turn out that way (even if we will never know why), "Catching Fire" also gives the cooking of meat over fire the character of necessity. In doing so Wrangham narrows down the diversity of the food as well as the cooking techniques. However, it is something different to say: "We all have to eat, but we don't eat everything we could."[8] That is because it is about preferences, the possibility of making a choice, and culinary diversity, which plays a significant role at least in a plate's appearance. That provides a culinary offering that aims to win one over to a specific conception of nutrition: "Dishes are ... pictures, cooking is creating a world concept (Weltentwurf)."[9]

A model such as the artist Dieter Froelich sketches, which approves of culinary enjoyment and associated diversity, could also offer new perspec-

---

evolution, says UC Berkeley anthropologist specializing in diet, in: *News Release*, 6/14/99, http://www.berkeley.edu/news/media/releases/99legacy/6-14-1999a. html, last accessed Jan. 31, 2017.

4 | Pollan: 2013, p. 27.

5 | Ekstedt: 2016; Katz: 2012.

6 | In ancient times the core of fennel stalks, whose embers lasted for several hours, even days, was used to transport fire.

7 | Thomas Sedlacek quoting Sallust in Sedlacek, T. (2013): *Economics of Good and Evil. The Quest for Economic Meaning from Gilgamesh to Wall Street*, Oxford, p. 108.

8 | Froelich: 2012, p. 11.

9 | Ibid.

tives from an anthropological point of view. The culinary triangle Claude Lévi-Strauss introduced in 1964, which mapped food in "raw", "cooked", and "rotten", and which also inspired Wrangham's "Catching Fire", cannot then be thought of as a model of a linear development from nature (raw) to culture (cooked), in order to rule out decay as a corruption process.

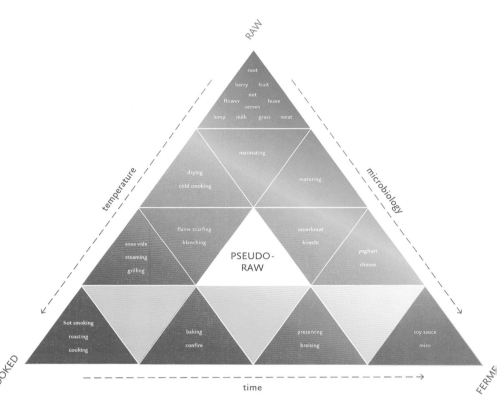

Fig. 1: Proposed advance of Lévi-Strauss' "triangle culinaire" for the allocation of plate imagery (Vilgis, further developed by NvdM and Isabel Lina Christen)

The culinary triangle provides a model for a more complex, cross-cultural matrix, in which the relationship between nature and culture is changeable depending of the cooking and decay process. Through the basic division of food into raw *(cru)*, cooked *(cuit)* and rotten *(pourri)*, and the refinement of this model by Thomas A. Vilgis into 'raw', 'cooked' and 'fermented', thus differentiating between the content, not only cultural and culinary forms, but also specific forms of plate imagery can be allocated. An elaborated version of the culinary triangle could also be a starting point for describing the components of a plate beyond their mere name and associate them with culinary and cooking dimensions.

HISTORICAL COMMENTS

However we reconstruct the origins of the human diet, not much imagination is needed to suppose that cooking preceded the plate, while the plate preceded the image of the plate. The more we move towards complex or reflected plate images, the more social and aesthetic dimensions come into play alongside the precision of culinary aspects. Systematic cooking presupposes cooking utensils.[10] Wrangham emphasizes that some animals, for example shellfish, supply the vessel they are cooked in, so to speak, themselves naturally and that from there it is only a short step to cooking receptacles.[11] However, this process must have taken place in long, slow steps. The very first pottery is probably 26,000 years old and as such was around 15,000 years ahead of the start of animal husbandry and agriculture.[12]

Fig. 2: Roman Plate: Roman Imperial Period (27 BC – 284 AD),
Museum Frankenthal, Germany

The historical developments from the bowl to individual plates and their relationship to trays for cutting up meals, to ritual offering plates and to joint plates have not yet been traced. One can assume, though, that shallow plates for individuals enabled social changes in terms of the relationship between individual and community, as well as culinary changes in terms of the type, structure, and number of foodstuffs. Furthermore, the shallow plate most probably developed from the bowl and, as opposed to the latter, made it easier to cut up and eat food, and arrange it separately on a plate. An approx. 5,000-year old shallow bowl in the Metropolitan Museum in New York indicates an early morphological relation-

---

10 | Gremillion: 2011, p. 66.

11 | Wrangham: 2009, p. 124.

12 | See Price, T. D./Bar-Yosef, O. (2011): The Origins of Agriculture: New Data, New Ideas: An Introduction to Supplement 4, in: *Current Anthropology* 52, pp. 163–74.

ship between bowl and plate.[13] There is an approx. 2,000-year old shallow plate made of molded clay in the Erkenbert Museum in Frankenthal near Mannheim, Germany. Not least of all it reveals how the standardized circular shape of the plate stems from the craft of turning and the circular movements of the hand.

In comparison with eating, little study has been conducted on the significance of the plate and *plating* in terms of cultural history. Art historical studies allow few conclusions, as their mostly iconological or social history thrust makes them little suited to illustrating the aesthetic design conditions for plates themselves and their relationship to cooking techniques.[14] According to initial studies, complex arrangements on plates go back to a development in the modern era. Though plates and arrangements on plates have been in use since Antiquity and were employed, for example, for the *cena* (lunch) in Ancient Rome, for the "banchetto", and for the multi-course feast (*convivium*), the separate accumulation of food in a receptacle or on a plate prevailed.[15] Not until the 17th and 18th century and the associated first steps towards "Haute cuisine" as there any striking change in the appearance of plates. The patissier and chef Marie-Antoine Carême, who also dabbled in architectural theory, apparently assumed a key role in the development of complex plate arrangements and their spread. Following Antoine Beauvilliers' major work *L'Art du cuisinier* (1814), in 1828 Carême published *L'Art de la cuisine française,* which together with works such as *Le Pâtissier pittoresque* (1828), created illustrative associations between architectural constructiveness and food arrangements.[16]

The historically decisive change can be traced to 1960s and 1970s nouvelle cuisine, on which Paul Bocuse was a major influence. A single plate gained in significance over a composition of plates based on a "still life". The closer links developing at the same time between Japanese (Shizuo Tsuji) and French chefs (Alain Chapel, Paul Bocuse) was of relevance for the arrangement on the plate. Inspired among other things by the traditional Japanese meal 'kaiseki',[17] simplicity, seasonality and plate arrangement had since the early 1970s been basic criteria of French nouvelle cuisine, and precise plating an important part of cooking.[18]

With subsequent avant-gardes such as "molecular" (since approx. 1990, Heston Blumenthal, Ferran Adrià) and "Nova Regio" cuisine (since approx. 2003, Stefan Wiesner and René Redzepi), the appearance of the plate has gone in different directions, though a scientific basis involving an aesthetic practice of cooking and plating is fundamental to both.

---

13 | http://www.metmuseum.org/art/collection/search/547264, access: 14.02. 2017.

14 | Bendiner: 2004.

15 | Schareika: 2008.

16 | See Trubek: 2000; Spang: 2001; Spence/Piqueras-Fiszman: 2014a.

17 | See Tsuji: 1972; Murata: 2006.

18 | See Halligan: 1990; Yang: 2011.

Fig. 3: Heston Blumenthal:
Macerated Strawberries,
with Black Olive and
Leather Purée, and
Pistachio Scrambled Egg

Whereas molecular cuisine's discursive and semantic references apply implicitly to complex (non-standardized) architecture and to post-modern, heterogeneous structures, Nova Regio refers implicitly to current political, aesthetic, and social discourses on nature, countryside, and agriculture. The quoting of nature that no longer is nature, a solemn gesture by means of blatant instances of movement and color, the gentle irony of the details, the Mannerist exaggeration of contours and the playing with the question of what it is are signatures of a post-modern aesthetic that associates molecular cuisine with postmodernist cinema and architecture.

Fig. 4: René Redzepi:
Little Forest on a Plate

When, on the other hand, Rene Redzepi says "we wanted to have a complete little forest on a plate", his reference model is nature or landscape, which on the plate is modelled to form an intact micro-landscape, and at a time when in many places landscape is experienced as fragmented: "Landscape fragmentation is the result of transforming large habitat patches into smaller, more isolated fragments of habitat."[19] On the plate a landscape thought to have been long since lost is modelled and is opened to gustatory experience. Molecular cuisine constructs the way the plate looks, whereas a Nova Regio plate tends to be modelled.

DESIDERATUM: TRANSDISCIPLINARY APPROACHES

Over the past few years applied research studies, in particular relating to experimental psychology, addressed the influence of shape, feel, color, weight, size and orientation of plates and vessels.[20] These studies led to a far clearer focus on the influence of specific plate arrangements on our eating behavior. Experimental psychology also drew attention to the fact that the generally neglected element of the plate has a deciding influence on what we eat and how we perceive the taste of food.[21] More recent studies point to the lack of close cooperation between experimental psychology and aesthetics/visual culture with a view to the better assessment of *plating* criteria.[22] The fact that putting food on or in a vessel (plate, dish, tray, board, bowl) is fundamental not only for western cultures is one of the interesting results of experimental psychology.[23] As such one can conclude that apart from pure functionality, *plating* enables an examination, appreciation, and increase in enjoyment of the food. Elsewhere, surveys revealed that a rising diagonal arrangement on consumers' plates tended to be perceived as positive and attractive.[24] As much as findings such as these provide interesting information about standardized eating behavior, they say just as little about the criteria according to which aesthetic innovation and a wealth of diversity occur on plates, and what influence cultural discourse has on the appearance of plates. Neither is ultimately based on consumer behavior alone, but also on aesthetic criteria, cooking techniques, the food elected, and social discourse.

19 | https://www.splendidtable.org/story/chef-rene-redzepi-of-noma-we-want ed-to-have-a-complete-little-forest-on-a-plate, last accessed Feb. 1, 2017; *Land-scape fragmentation in Europe*, Joint EEA-FOEN report, EEA Report No 2/2011, p. 9.

20 | See Piqueras-Fiszman/Spence: 2012a/2012b; Piqueras-Fiszman/Harrar/ Alcaide et al.: 2011; Harrar/Piqueras-Fiszman/Spence: 2011; Levitsky/Youn: 2004; Marchiori/Corneille/Klein: 2012; Michel et al. 2015; Spence/Michel et al.: 2015.

21 | Spence/Piqueras-Fiszman: 2014a, p. 115.

22 | Spence: 2016.

23 | Spence/Piqueras-Fiszman: 2014a.

24 | Michel et al.: 2015.

In the above-mentioned studies, multi-sensory aspects, in other words the interplay between sight, touch, smell and hearing were not taken into consideration. Other more recent studies examine *plating* from the point of view of chefs and cooking practice. In this context *plating* is regarded as central, although the quality of the menu cannot be reduced to its appearance, and experienced chefs can assess the freshness of the produce, quality of the taste, and the cooking technique without touching the food.[25] Contradictions such as these show that the criteria for plate imagery cannot be determined by application-oriented studies alone, but require dialog with the natural sciences, aesthetics, and visual culture. The last two disciplines lack scientific as well as culinary knowledge, making a trans-disciplinary perspective necessary for more accurate findings

IMAGE AND TRACE

No matter how delightful it may be, the appearance of a plate retains its attractive character for a short time only. It is unstable. We can ask ourselves when the appearance of a plate is finished: as soon as it has completed the long process from the initial idea and the drawing up of the recipe, to the cooking stage and ultimately the *plating*, or only when a guest has assimilated what is on the plate? The moment of direct encounter or touch between guest and plate is preceded by a process of constant rapprochement, which on the part of the guest is associated with a growing expectation, while the cooked food assumes its most stable form at the moment of plating before being chewed to pulp in the guest's mouth. Even before becoming visible the smell of the food has laid a track. However, the appearance of the plate is not or not only designed to be just seen, but at the moment it becomes visible triggers a longing that leads to tasting and eating. This is one of the punchlines of the plate's appearance, namely that though it is made to be beholden it is only in the act of being tasted and assimilated that it becomes complete. The appearance of the plate is procedural. It culminates during the course of its deconstruction. With the guest sitting in front of the plate its appearance is soon split into an assimilated, chewed pulp, and a trace the person eating the food leaves behind on the plate. The trace of food is legible as a "surviving presence of remains",[26] which subsequently says something about the type of food on the plate and its consumption. No one trace resembles another. A plate's contents that have been assimilated remain an image. Like any trace, it requires interpretation. For this reason it is not enough to read the plate's appearance from the point of view of *plating* (and the preceding recipe), but also from the trace it leaves that has to be interpreted.

---

25 | See Fernandez, P./Aurouze, B./Guastavino, C. (2015): Plating in gastronomic restaurants: A qualitative exploration of chefs' perception, in: *Menu, Journal of Food and Hospitality Research*, 4, pp. 16.

26 | See Derrida: 1997; Kogge/Krämer/Gruber: 2007.

Fig. 5, 6 and 7:
Tanja Grandits: Fillet of deer,
ginger, quinoa, red cabbage,
blackberry pickle and pea
blossom, 2016 (Appearance
of plate and trace on plate)

The plate displayed here by Tanja Grandits (Restaurant Stucki, Basel/CH) comprises three basic components: deer, quinoa, red cabbage. In addition to which there are smaller elements that extend the aroma complex, such as blackberry pickle and ginger. The way the components are arranged on the plate allows several combinations or what Vilgis terms "projections" on it. The plate's appearance can be said to be coherent, if gustatory and visual elements produce an overall picture. Bu how do the gustatory and the visual really reference each other, as they do not really develop in each other? It would be worthwhile interweaving formal aesthetic qualities such as deep/shallow, architectural/organic, concentrated/dispersed with gustatory qualities sweet, sour, salty, bitter, umami in a joint and "thick" (Clifford Geertz) description. Not in the sense of homogenization, but development of the visual through taste. The taste component is not only built into the appearance of the plate, the taste helps shape the appearance. Here, the three parts into which what is on the plate are frequently divided are concentrated or as one. The separation of the elements and the associated opening of the triad would produce an open form and a completely different picture, and also increase the complexity, as the guest is confronted with higher requirements in terms of the combination of the elements. Tanja Grandits' plate comes with ways of finding one's way round the plate, for example by the overlapping of quinoa and red cabbage, or by positioning red cabbage and fillet of deer close together. At the same time though the guest is advised to combine several, at least two elements in his mouth at the same time.

The color modulation brown, red, violet, through to black conveys great painterly coherence with appealing warm hues. The proximity of pink pea blossom and blackberry to the guest reduces the dominance of the meat on the plate. To a certain degree the taste modulation breaks up the color unity with a broad spectrum of nuances ranging from sweet (meat, red cabbage, quinoa) to sour (blackberry pickle, ginger, red cabbage). Visual and gustatory modulation do not blend here. In other words: Though taste and aromas are part and parcel of the plate's contents, the latter do not develop them on an equal basis. We often experience the taste through the contents and from there describe differences and relationships between taste and contents. The food moves from the contents to the taste and melds with the texture.

Like an abstract picture by Kandinsky, which can be viewed several ways, the plate's appearance shows very accurately that interaction between guest and plate can be very different. The question of whether one prefers to taste components combined or experience them in isolation is pivotal in terms of whether to a certain degree they are "pulled apart" or kept together. The trace on a plate that has been eaten clean reveals whether the emphasis was on isolated or combined consumption of the components.

Scale Patterns (Together with Thomas A. Vilgis)

At molecular level, dimensions of taste and smell that are relevant for aesthetic perception (and as such for *plating*) become tangible but often cannot be described linguistically. A hypothetical scale enables aesthetic and physiological, as well as taste and visual dimensions of perception to relate to one another.

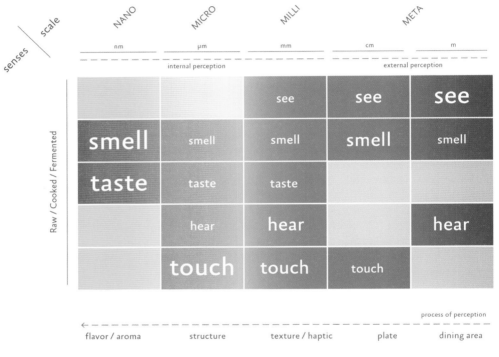

Fig. 8: Hypothetical model of the physiological and aesthetic perception of plate imagery (Vilgis, further developed by NvdM and Isabel Lina Christen)

The perception and consumption of the plate's contents can be thought of in terms of length scales. Taste and aroma, which are perceived by means of taste receptors on the tongue and olfactory cells in the nose reference atomistic scales. Ions and aromatic substances interact with corresponding proteins on the tongue and olfactory bulb. These senses are triggered directly by readings on the scale of typically 1 nanometer. Preparation techniques used in classic as well as avant-garde cuisine take effect in the length scale between 10 and 100 nanometers.

Tactile receptors on the tongue are in a position to detect the smallest of differences, for example in the flow behavior of liquids or in the breakage behavior of crispy elements. The texture, sequence, and superstructure of proteins, carbohydrates, the distribution of fat and water, all of which are present in raw and cooked foodstuffs, range from micrometers to macroscopic measurements, which even now affect the form and shape of the elements on the plate. As opposed to nano- and microstructures, they are already visible.

Plating, serving techniques and the visual styling of a plate are now decisive. Nobody would think of serving two liquids (sauces, juices, etc.) close to each other on a plate if they had identically low viscosities. They would mix their individual aroma in an uncontrolled fashion. Plating is for this reason not only motivated by aesthetic and sensory intentions, but also pre-defined by the physical and chemical parameters of enjoyment: taste, aroma and texture.

According to theory, the meta-scale begins on the length scales. There impressions are touched on that relate to sensual perception. In addition, light, the room, and acoustics effect the plate imagery. The two levels, physiological perception and aesthetic perception become clear. At the meta-level the whole external impression is recorded, before the plate and its sensory content is noticed. This involves the room, its acoustics, noise, music, voices, lighting, colors, architecture, and interior design.

Fig. 9: Guestroom, Plate, mouth in relation to the perception levels (NvdM, Isabel Lina Christen)

The way the plate is styled is perceived at table. The style of cuisine can be recognized at first sight, the difference between classic and avant-garde cuisine is obvious. Chefs' different ideas become visible. In each case, elements and components are served differently according to colors, textures, food groups, flavor aspects, and temperature. In terms of smell the first "scent blends" can now be perceived. The mixture of aromas that make up the fleeting fragrances defines the basic direction.

After evaluating the meta-scales of the plate's appearance, the guests devote themselves to the sensory aspects in their mouth. In their brain these, together with all the impressions of the meta-scales, are put together to form the "flavor".

LIVELINESS AND THE PLATE'S APPEARANCE

Lots of people have experienced this: If the host, room, plate's appearance and food come together perfectly, the experience becomes an aesthetic one, which with regard to concentration, power, and sustainability otherwise only occurs this way in art. The arranged plate then has the character of a "gift"[27] because it is never to do with me alone. The arranged plate is more than something that can be just settled up by means of payment, as apart from the eating aspect it creates a surplus of meaning.[28] The gift goes back to a gesture of giving, which is not countered with money, but with certain customs and rituals. Acceptance of the gift, the contents of the plate, is answered with thanks, trust, commitment, and a sense of community. It creates feelings such as enjoyment, satisfaction, warmth, and happiness. But what is it that makes a perfect meal such an intensive experience, and what significance does the appearance of the plate play in this?

My hypothesis is that the aesthetic experience of eating tells us something about aesthetic experience in general and that eating (at least in the way described above) assumes a paradigmatic role in this context. A phenomenological view of aesthetic experience and the *enargeia/evidentia* discussion conducted a good ten years ago in the field of cultural studies and visual culture[29] offer an important starting point in terms of understanding. *Enargeia* suggests that the rhetoric of illustration, be it written or visual, cannot make do without a moment of liveliness running from the aesthetic object in the direction of the person perceiving it. The intended impact of *enargeia* is animation.

With regard to food and the appearance of the plate, this intended impact has a very concrete thrust, not just because one is hardly able to resist the attractiveness of a perfect meal, which can be experienced through smell, look, and taste, but also because the moment of the metaphorical *being touched* takes on a concrete, physiological side through the impact of

---

27 | Mauss: [1923/24] 1990.

28 | Waldenfels: 2008.

29 | Campe, R. (1997): Vor Augen-Stellen. Über den Rahmen rhetorische Bildgebung, in: Neumann, G. (ed.): *Poststrukturalismus. Herausforderungen der Literaturwissenschaft*, Stuttgart/Weimar, pp. 208–225; Belting, H. (2001): *Bildanthropologie. Entwürfe für eine Bildwissenschaft*, München; Boehm: 2003; Bredekamp, H. (2007): *Theorie des Bildakts*, Frankfurt/M.

enargeia during eating. The transformation of goods into enjoyable dishes, which makes a statement about a certain understanding of nature, community etc., leads at a metabolic level to an energy reserve provided for the person, which literally has an animation dimension which, however, goes beyond just usable energy. As such there is a literal and a metaphorical dimension, to touching and being touched through eating. The metaphorical dimension is often seen too little, because at the theoretical level is predominantly related to the satisfaction of primary needs.

Even if there are initial signs of being touched through food by the smell and sight of it, the pivotal moment is when it disappears from our field of vision and touches our tongue: "The object of taste is a form of the tangible; ... for no more is it so with touch", Aristotle writes ("De Anima", Book II, 10). Tasting always also has a tactile dimension. This too is given little attention in the current discourse about the aesthetics of eating. But is it touching or being touched? And if it is both, do both occur at the same time? Maurice Merleau-Ponty calls the associated criss-crossing of subject and object a "chiasm" and describes it as a "reversible" interrelation. The example that Merleau-Ponty gives is touching one's own hands: "If my left hand can touch my right hand, while it palpates the tangibles, can touch it touching, can turn its palpation back upon it, why, when touching the hand of another, would I not touch in it the same power to espouse the things that I have touched in my own?"[30]

When I touch one of my hands with the other, I cannot at one and the same time feel my hand is the one that is touching and being touched. And the fact that simultaneously experiencing something as subject and object is not possible also applies to other senses. I cannot, for example, observe myself as subject and object at the same time. There is no coincidence of sight and visibility, of touching and touchable, but only a reversible interrelation or criss-crossing. Although this is no different in the case of tentative tasting, the transition from seeing the food to tentative tasting can be described as the maximum convergence point of that reversible chiasm of touching and touchable, of tasting and tasted. Because directly beyond this perception the non-simultaneity of the perception of subject and object disappears, as in metabolism the object is assimilated in the subject. The phrase "The way to a man's heart is through his stomach" is a reminder of this. It states why like no other field of perception, tasting as enjoyment is associated with the possibility of bridging the hiatus and here is paradigmatic for what is known as aesthetic experience.

---

30 | Merleau-Ponty, M. (1968): *The Visible and the Invisible*, Evanstin, p. 141.

Decay and Other Flip Sides

Gastronautical Ramblings

About Post-Culinary Design Possibilities

International Gastronautical Society

We 'gastronauts' are convinced that fast food, the mass rearing of animals, and discount food is not an ethical question, but rather a question of sensory properties. Whereas mankind has for centuries been sharpening its "view" of things, taste faded. Tongues and noses are detached from our brains, and sophisticated taste combinations form the height of our culinary reception. Mankind has only just begun to design food and to train the associated senses as an intellectual tool. But what is food? And in particular, what will food be in the future? We cry out for local produce, and we like the taste of the goods we get: thanks be to labels. We cry out for fresh produce and are glad to see short expiration dates. That said, we would need to address putrefaction in order to recognize freshness not just by color or the droplets of water on the advertising photo.

In a work for a surreal documentary by Florian Bitterlin (camera: Garrick J. Lauterbach) about a social, psychiatric art workshop called 'artSoph' we, the International Gastronautical Society, arranged, at intervals, a giant table full of food and exposed it to decay. Apart from photographs and a film sequence, this gave rise to a temporally unstable work that depicted decay as a process, while we influenced the form it took:

For 80 days we nurtured a fairly demanding, fascinating monstrosity whose smell was constantly changing. It all began innocently with a table laid in white that was almost full of top-quality fresh vegetables that a wholesaler was no longer able to sell. Ready-made pizzas, tinned peaches, French fries, cartons of yoghurt complemented the scene. Little happened for quite some time.

It is March, and things are still fairly fresh in our half-open work space in a rear courtyard: The lettuce is becoming a little wilted, the bread somewhat dry. Our objective though are cloudy mountains of mold in all forms, colors, and textures. We are under time pressure, on account of the date for filming. Though the outside surfaces of the food are changing slightly and becoming a bit greasy, they are still sealed rather than bursting, as if ashamed of their insides. There is a slight acidity in the air. Only the bananas are really brown. We moisten the table of food every day with stale beer and water and hope the process will speed up, which fails to happen. We set up heat lamps to raise the temperature of the sculpture: The goods now begin to get softer, on their insides something really seems to be developing that gently oozes out of certain cracks. We keep on adding on new produce to illustrate the decay time. Maggots are now beginning to live on the bottom of the loaves of bread. The day of filming is getting closer, the smell is becoming more intense, but visually the table is no more interesting than a pile of forgotten loaves of bread in a cupboard. We wrap the entire sculpture in thin plastic film. That brings about the breakthrough: It is as if the goods' rotten inside now dared venture outside because of the protective foil. Everything gets going! The mold grows rapidly. From inside to outside the French fries turn first deep black, then green. The neighbors complain about the stench and we can hardly bear it when we are working. We buy breathing masks. But the challenge is yet to come:

The entire range of produce, from the freshly cut fig and the half-wilted lettuce, to the egg plants, which by now are almost humus, are ultimately intended to be presented in one sweep of the camera along the table. As such we have to arrange the rotting material. Brown slime with brown slime, green mold with green mold, semi-decayed with semi-decayed. And for us on the set the stink suddenly becomes not just a stink: Hours later we begin to notice hints of yeast, like in champagne. We can suddenly make out different vinegary odors. The sweetness of the decay has astonishingly varied nuances of sweet, which linger in our noses long after we have left the studio. We saw to it that we were capable of the task, but are no longer sure that we can tolerate this capability.

With the series of images that were made of the work we as 'gastronauts' assume responsibility and attempt to actively design the decay of food, because only if you are familiar with putrefaction can you judge quality. Culinary design does not begin with cooking and end with eating.

For the sake of all-embracing design we want to elegantly push the boundaries without erratically going overboard. That said, we see the boundary not just as a spatial, but also a temporal limit to culinary experience.

By way of example we display on the coming pages post-culinary design possibilities in the form of mental games, and in linguistic macro-recordings describe our impressions in light of this marginal work of stylized decay. The photographs offer visual evidence of what we thought, saw, and suspected when working on the mode.

Text: International Gastronautical Society, Felicia Schäfer and Leon Heinz
Photos: Zeitversiegelung, Florian Bitterlin

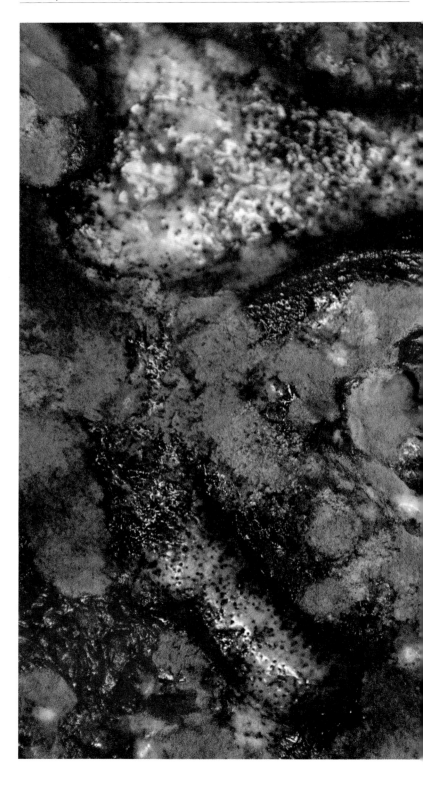

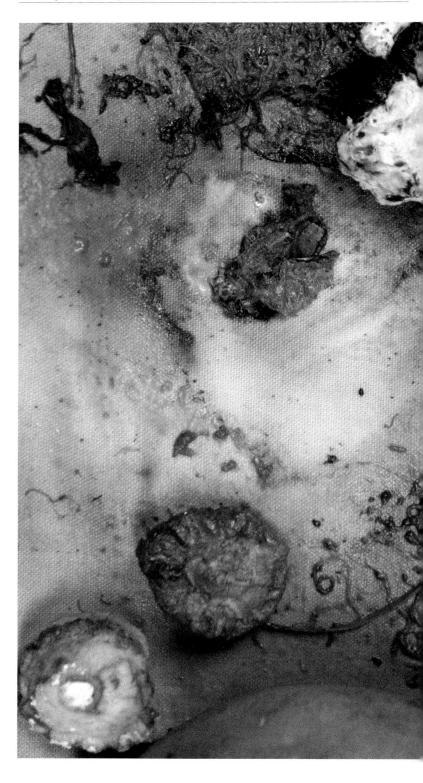

The increasing beauty of the table over the course of time engenders a smell that is tasty! Glances begin to exist on our tongue. The foods on the table themselves, on the other hand, are now only visual theories of their past. Anyone facing the table begins to experience nervousness: Looking at it, its current state penetrates the soul, and as when we breathe the mouth. Our eyes, savoring the food as well, look towards a new dimension, swallowing as they do. Our nose becomes our tactile sense, a touch for composure. At the sight of the table our thoughts become a confusing form of consumption. Through breathing alone our mere presence becomes an act of chewing.

Are we shaping the table or is the table shaping us?

A fart does not smell of excrement. Or only as strongly as milk smells of cheese.

In the Elugatic provinces farting is good manners. What here we have to be ashamed about was cultivated there. An elugatic epicure knows exactly how much caraway to sprinkle over the rind to particularly enjoy a post-culinary fart. This means that a connaisseur Elugate makes more of his culinary design possibilities than a European, who discreetly tries to conceal the potential fermenting in him. Where an Elugate, by virtue of his being conscious of and steering his bodily possibilities, exerts great influence on the form his food takes, a European flushes a bucketful of design possibilities down the john: If an Elugate were to do that, it could be a statement. "Action digesting", as a form of expression of abstract post-culinary expressionism, for example. But here in the West, where, ashamed, we sit down on the white bowl to get rid of our potential as quietly as possible, we can at best call it propriety.

And what is with our chefs? Do they perhaps think further than we believe and wait in the kitchen until the liberating fart in Elugate fashion is the talk of the town here as well? Or do they run away from their own flatulence, like the rest of us, and for this reason never really know what they are doing?

The moist evening air is pointless. Fresh underwear is pointless. As pointless as traffic with that smell of its own, which only brings some relief. The table has become embedded in your nose! It lingers: invisible but present. Sweeter than sour and at the same time sourer than sweet. An olfactory contradiction.

Anyone who has entered the space only really leaves it hours after they actually left. What remains in our tiny nose hairs? What lingers for so long in the air – and where?

When, after several hours of nasal tinnitus, the nose fetter loosens, the impression has not gone entirely, as there is a hint of putrefaction everywhere – and you can smell it now. The contradiction becomes a cycle.

And yet: time heals all odors: As it passes through our metamorphic respiratory tract the table enters a vale of tears before leaving it again later. Its smell through time is the dramaturgy of decay. On route to becoming what we never want to smell the first thing that the smell of the table develops is stinking putrefaction.

Then, very gently, after days of chaotic, almost unbearable stench, hints of vinegar, yeast aromas, and ultimately geosmin and petrichor begin to emerge. And we ask ourselves: are we smelling the table better, or is the table smelling better?

Eating slowly keeps you healthy. Keep to the right rhythm! Chew well! Produce lots of saliva! Lick your lips with your tongue after swallowing. And do not forget your lower lip. And then count. Count caudalies.

Caudalies? A caudalie is a unit used for measuring the number of seconds a taste persists. You count them (if you do at all) at least with wine. As proof of quality. One caudalie represents one second of a wine's finish. The more caudalies the better.

In Vino Veritas. As such:

If you eat caudalie-style, you eat well. It is not about producing lots of saliva and chewing well hundreds of times. It is about waiting. And waiting is easiest when you are eating, especially if the delicacies have lots of caudalies. Then you can while away the time with them and slither along the aroma curve.

So even when you are cooking take care to add lots of caudalies to the food. It is healthy and is only entertaining later on! When preparing the food, ask how many caudalies you have already had in your life, how many caudalies, on average, you eat every year? Is it possible that this average correlates with your life expectancy? Can being be measured in terms of caudalies?

They shimmer, gleam, and sparkle: Sit cheekily, like dewdrops, on lettuces and tomatoes – and the smallest of them cling to the soft little hairs of fluff. They are condensation pearls. We know them as the tears of decay. They form beneath the plastic cover over the table: They move from the vegetable to the foil, then back to the vegetable. Again and again, becoming bigger as they do. So big that ultimately you can see them with your naked eye.

The fact that for maggots these droplets are a refreshing pleasure is no reason to be disgusted: It is a quality seal. They are the distillate of putrefaction, and as a distillate (like all distillates) are superior to other drops and droplets. Anybody who notices them is amazed. Who has ever tasted the dew that clings to the top of the packaging containing blue cheese?

We then miss the moment at which the end becomes the beginning. We are not present when the rotting process comes to an end and a new being manifests itself. It is not tangible, the moment between death and rebirth, at which everything becomes reversed.

We can shape the end, but not right to the end. We can shape the beginning, but not right from the beginning. We influence colors and smells, which in the course of the rotting process become ever more specific. The spectrum is narrowed down by shaping: Colorful becomes monochrome, but in a thousand hues. And a thousand possible instances of monochrome always ultimately become brown. Dust and brown earth. With brown, we lose control. With brown the designer becomes an observer.

Until something grows from brown again that is designable and colored. Colored like mold or colored like fresh fruit.

Some people wash their hands when they are in a restaurant. Some use soap after eating out.

Expensive restaurants have expensive liquid soap in the bathroom, while in standard inns the soap is, as a rule, cheap, and when washing their hands lots of people possibly have the mint in their mouth that they got with the bill.

Perhaps in this or that inn some benevolent thoughts have been given to these moments after a meal. But only in very few cases were these deliberations made specifically with the intention of post-culinary design.

In the unconsidered way it is presented, the mint may well even be the pinnacle of anti-design: After all, it is used to neutralize the preceding (designed) meal.

If you kiss somebody now, with your minty breath, you become a container, the host's crockery and source of aroma, the plate for a culinary expression (or anti-expression), but because you are not a plate you can guess what being a plate is like.

Are you now a medium or still a consumer? Can one be both at one and the same time? And anyway: What is a medium when you are eating? Everything? Is a really attentive host one that gives you toothpaste that suits the meal as you leave?

We ultimately fell in love with the table: In front of us there was true beauty. Having seen far too much of it, we still look at it. Allow our eyes to wallow in its appearance. Still see more colors. Still see more shapes. See more and more.

As beautiful as the table looks, it feels just as ugly to the touch. What we allowed to grow, we have to dispose of. What we made pictures of we now have to put in sacks.

Brooks of rotten juice pour forth from the rotten tablecloths. We scrape buckets of slime from the rear of the decaying matter. Heavy sacks, almost fluid are the result of the results. And yet everything is driven by this moistness. Without moistness everything would only have dried up, whereas instead it all adopted a new form.

We would not get ill, and we would smell no different whatever, if always after eating food and shortly after its excretion we were to put on rubber gloves and knead our excrement for a short time. But we would certainly eat differently: We would perhaps have long since realized that cucumbers influence the consistency of what we discharge – or that in its post-culinary state, cheap pork smells horrible.

Culinarily speaking everyone is nowadays omnicompetent: It goes without saying that on any street corner you can buy crisps with cider vinegar from Brittany and pepper from Andalusia. We have great discussions about wine with our contemporaries, and there is Himalayan salt on every kitchen table.

Only when you are having a shit is it good, if it is not bad. Are we too modest? In the past twelve months what was the food you discharged noticeably good feces after? And what is good anyway? How do you describe it? What would the culinary world be like if by reflex you did not put the question to a physician but rather a chef?

Mold, however beautiful it may be, is only ever ugly in waste sacks. Disgustingly heavy. So dead and yet threatening. So leaden it almost makes you frightened. The table, no longer a table. Now only a board. The end, as concrete as it should never have become. With no vibrations whatsoever, just as the end should not be. An end without an end or a beginning. All you want, in the true sense of the word, is to dispose of it. A stationary end – waste – and for that reason so ugly.

On the Sensation
of Freshly Grated Lemon Zest

Anneli Käsmayr and Thomas A. Vilgis Talk About

Food Innovation, Taste and Emotion

AK: *Mr. Vilgis, I would like to start this interview with a personal question that stems from my work as an artist. For the 'Sound in Savor' series I am compiling gustatory memories from people I talk to in a taste archive.*
What is your strongest taste memory? Can you describe it?

TV: It is undoubtedly a memory from my childhood: Sour tripe. It is a taste I can always recall and which I still miss as much as ever since I moved away from southern Germany.

AK: *Tripe is a regional specialty which I imagine not everyone is familiar with. Can you describe the taste more precisely, i.e., what is the consistency like, the aromas – what do you taste first?*

TV: Plain tripe, part of the digestive tract of bovines, is something a lot of people find disgusting. But if the tripe is cooked well then its surface is extraordinarily soft and a little rough, because the structure of the stomach remains intact of course. It releases a delicious flavor that is somewhat reminiscent of offal, but is also very meaty. It has a subtle acidity and the long stewing process produces a consistency that is hard to find in virtually any other food. For us in Swabia it is of course always served with spätzle and the dish is indescribable – even as I talk about it now, it triggers a feeling of longing.

AK: *Yes, I can well imagine. Favorite dishes like that have a strong emotional component as 'soul food'. But back to the taste. Is there tomato in the sauce too?*

TV: For us in the Swabian Alb region there has generally been very little tomato, but more vinegar for the specific sour tripe recipe. There are regional differences of course. In Italy, for example, the proportion of tomato is considerably higher, and the same applies in southern France where you can also get tripe. The way we do it is to stew the classic stewing vegetables – onions, some celery, carrots – along with it for a long time. The vegetables are then broken down and the thickness of the dish comes from the release of the collagen in the tripe. It is really delicious, with a slight stickiness, the "viscoelastic part of strong umami flavour", or 'schlotzig' as we say in Swabia.

AK: *Does that mean proteins change as a result of the enduring heat?*

TV: Yes, this veal tripe of course contains a large amount of collagen, which turns to gelatin during cooking, but it also has a very fine meat structure between the collagen fibrils. The muscle meat consists of very short fibers with a lot of connective tissue, meaning it is very flexible so that the bolus, i. e. the grass, is kept in motion. It is a highly complex food if you consider the biology and the physiology of the animal. It is also a very juicy meat.

In our recipe we add normal wine vinegar, although you can play around with it a bit in gastronomy of course and develop the dish very rustically. You can add wine or fine vinegar to it. This can be added in several stages during cooking so that the cooking process is controlled accordingly. In the classic cuisine I enjoyed as a child, however, that was not an issue of course, and we would just add a dash of vinegar at the beginning of the stewing process and another at the end and it turned out great. You ended up with a lot of sauce – that is the way Swabians like it.

AK: *What difference does the acidity make when it is added before and after the stewing process?*

TV: The acidity added before the cooking naturally ensures that some proteins break down, denaturate and hydrolyze more quickly as a result of the acidity. It is purely about the technicalities of cooking, although my mother did not know that of course – it was just passed on through the recipe. The final dash of vinegar adds to the taste, with the addition of salt and sometimes parsley or whatever other herbs were available. Allow to cook for another 5–10 minutes and then you have got a mouthwatering dish. These days of course you can do it with lemon or lime juice too, but this was back at a time when there was no other option in the Swabian Alb region.

AK: *How often did you eat the dish?*

TV: At least once every two weeks; it always depended on when the local butcher's slaughtering day was. I come from a small town and if the butcher got a fresh cow then first he would get the offal. Then once he had removed that, the stomach, the tripe, would be cleaned and cooked. It was not like today when everything is available all the time, it was only on the slaughtering day. Then there was the blood sausage and liver sausage and everything we would call 'Schlachtplatte', meaning 'slaughter plate'. In fact it was a relatively easy dish to cook; you can leave it to simmer gently on the stove, you cannot really go wrong with it. And that is something we would do often, for example if it were laundry day and there was not much time for cooking.

AK: Do you sometimes deliberately relive this taste experience just to indulge yourself?

TV: Absolutely. Back then I moved to the UK after my PhD defence, where you could not get it of course. Then I came back to Mainz and asked about tripe, only to be told "We do not have that here at all, it is pet food". I was initially shocked to discover there is something of a 'tripe divide' straight across Europe: You can only find it to the south of a line level with Heidelberg, i. e., in Saxony and in southern Thuringia, then up towards Poland. And at the time this was not clear to me, because for me it was a little delicacy, something extraordinary, and so I wanted to eat it again but could not get it. Since then I have always bought tripe when I have seen it, be it in Strasbourg or in southern Germany, or even in Provence. Wherever I get it, I always cook it at least once. But not like it was back then, I could not recreate it, but I use my own ideas so the taste varies – you either bring in the acidity differently or add mustard to it depending on the market conditions and your own preference.

AK: How did you as a physicist actually end up in the field of taste research?

TV: I spent many years conducting research into polymers, i. e., soft systems: plastic materials, rubber, non-metallic materials, which can be worked and molded with low levels of force. Emulsions and paints are included here, as are fillers and absorbent materials for diapers, for example, or even car tires, adhesives and dissolved polymers. Then later I became interested in proteins, and at that point you are actually quite close to foodstuffs. Then there was the huge boom in molecular cuisine and I changed tack entirely. All the knowhow from soft materials can of course be easily transferred to foods, and then it does not take long before the idea emerges to work on taste, too. With normal materials it is not about the taste. It is true that the molecular structure determines the macroscopic properties, i. e., if I want to improve a bicycle tire so that it lasts longer and suffers less wear, these properties can be traced back to the molecular structure on the nanoscale. Here there is always a structure-property relationship, which is a concept in materials research that has played an important role for a very long time. And it is similar with foods: In addition to the elements that fundamentally change, i. e., texture, mouth feel and firmness to the bite, there is the connection of the taste to the molecular structures. More precisely, the speed at which taste is released based on specific molecular processes is the be-all and end-all. And in that regard for me it is crucial to link up the expertise from both areas.

AK: *Specific processes in cookery that draw on knowledge of physics have been known for centuries. Can you actually determine a point at which cooking was changed by science?*

TV: Food technology has existed for a long time. However, it was not until the 1980s that people began to consider molecular structures. Back then there were so-called 'molecular gastronomists' who dealt with the topic in more depth and tried to establish what changes during the cooking of a puree, why pasta dough works so well, why bread has nice bubbles and a structure, and how this can be controlled. This was long before the hype about molecular cuisine, as driven by Ferran Adrià.

My own experience during my studies in the early 1980s concerned meatloaf. I had encased a hard-boiled egg in minced meat and then, whilst the whole dish was being cooked, it fell apart completely and there was no longer any meatloaf, but rather mince. That was whilst I was doing my doctorate. Here specific adhesive properties of the bits of minced meat had failed and it became clear to me that there was undoubtedly more to it than that which I had gathered from home. That is a point I like to remember, because there is a lot of materials research in cooking too.

AK: *Recently there has been a stronger focus in research on the artificial (re)production of foods, for example the production of meat in a laboratory, which has caused quite a stir of late. In one of your last research projects you looked at the production of soy milk. I would be interested to know: Could you theoretically produce cow's milk artificially too?*

TV: It would be very laborious technologically. You can of course create a product similar to milk, but in terms of the microstructure, it would never equate to what a cow is able to produce. In raw milk the fat is encased in a phospholipid layer, which creates another complete membrane around the fat particle, a lipid bilayer that stores enzymes and proteins as can be found in any cell. The main task of this milk is to pass these substances onto the calf, the offspring of the cow. Of course that is something nature does unbeatably well. Creating such things in the laboratory – no one would be able to afford that sort of milk.

AK: *Madness.*

TV: Yes, it is crazy. You can actually recreate the nutritional value; you can take the milk fat and assemble the proteins, but creating the structure is virtually impossible. You really have to hand it to Mother Nature and her ingenious biological processes.

AK: *In your scientific work you disassemble fundamentally natural structures. How are your feelings towards nature changing here?*

TV: As before, I have tremendous respect for nature. Personally I am a huge fan of natural foods and I really love cooking. Of course it is true though that research permits a great deal of insight into foodstuffs. At the Max Planck Institute we carry out fundamental scientific research, so we aim to understand the molecular correlations. This permits a different way of looking at foodstuffs and food itself. There is a great deal of ideology in the various teachings on nutrition, and naturally research puts this into perspective, so you get a feel for how things happen in nature and what benefits we get from that. Up until a few years ago I still did not even know how much physics was involved in human beings digesting droplets of fat from emulsions. Or what role bile acids play – it is thoroughly fascinating when these phospholipids are replaced and suddenly fat is released. Through this research you become ever freer of ideology and you no longer believe what all the nutritionists love to preach concerning what is healthy or unhealthy.

AK: *What sort of topics are you talking about here?*

TV: Gluten, for example, which is currently so vilified. From a scientific perspective that makes no sense at all. There is a small percentage of people who cannot tolerate gluten and/or its by-proteins. Gluten is a very long protein that generates rubbery properties. This has the advantage that bread dough, for example, is very elastic. This is also evident in how difficult it is to produce baked goods that have the same mouth feel and baking properties but do not contain gluten. But really our bodies do not care at all where the amino acids come from.

AK: *What I find very exciting about current nutritional trends is their dichotomy. On the one hand we have Slow Food, neighborhood gardens and a now extreme regional trend, on top of which the last few years have seen an increasing trend towards street food and, on the other hand, the laboratory meat we mentioned or the lifestyle product* Soylent, *which is being hyped as the modern food replacement or, as you can see on the website, as "simple, efficient and affordable".[1] The idea behind this is that you pack all the nutrients human beings need to survive into a liquid. What is your take on that?*

TV: That is possible from a scientific perspective of course, but the question arises as to how our stomach and digestive tract will react after a long period of having nothing to do. In evolution too we see that if, as the paleo movement proposes, we were to have a diet like our ancestors 50,000 years ago, there would be foods we are no longer able to digest because we no longer have the bite for them and because, over the course of time, our intestines have shortened, and the enzyme situation has changed. *Soylent* is a step further: Why would I need peristalsis if the digestive tract no

---

1 | 'Soylent' lifestyle product: www.Soylent.com (accessed on Apr. 15, 2015). The slogan now reads: 'Healthy, convenient, affordable food'.

longer needs to move semi-solid boluses through it? What happens with enzyme production, the pancreas, if the proteins have already largely been broken down? It would not have anything left to do. The physical components of digestion are largely redundant with this sort of nutrition, and I cannot say whether the intestines would become slacker or even shorter in that case, but I imagine they would. The reason I find this *Soylent* funny is that it would represent the end of an eating and cooking culture and that is something I would fight until my dying breath. I want to see my food in advance, to taste it in all its facets and to prepare it in all sorts of different ways. For me *Soylent* is something that is strongly reminiscent of food for the elderly. I became familiar with this field when my father was in a nursing home and it ultimately resulted in a book on nutrition for those who have difficulty swallowing.

It tackles the issue of how you can actually keep older people eating independently for as long as possible and thus contributes to maintaining a feeling of self-worth. Similarly to *Soylent*, there are liquids like starch and sugar cocktails that contain everything the body needs: trace elements, vitamins, essential amino acids, minerals and the right quantities of fat. For me and my food biography and culinary future though, *Soylent* is of no interest.

AK: *Yes, I agree with you on that.* Soylent *makes no sense at all when subjectively I can see that it is first and foremost the aromas that really speak to me in cooking. Freshly grated lemon zest or a sprig of rosemary – for me these are the experiences that make me enjoy cooking.*

TV: In reality cooking actually begins when you buy the products at the market. If you can tell the season and sense that now asparagus, for example, is ready and the first beans start to appear, then that is something I long for, because I have a certain sensualism with regard to food and cooking. And neither do I need tomatoes in winter. They do not taste of anything; they are hard and have a consistency that makes you want to run a mile! In winter I have entirely different flavors in mind, so you can really make the very most of a cabbage in all possible variations. As soon as the spring gets underway again, you go back to thinking precisely about lemon zest, the first sprigs of parsley, the first chives …

AK: *Rhubarb, peas!*

TV: … Exactly. Then you suddenly start to live very differently again. And all that is something I do not want to miss out on or replace with any sort of groundbreaking nutrition drink or smoothie. It is already happening with these energy drinks, which is a load of nonsense.

AK: *What I find extreme about* Soylent *is the fact that there is only one taste sensation[2] and I actually ask myself what that does to you? But with* Soylent *it is not exactly about the taste, it seems. Nevertheless, if I look at how closely emotion and taste are linked, i.e., how sensory satisfaction can actually also be a pleasurable experience, then I find the idea of only ever experiencing one taste as very menacing. You initiated a research project on the correlation between emotion and the gustatory stimulation of a dish with researchers from Humboldt University Berlin. What exactly is being studied there?*

TV: The idea for that came to me because I really like going to eat at top restaurants. I was interested for various reasons and I am always curious about the cook or chef's thought process behind the dish. It struck me that personally I get a feeling of extraordinary satisfaction from a complex plate rich in components, yet without the feeling of fullness that comes from having too many calories: a profound satisfaction, although the number of calories is actually much smaller. And it struck me that I actually do not put weight on with this sort of cuisine. I am also able to resist feelings of hunger without any great difficulty if I know something great is coming up. I was therefore interested in whether a direct correlation might exist between the feeling of satiety and the complexity of a meal. Together with Professor Werner Sommer, a professor for cognitive psychology at Humboldt University in Berlin, we conducted some simple experiments relating to this involving two meals with the same caloric content, one presented in deconstructed form and one normally. The study has just been evaluated.[3] Actually the eating times change with increasing complexity, and it is also possible to see a slowing down of the increase in glucose. The paper has now been published in open-access form and can be viewed by anyone who is interested.

AK: *It would make sense that through some kind of archaic imprinting we are compelled to consume a variety of nutrients and are therefore always looking for different tastes.*

TV: Yes, exactly. It is the same as the idea that you should eat a varied diet or consume 'five a day', but evolution has also taught us that we have not always been able to get hold of all nutrients at all times. Back in the past too we ate a variety of things that were available at the actual point in time in relation to the seasons. Evolution showed us what we have to eat, otherwise humanity would not have developed the way it did. And it is also through trying different things that man has discovered what is good for him and what he can eat. Thus a plate rich in different components is not only important for the reward center, but is also linked to a variety of nutrients. If you do that regularly then it makes no difference if you do not eat

---

2 | In December 2016 *Soylent* introduced new flavors of their drink products (available in addition to the powder in the product range).

3 | Łuczak et al.: 2016.

an orange on a particular day. It is all about the variety. You should never look at these things in isolation, but rather in relation to everything else.

AK: *That fits in very well with your taste-physical reinterpretation of the culinary triangle of Claude Lévi-Strauss,[4] which has also found enormous resonance with cultural theorists. What does it mean?*

TV: I was not familiar with the culinary triangle until a few years ago either, but I think it is a thoroughly wonderful clarification of the transition from nature to culture, where cooking and the utilization of fire play a huge role for human nutrition. Previously people only had uncooked food available to them, but the cooking process suddenly permitted a huge availability of energy, greater diversity of taste and the development of social culture. For me this was an interesting idea that still represents the very essence of cooking today. There is raw food, cooked food and fermented food, which Lévi-Strauss dubbed rotten. Take the example of cabbage: There is cooked and raw cabbage as well as sauerkraut. The old and modern cooking techniques that we acquired even in molecular cuisine fit precisely into this triangle. The food has a raw structure, through heating something changes, and fermentation changes something else. And then of course I end up back in the depths of my materials research. Thus when I cook purposefully, I also change the food to that extent. For me that was a fundamental clarification, which forms the basis of my fascination for this culinary triangle.

AK: *Is it not also the case that every culture has cultivated dishes in all three categories for millennia? Fermentation plays a role everywhere, albeit in different ways.*

TV: Fermentation has been around for a long time. Its oldest-known applications date from around 9,000 years ago. Yet fermented foods were around even before that. People could find fermenting fruits – a valuable foodstuff – and in some regions early humans even developed enzymes so that they could actually eat them. Long before the birth of Christ people began to ferment foods in order to preserve them or make them palatable – examples include phytonutrients and even milk. In the beginning people were very strongly lactose-intolerant, because they were dosed with lactose as a source of energy through the mother's milk. If you then eat normally, the enzyme is no longer necessary and breaks down. That is the case with all animals, and humans were the same. It is only over the course of time and through adaptation that the enzyme has redeveloped in specific regions, although not in all, hence even today there are still many people who are lactose-intolerant. In parts of Asia, for example, cow's milk has never become fully established, and in the African and European sphere it has been proven that the settlement of people correlates to the

---

4 | See p. 154 f.

developed tolerance of milk products. Here the acidification of milk was an obvious way to break down all the lactose. Anyone can eat yoghurt and cheese as long as it is well fermented. Hence through the fermentation process, people also learnt to preserve things.

AK: *The bacteria that are involved in the fermentation process are very beneficial to human health too. A large part of our immune system is found in the flora of the gut. Over the last few years, so-called 'effective microorganisms' or EMs coming from Japan have become very popular and have not only been adopted for health reasons, but also offer huge benefits in agriculture. In New York it was brought to my attention when examples for waste reduction in big cities were presented as part of a festival held by the New Museum in 2011. One of these was a Japanese compost known as Bokashi, which uses EMs to break down matter particularly quickly without putrefaction processes. The pleasantly acidic smell of this compost really struck me.*

TV: That was undoubtedly a form of lactic acid fermentation, which is non-toxic. That is why in food production you always need to add sufficient salt, because the salt prevents pathogenic microorganisms that produce specific toxic products from building up in the first place as a result of putrefaction. If something smells pleasantly acidic then that is always an indication that lactic acid bacteria and yeasts predominate. Nevertheless I would be wary of simply ingesting these sorts of foreign microorganisms because you do not really know what is happening there. First you need to understand exactly how our gut flora works. Of the billions of bacteria, these are at least known in terms of their genetics, yet every individual is entirely unique in this regard. Actually you would have to make a specific cocktail for each human being.

AK: *On the other hand, there are many studies into the fact that our gut flora have changed for the worse as a result of our diets, use of pharmaceuticals, etc., and thus specific fungi like candida and also skin diseases are taking hold.*

TV: There I also see the connection to Lévi-Strauss: If your diet corresponds to the regularities – raw, cooked, and fermented – then people have actually always eaten this way, so it is good for you. That is why I would advise staying away from convenience products, the sort of highly processed and therefore no longer naturally balanced foods. These are non-toxic, but we do not know what the long-term consequences are on the ecosystem of the gut flora, for example, if you consume these exclusively. The same also applies to *Soylent*. You cannot get any more processed food than this product. That could actually have long-term side-effects in microbiological terms too, in the form of fostering diseases, changes in the flora and hence shifts in the standard of health. And if I no longer need to chew, then it may be the case that my teeth fall out at some point. But before that happens, I would actually be much more concerned about 'social neglect' if the eating culture were no longer perceptible, as can currently be observed in our highly industrialized society. I do not want to say that everything was better before, but it is true that the sociological function of eating was more strongly rooted in society. If you sit down with other people at a table morning and evening, that is naturally going to mean more than simply the consumption of food. It gives structure to the day and provides for varied meals and encounters. The function of eating at McDonald's these days is an entirely different one, because there the food becomes a side issue. And in all these discussions we are currently having about diet trends, be they vegan, vegetarian, paleo, pegan, raw food or even *Soylent*, this is entirely forgotten.

AK: *In contrast, what I find very stimulating about the trends such as specialty coffee or the enthusiasm for spirits like gin, vermouth or vodka and even fruit wines and craft beer, is the taste diversity that develops. This perhaps, in turn, represents a countertrend to* Soylent: *the need for regional specialties, for varied aromas, the success of very small-scale producers. Or even the concept of the German association 'Educated drinking'.*[5]

TV: People always used to laugh at me when I said I get my beer from Belgium or France. For me personally, beer is actually comparable with wine when it comes to enjoying a meal. For many people who eat at home, alcohol has to have a certain function; it has to match well with the taste. And here beer has long been underrated – perhaps partly because of the German purity law. The craft beer movement is now shifting away from this; with the use of aromatic hops or ingredients that actually do not correspond to the purity law requirements and cultured yeasts you can suddenly discover entirely new aromas. And that is another hype which, like other trends, will also disappear eventually. In Great Britain, gin is 'the' national drink. And that is also the great thing about it, because lots of people explore these things which also represent the manifestation of a piece of regional culture.

AK: *For years you have also been pursuing the idea that you do not always need to be drinking alcoholic beverages if you want something interesting to drink with your meal (including at home). I am particularly pleased about that because for some time now I have been involved in a working group on the topic of 'Non-alcoholic Enjoyment'.*[6] *In the 'Foodpairing' book you placed a great deal of emphasis on non-alcoholic accompanying drinks, something that I had previously only ever seen with any degree of consistency in the German-speaking region with Roland Trettl and his columns in the magazine 'Lust auf Genuss'.*[7]

---

5 | Website of 'Bildungstrinken' ['Educated drinking']: http://bildungstrinken.com/ (accessed on Jan. 5, 2017).

6 | Website of the working group 'Genuss Alkoholfrei' ['Non-alcoholic Enjoyment']: http://www.genuss-alkoholfrei.de/ (accessed on Jan. 5, 2017).

7 | Trettl, R.: Columns on non-alcoholic drink pairing, in: *Lust auf Genuss*, issue 8/2012 – 1/2014, Offenburg.

Unlike premium gastronomy, where many places are now offering non-alcoholic drinks pairings.

TV: Sometimes wine is simply essential – it is of course the classic drink to enjoy with food, but there is this idea of bringing to bear the aromas that are in the food with a light drink. What I found problematic was that the options for non-alcoholic accompanying drinks were either water, non-alcoholic beer or some kind of fruit juice, but a juice with a proper, high-quality meal – that sends shivers down my spine. It is simply too sweet and too viscous, even as a cocktail, it just seems wrong. That is why we thought it has to be done differently, it should be easy. One aspect of wine is not only its aromatics, but a certain astringency. This astringency is good for us, but it cannot really be achieved with food. I had a formative experience in this regard in encountering Asian culture, in which green tea has this same astringency. It is a watery drink that acts as a carrier for aromas. It was from this idea that we developed ideas for drinks that are light and highly viscous – they have to be drunk like a wine or a beer. And it is precisely in this direction that many new restaurants are now heading with young chefs full of innovative ideas – you need only think of names like Nils Henkel, Sebastian Frank or Felix Schneider.

AK: *These ideas are of course sometimes a little more costly to put into practice, but are really exciting in the way they enhance the aromas. I am convinced that in five to ten years' time there will also be finished products on the market here.*

A further future trend I would like to talk to you about is the consumption of insects, which are considered a good source of protein. At the beginning of 2015 an article appeared in Brand eins *business magazine about food hacking in Silicon Valley, which included details of a start-up that produces cookies as a low-allergen product using insect flour.[8] You have already experimented a little using locusts and maggots, for example as part of a cooking project at the University of Osnabrück. Does that excite you from a culinary perspective?*

TV: You can fry the insects, which makes them delightfully nutty and crispy. And if you extracted the proteins from them you could even make substitute products like tofu or something similar. But you also need to account for the fact that a mealworm is around 1–2 cm in size, so you need a lot of them to make a full plate. If you want to feed a family of four or five, then you need an appropriate amount of matter. A cow might bring 800 kg of meat to the table, so only one slaughter is required and you can live for a long, long time on the result, but with mealworms you need to kill millions of them to feed a five-person family, which raises some questions with regard to animal ethics. What I find tricky though is the

---

8 | *Lecker Grillen-Kekse, Brand eins* (issue 02/2015) - *Was Wirtschaft treibt*, available online at: http://www.brandeins.de/archiv/2015/marketing/food-hacking-silicon-valley-beyond-meat-bitty-foods-hampton-creek-lecker-grillen-kekse/ (accessed on January 26, 2016).

reduced variation in taste. You can smoke and salt the mealworms but at some point that becomes boring, because the food does not have the same potential as a vegetable, for example. The aromatic possibilities of a vegetable are extremely diverse – meat is already limited here because of its molecular structure. One is based on pectin-cellulose, whilst the other is protein – they have different temperatures, and the maggots and insects are undoubtedly the most boring. That is why I think that it might work in the food industry as in the example of the cookies, but not in "family scale" home cooking. I have some serious doubts there.

AK: *On the subject of vegetables: You talked about the particular diversity of aromas in sous-vide preparation in relation to the culinary triangle. Might that be something that could make it into the realm of home cooking?*

TV: Yes, most definitely. I can cook food at home this way even without a sous-vide appliance – I can easily do it in the oven, for example. I recently cooked a whole celeriac sous-vide, so the entire bulb in the skin with some Tonka beans, Ethiopian coffee, a little sugar and salt for the osmotic effect and some butter so that the aromas are released in the fat, in one of those plastic bags. It then remains in the combi-steamer for an hour and a half at 87 degrees, is then chilled in water and simply marinates for up to two weeks in the fridge. It is an unbelievable experience! It is only with recipes like this that you realize just how much you can do with vegetables – more than you would ever dream of. Hence for me food trends are somewhat secondary; I observe them and have fun with them, but as long as I have food from the garden or can buy it at the market or in the countryside around Mainz then that is trend enough if I approach it with my own quirky ideas.

AK: *So to use the words of* Michelin-*starred chef Vincent Klink: "Voll ins Gemüse!" – Vegetables are the way forward!*

TV: Exactly!

AK: *Through your job you have the extraordinary opportunity to explore what fascinates you in scientific terms. What other topics are you particularly interested in?*

TV: One example is the question of what else you can do with the fat particles of nuts and soy beans. Or what you can do with specific plant sugars, these types of oligofructose that make up all root vegetables, for example, from chicory to parsnips. These are very specific short-chain sugars that are not built on starch but rather on fructose, which are probiotic and yet are not digested by humans. These are the sorts of interesting physical phenomena that I am looking at in my research.

AK: *Your popular science books convey a lot of knowledge and get people excited about letting loose and discovering new taste sensations. Your latest book 'Kochen für Angeber' ('Cooking for Showoffs') in particular – the title of which was perhaps chosen a little reluctantly – represents a very humorous and inspired approach to aromas and techniques in avant-garde cuisine. Even just the graphic integration of the seemingly handwritten comments on the texts in the book is really fun. It takes your book 'Aroma', which was presented with the highest accolade by the Gastronomische Akademie, to the next level in a practical, user-friendly way. How did you end up getting interested in aroma pairing?*

TV: Classic food pairing has been around since about 1990, when people assumed that you could match up two foods if they had the same key aroma. But for me that was too narrow; it lacked aromatic contrast and so I took a new approach to the whole area. What it was really all about for me was the fact that the mere existence of an aroma did not really express anything. In coffee, for example, you have a sulfuric aroma that can also be found in salmon, so it is said that you can combine coffee and salmon. Personally though I am not sure that this is the reason why the combination tastes good. It is not just the one aroma, which is released very differently by the coffee of course than by the salmon, and most importantly it depends on how I prepare a food so that the aroma actually reaches my nose in the first place, and how quickly it is released and what exactly this odor-activity is. There is a whole series of structural questions: What does the molecule look like? How is it released from the food? That means that here there is a lot more to take into account to emphasize the food pairing than the mere existence of aromas. And that was the idea behind the book 'Aroma': working with aroma groups to understand the pairing using herbs and spices. This opened up a whole new world to me. And the 'Foodpairing' book was based on the same idea, but here the aroma groups were not limited to herbs and spices, but to food as a whole. It is true that it is highly complex, but it worked there too and it was simply logical. Classic food pairing is therefore the combination of the same things, but of course you also need to create contrasts to keep things interesting. For example cucumber, melon, borage, salmon and goat's cheese all have an identical aroma. You can combine these and make a great salad out of them, but the salad is not that exciting and after the sixth forkful you know how the seventh is going to taste. If I add some contrasts to it, however, then it suddenly becomes exciting.

AK: *At the beginning you said that you have many reasons for visiting top restaurants. Can you elaborate on that?*

TV: It is curiosity for one thing. Visiting a top restaurant is a huge experience for me and is actually a piece of culture – it has a similar value to a music-lover's enjoyment of opera. For me it is a veritable culinary opera when there are several courses. And what I also find interesting is the development: What changes, for example, with molecular gastronomy? On top of this, I like to see the particular signature of the relevant actors in the kitchen.

AK*: Does the overall presentation also play a role for you personally? I. e., how the space is designed, what sort of atmosphere there is?*

TV: No, not at all, I only have eyes and all senses for the plate. For example, I could never have a business lunch in a top restaurant, because my discussion partners would take up far too much of my attention. Then I would consume my dish without focusing on it, which for me is a travesty in cultural terms. In that regard I prefer to go with like-minded people who can also keep quiet for ten minutes and immerse themselves in the taste. I am also very happy to go for dinner on my own when I am traveling for meetings or conferences. It is a great experience to be entirely alone with the plate and the service and the chef (in the kitchen), so you can dedicate yourself entirely to the food. Some people like going to the theater or to a rock concert – I like going out to eat. I simply like the discovery element of it, entering the unknown. I want to know what the people there do and I am open to various ideas. Unfortunately there is just not enough time – I work 12-hour days – but when I am retired then I will catch up with it all. Hopefully.

AK*: I will take your word for it. Thank you for talking to us.*

The interview was recorded on April 22, 2015 and was revised in December 2016.

Perfume and Cooking

Anton Studer

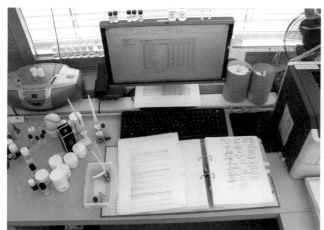 

When a chef and a perfumer work together, this can result in a riveting dialogue on aromas and the translation of moods into taste and smell. Even before we met, chef Stefan Wiesner had used perfume to accentuate his creations a few times using the same herbs and spices as in *Le Male* by Jean Paul Gaultier in an ice cream. In a radio feature Wiesner then mentioned that he would one day like to work with a perfumer. Since I had grown up next his home village of Escholzmatt it made sense to volunteer my services. And that is how our shared story began.

We debated, inspired and analyzed one another. My knowledge of chemistry – and to a certain extent also of physics – helped me to better understand, and in some cases even just begin to understand, the common processes used in cooking. The incentive for this kind of dialogue was to discover just how the other person thinks and to open one another's eyes. An encounter between a perfumer and a chef is a meeting of two different worlds, each one new to the other. Perfumers think and work quite differently from chefs, since we are merely able to examine our raw materials and creations in bottles, on scent strips and ultimately – and most significantly – on skin. A perfumer spends two to four years of his career by simply studying, memorizing raw materials, without actually creating anything. Later he creates simple accords by using two or three components. The focus hereby is not on creating a masterpiece, but on learning and gathering knowledge.

Smell is not taught in schools the way singing or drawing are. It is therefore very important to train the sense of smell – perfumers learn this at special schools, but graduates will then always also have to undergo a perfume house's own internal training courses.

Right from the beginning, fantasy is an important "component" of the perfumer's work. And this involves smelling and tasting without seeing at the same time first and foremost. This "blind" tasting and smelling stimulates fantasy and fosters the imagination. Few people are able, for example, to identify orange oil or mandarin oil on a scent strip, because the accompanying peel or fruit is not visible. In our day-to-day lives, our sense of smell relies strongly on our vision. Perhaps when smelling "with their eyes", very few would recognize lavender in a yellow-colored shower gel, while a violet shower gel might prompt an immediate identification of lavender. Colors and shapes help us to perceive and recognize odours and flavors better. This in turn helps us to understand the complexity and the multifaceted flavor of fruits, vegetables or meat. One example is mandarins, where we can discover facets of lime and orange blossom, amongst other things.

A chef is far less likely to conduct extensive studies of all his possible food ingredients than a perfumer is. During the chef's training, he prepares or helps prepare meals right from the beginning. Right from the start he sees how his dishes will look, what forms, colours and tastes will characterise the meal. Scents are everywhere during the cooking process. Starting by peeling, chopping of vegetables and fruits, later frying, stewing, boiling them, are resulting in complex odour accords. An interesting point here is that everything one perceives in the air is no longer in the dish. It has evaporated.

Taste is perceived via the tongue and nose. The typical aromas of meat, fish, nuts, fruits, etc. are identified via the olfactory organ. Some scientific studies show that the proportion of scent involved in taste is up to 80 percent. In turn, knowledge or recognition of scents helps a chef to "discern" dishes more accurately, i. e. to perceive the full complexity of the culinary creation better and more intensely. This gives him ideas on how new combinations might ultimately work, how they can be developed further, or about finding out why the dish he has created is harmonious. In a pear, for example, we can taste, smell facets of quince, cognac, lily-of-the-valley and freshly cut grass. Recognizing these facets of the scent accord 'pear' requires years of acquired knowledge and precise analysis.

In contrast to a customer who gives the perfumer detailed instructions for a perfume, cooperation with a chef is very different. Stefan Wiesner generally begins with a dish, with the intention of then creating variations of this in smaller or greater combinations. What might go well together, what can be used to complement the dish, which reductions can be made and to what? All this requires a great deal of work and plenty of trial and error. Often, as the dish progresses, one notices that one or the other component no longer creates the effect one is actually seeking.

The common features in the work of the chef and the perfumer lie in the experimental testing and approximation, and the constant sampling of new possibilities. One has to simply try out new things – they cannot be developed according to a reference book, but they can be an excellent start or source of inspiration.

But the differences between the chef and the perfumer are also obvious: the chef needs to perform outstandingly each and every day, always creating something afresh. Every day he has different guests, each guest expects the same excellent dish, and perhaps will even come back because of it. Dishes appear to be far more complex than perfume. They have to be served at specific temperatures and with specific textures; smell and even taste are just two aspects. Visual appeal is part of the experience of eating, so the colors in a dish have to go well together and the presentation must be appetizing. The tongue wants to be indulged by sweet, sour, bitter, salty and umami, whilst the nose likes to be seduced by roasting flavors, different fruits, vegetables, spices and herbs. A perfume on the other hand is developed, sold and then produced in quantities of millions, without the perfumer continuing to be involved in the distribution process. He does not hear what customers and consumers say about his perfume at the sales counter, how they criticize it or comment on it. At most, he might see a bottle on display in a store now and then, but his work essentially ends with the basic formula.

For Stefan Wiesner's perfumes, which were named after ancient runes to reflect his interest in their meaning, we initially sought scents whose accords could easily be incorporated into dishes. 'Bay Rum' is an old classic, developed in the Caribbean. The main components are all native to the region: rum, orange (peel) and West Indian bay leaves (not to be confused with common culinary laurel leaves, one bay leaf is sufficient for ten liters of stock). With these three components, Stefan flavored/modified a fish dish, and they are also the main accord of the perfume *Fehu* (meaning fruitfulness or genesis). The perfume *Sowilo* (sun, Kundalini) was inspired by a classic Eau de Cologne, supplemented with basil, cardamom, caraway, lavender, rosemary and thyme (all of which are aromas also often used in cooking). *Gebo* (gift, harmony), the third perfume, is inspired by what is probably the most elegant and luxurious theme in perfumery, a chypre. The chypre is the "fur coat" or "diamond necklace" of perfumes. It is not worn every day, but only for special occasions. I think it is a great addition to *Fehu* and *Sowilo* and thus forms a beautiful bridge to perfumery. All three perfumes do not differ from industrially-produced scents.

The development or creation of a scent can take various forms. One can draw on works from the past (known as 'formulas' or 'recipes') that fit with the idea or brief, and often a new scent is based on one that has been successful in the market. Generally, the marketing also describes precisely what impression or desire is invoked in the customer. There are new raw materials or new themes that can be incorporated.

To get everything just right – top notes, middle notes and end notes – a great number of attempts is often needed and this work can be frustrating at times. It is a question of patience; over 95 percent of our experiments end up in the bin. But once the work is complete, the sense of achievement is magnificent.

This means the first impression a perfume gives, the top note, should immediately draw the consumer under its spell. The middle or heart note is crucial in defining the character of the perfume, as well as for the "scent" you perceive when someone wearing it walks past you. This part of the scent is also influenced by the end notes, the fixing. These are responsible less for the character of the scent than its enduring nature. Since they have a low volatility, they evaporate slowly and therefore stay on the skin for longer. However, an overly high proportion of fixers can negatively affect the intensity and radiance of the perfume to the extent that the customer gains the impression of it being weak and not lingering.

That said, let's get back to the cooking: not all aromas found in the kitchen can be translated into pure scents. Milk, chard, lime and bay leaf are all things I can interpret in perfumery, but pig's head is trickier, possibly with aldehyde notes for the fattiness. I would think sardines simply cannot be interpreted in perfume form. Aside from meat and fresh fish, pretty much anything can be interpreted as a scent composition. Whether there are consumers who would be interested in such scents, though, might be doubtful. For example, to recreate a simple dish like pizza as a perfume for candles, I would begin by analyzing the individual components. I can create cheese, oregano and tomato; representing the pizza dough, on the other hand, is quite a challenge. The most difficult thing is finding the balance that makes it possible to smell all the components clearly. Thus hot, sharp spiciness cannot be smelt, because it causes a stimulation of the pain nerves and is not a smell on its own.

Scent has always accompanied cooking right from the beginning, even when humans cooked their food in caves on open fires. You can even smell whether it is pork or beef sizzling on the grill. Scent was always present, but oftentimes overlooked.

However, for some years now there has been an increased interest in a pairing between perfume and dishes. Perfuming the air whilst eating, however, is somewhat difficult. It can mislead, interfere and in fact be very unpleasant. What does work well though, is if various aromas are sprayed in the air during consumption of, for example, weakly salted mashed potato. This leads to a more sophisticated perception of the mashed potato.

If, on the other hand, like Stefan Wiesner you aim to recreate a perfume in the kitchen, then the dishes should be based on the perfume's top notes. The composition and ingredients of a perfume are often indicated in its publicity and marketing material. It is therefore relatively easy to identify the main components of a scent. You can then try to combine the herbs, spices, etc. to create a harmonious mixture in order to subsequently incorporate this into a mashed potato, an ice cream, a dessert cream, a soup or a sauce. Of course the finished product should taste like a dish and not like a perfume, so the components should be used in moderation. It sounds pretty easy this far. However, if you want to get more complex a little imagination is required, so you can use coriander leaves to simulate the aldehyde notes, apricots as freesia or feta cheese for the costus root. We perfumers also have a secret weapon, a gas chromatograph (GC) with a mass spectrometer (MS), abbreviated to GC/MS. This is my "brain", so to speak, because I use it to analyze essential oils. I can clarify structures, check whether suppliers are selling counterfeit products, analyze market products, see what makes a product so successful, etc. The GC/MS is not however limited to the analysis of perfumes (it is thanks to this gadget that I have "insider info", secrets or new raw materials the perfumer might have preferred to keep to himself, without informing customers or marketing), but can also be used for rare or new herbs and mixtures of herbs. A few years ago I tried to produce a list under the title "foodstuff compositions". That also shows that cooks and chefs have always come up with combinations of herbs, spices etc., in which scent plays an important or a primary role. Curry, for example, is centuries old.

A primary concern in the kitchen is to avoid "over-composing" – i.e. not make the whole thing so complex that it is no longer possible to perceive a character or the character is simply too boring and inexpressive. Hence a tomato soup must remain a tomato soup and not become a basil soup. A basil soup does not necessarily require tomatoes. Thus Stefan Wiesner and I began calling herbs and spices 'modifiers', as is common in perfumery. Modifiers are used to make creations appear more beautiful, radiant, intense or interesting. They are added sparingly enough for a clear effect to be perceived, but without it being possible to actually discern the fact. So-called "creatives" often struggle to contain themselves, adding an endless amount of different modifiers and thereby achieving almost thoroughly disappointing results. For me, this has nothing to do with complexity or creativity, but rather with the fear of forgetting something or avoidance of precision. Here, the precision is precisely what is interesting, and this is where Stefan Wiesner is a master. A perfume always "represents" something, tells a story, allows us to dream, transports us to the seaside or the mountains, or gives us a sense of cold/warmth, just like a taste composition can. It combines certain themes, complements them or creates contrasts.

In my view as a perfumer, it is important to make clear to the person cooking just how complex the tastes of the individual foodstuffs are, how they can contribute to the complexity of dishes and in what way this stimulates the variety of combinations and the level of creativity. That is why blind tasting and the practice and discovery of scents are so important, including – and indeed precisely – for laypersons at home. But the most important thing here, I believe, it's more fun being a gourmand than an analyser.

Culinary Criteria Creation in an Open Society

Jürgen Dollase

Fig. 1

Fig. 2

EXPOSITION: THE TWO PYRAMIDS

One could perhaps imagine the most important developmental phase in the culinary arts, a series of events from about the beginning of the 90s, with a single image: two pyramids. The first is a perfectly normal pyramid. It mostly stands for the long-dominant classical French cuisine. Participants of this system were in complete agreement about what was at the top and what was at the bottom, what quality meant and how one could reach the pyramid's tip. That is still more or less the case today, especially in this cuisine's country of origin and among chefs who for the most part are involved in the system. When a chef sets off to conquer the summit, he has got clear criteria to follow, quite obviously the same criteria that the *Guide Michelin* followed. These criteria developed within a close relationship between the chefs and their critics, whereby the critics' greater leverage was a mere illusion. In fact there has been and still is a kind of joint policy that should never be underestimated, one made by many (but not all) participants and that entails the influence of renown chefs and other professional opinions on the applicable criteria – for instance, the requirements for becoming a three-star chef. On top of that, for a long time in France this system was in no way as "lofty" and professionally self-contained as it might seem to us today. One must not forget that the basis of this system, the criteria for culinary quality were very widespread. The first three-star restaurants in the environs of Lyon (like the two chefs Eugénie Brazier – "La mère Brazier" – and Marie Bourgeois – "La mère Bourgeois") were essential restaurants for refined yet traditional bourgeois cuisine. One used the finest products and embellished them regularly with delicacy ingredients, from truffles to foie gras, but never left the solid staples universally considered to be "good food". Right up to today, one can observe that the best restaurants of the French provinces use regional dishes and corresponding images of taste and that they are part of a coherent system as a rule. What they do well is something almost everybody knows – even when they can only afford the rare visit to such a fine establishment. In any case, for big celebrations, one knows where to go and can be sure that the criteria in play will indeed be the kind which one understands. Seen thusly, there is hardly any pressure "from the outside" to be exerted in this system – such as a critique of a course that is too modern for a restaurant. The best venison, the best pikeperch with sauerkraut, the best foie gras and the best paté en courte d'Alsace is to be found in the 'Auberge de l'Ill' of the family Haeberlin in Illhäusern – and maybe at one of their high-ranking competitors.

The second pyramid stands today – inversed – with the tip on the top of the first, opening upward. This one symbolizes the opening of the culinary arts into a space without limitations, with an unknown goal and headed in all directions at once. We have been experiencing this opening for about twenty years – so not since Nouvelle cuisine, which was part of the old system, but rather since the beginnings of a creative cuisine, one that either overcame the rules of classical French cuisine peu à peu or extrapolated them ad absurdum. This development has seen a particular thrust in the last years, and that from whom but none other than the *Guide Michelin*, long synonymous with the old system. What happened? The big break came with the international expansion of the restaurant guide business, driven by Michelin itself. The decisive change happened in 2008 with the publishing of the Tokyo guide. Even though Japanese haute cuisine already enjoyed a legendary reputation among top international chefs for its product fetishism and minimalistic presentation, the French were extremely surprised by the number of three-star restaurants that the testers in Tokyo featured (there were eight and then 25 two-star restaurants and in the current guide for 2015 there are already twelve with three stars and 53 with two). This was not just recognition of an equally highly sophisticated cuisine, it also went against what the rest of the world knew as a synonym for high cooking culture. Could one really rate sushi bars with the same grades as Parisian luxury restaurants? Can one chef and a couple of helping hands be as good as highly developed kitchen machineries? Will it really be possible to succeed in the future in a small restaurant serving uncomplicated cuisine and working with mostly raw products?

In these discussions, which are partially still ongoing, primarily culinary criteria as well as a kind of gastronomic criteria are blending together for the first time in a really striking way. When it was really about the culinary arts in a narrow sense (i.e. criteria like product quality, product-related preparation, aromatization, culinary construction) not much could be excluded from this extension of *Michelin*'s definition of what is good. But how should one react and can such a development be without consequence for the classic French haute cuisine and all the values that come with it?

THE CHANGE AND EXPANSION OF INTERNAL CULINARY ARTS CRITERIA: STABILIZING OR DESTABILIZING?

The relativity brought to the values of the classical French system through the strengthening of a significantly different kind of cuisine limited to the Asian region might not have been a huge problem for the traditionalists. But there were other problems, coming in from the various "fronts" at the same time. For instance, there is the British list of 'The World's 50 Best Restaurants' in which the best restaurants worldwide have been identified in a global scope since 2002. French restaurants play only a rather minor role – at least in view of their traditional self-image. They play such a minor role that the list makes certain people see red: this list – which came about under very questionable statistical conditions like all such lists – turned the culinary world upside down with names at the top of the list that would never have been allowed by traditional standards. It is very characteristic of the situation that the current number one, the 'Noma' by René Redzepi in Copenhagen, has already gotten first place four times in a row although it only has two *Michelin* stars. Besides the top 50, there has also been the problem of the long-standing dispute about Spanish modernism. Ferran

Adrià's Spanish avant-garde makes for particularly heated discussion. To some in France, the scene is very controversial and quite often receives openly aggressive reviews. Despite the fact that a few top French chefs have meanwhile praised Adrià, this cuisine mostly incites polemic even today. The issue is the use of "chemicals" (mainly texturing material), which is invariably called a health hazard. The fact that French star chefs like Yannick Alléno and others resort to Adriàs research for almost every dish is something that is studiously ignored.

Parallel to these developments, the *Michelin* people began to draw conclusions, especially from the Tokyo reviews. Up until now it has been considered gospel that a restaurant with a *Michelin* star had to look like a gourmet temple. Although the guide always maintained that their star ratings were given only in relation to the food, in practice a certain luxury, expensive glasses and all sorts of gold and silver had a lot to do with which restaurants were awarded stars. Recent *Michelin* reviews in various countries, however, have shown quite clearly that "boutique restaurants" – small to tiny establishments without ostentatious luxury but with a good kitchen – have gotten good ratings, as increasingly do restaurants whose cuisine is no longer so strongly influenced by French haute cuisine in the classic sense. Within a few years, all of the sudden there were molecular chefs, vegetable minimalists, tiny and austerely equipped establishments and busy "in" bistros all receiving *Michelin* stars.

The decisive culinary factor was that these ratings, which are still accompanied by prestige and increases in revenue, are obviously no longer based on the classic sauces, the aroma spectrum or the constitution of a typical haute cuisine dish. Rather, they are awarded according to the sort of purified criteria for the culinary arts that is seen as being more precise. Product quality then is not about the luxury products of traditional gourmet restaurants any more. What it potentially comes down to are a few fine quality herbs or some heirloom vegetable varieties that had been considered totally marginal until now. The typical spice spectrum of classical cuisine, for example, has principally comprised of the spices that are allowed and the ones that are not allowed for as long as anyone can remember. On the one hand, no one minded much that any and all elements of a composition could be dusted with salt and pepper. On the other, however, a plate of bacon ice cream and tonka beans was quickly considered a deviation from the norm and thus given a bad review.

People in other countries – the Germans especially – started to reflect on a structural view of the culinary arts. Suddenly, the characteristics of classical French cuisine were critically divided into a sort of immutable principles (e. g., cooking times and product qualities) and more specifically regional, national, or in the broadest sense "fashionable" characteristics such as certain sauces (particularly those whose binding elements were cream and butter). This clarification, which of course also had something to do with the new global view of cuisine, led to considerations regarding what a universal canon of criteria for good cuisine might resemble. In 2007, I presented my "stage theory for culinary art" in which there are five primary stages: product selection, product preparation, aromatization, varying the states of aggregation and the culinary construction. Every cuisine type in the whole world fits into this evaluation grid and hence can be described based on how pronounced it is for each stage. It shows for example that the Japanese "product fetishists" are more intensively engaged in product selection and product preparation than Europeans, the aromatization of classical French cuisine finds its limits but is much more broadly employed in the Middle East, India or China, and that the Spanish avant-garde has a lot to do with an extremely expanded form of variation in aggregate states. Even the classic grandmasters can suddenly be quantified in relation to others in the light of newer criteria that as of yet has not been observed to this degree – such as sensorily harmonious culinary structure that gives each product its place and can greatly improve the quality of the dishes. Something that one begins to notice quite often with the new criteria is, for instance, unhappy proportions of the elements render whole dishes incoherent when it comes to overlapping that makes no culinary sense.

And thus in the culinary arts today we find ourselves internally carrying out a revisionary process, laying new foundations of culinary criteria. What shows that this process is still in full swing are the reactions of many restaurant guides, which obviously have difficulty with the newer developments. Until a few years ago it was considered among chefs that at best every dish that leaves the kitchen should represent the level of the restaurant. So if a chef sought a second *Michelin* star and in some way hinted that he had the potential to achieve that goal, he endeavored to make each dish – even the smallest appetizer – muster what it takes for the two stars. In the internal discussions, comments are often heard like "but that is not a three star dish" or "he has got a number of three star dishes but also a few that are not worth more than one." This old obsession with the typical '*Michelin* image' is in recent years increasingly butting up against its limits. The ones who deserve thanks for this development are the younger and more creative chefs who have a loyal following among the global gourmets. Namely, they are in the habit of offering menus with a whole series of small courses (sometimes far more than twenty), where the individual dishes often only consist of a few items and there is no such resemblance to one of the more luxuriously decorated dishes of classical provenance. The question of whether a tiny filet of mackerel with a little cube of some vegetable and a vinaigrette could attain "three star quality" is obviously still not resolved by many guides. Their catalog of criteria comes from bourgeois gourmet cuisine with all its various parameters that are largely merely reminiscent of traditional bourgeois cuisine and only apply to creative gourmet cuisine in the rarest of cases. That one would have to evaluate the talents of chefs like René Redzepi or Kobe Desramaults ('In de Wulf', Dranouter, Belgium) or Alexandre Gauthier ('La Grenouillère', Montreuil-sur-Mer, France) en bloc, so to say, because they use completely different forms of presentation and menus, just has not really prevailed. Thus, the expansion of criteria for a good cuisine has so far provided for considerable destabilization within the culinary arts. This destabilization might be around for quite a while, however, because – at least for us in Europe – it is the result of the developments of two fundamentally different approaches, namely those of the bourgeois and the creative gourmet cuisine. If assurance and confirmation of the expectations of the public is up against an expansion of experiments and positive irritations, if the new is considered suspicious on the one hand, and on the other every creative idea is anticipated with excitement and interest, the distances between the two visions are often quite considerable.

INTERNAL AND EXTERNAL CRITERIA: THE ART OF COOKING UNDER THE INFLUENCE OF SOCIAL MOVEMENTS

It could very well continue along this path, as has been the case for other art forms. The modernists could continue to evolve under the pressure to innovate that is typical of constant global communication, as has been the case in broad swaths of the contemporary art world, for example. Thus, one could increasingly invest in a subculture, "do one's own thing", worry only about the stability of one's own community and forget about the rest of the world. Then, one would only be understood by a small few but would have a stable niche that sustains itself and makes further work possible. But for the culinary arts, this trend has its limits. Part of the reason for this is that culinary artists must largely fund themselves. In contrast to the other arts, there is a lack of public funding that makes things possible in music or the visual arts that are simply not capable of financing themselves.

Beyond that, culinary goods are not of the sort that – like a work of visual art – can be sold at horrendous prices. Hence, the culinary arts still have to tend to their audience directly and maintain a certain mercantilism day to day. They must stay principally open to society – whether out of necessity or not – in order to survive.

It is precisely within this somewhat tricky situation that impulses come directly from society, which might be considerably relevant to the culinary arts as a whole. On the one hand, the guy on the street, who knows nothing about or has only had fleeting contact with the art of cooking, can hardly understand its culinary criteria today. In the "old" closed system that was, however, also characterized by social feedback taking its cue from the French model, things were significantly different. On the other hand, "new" criteria are increasingly developing around nutrition; for a long time these criteria were not really situated at the center of the chef's efforts from the point of view of the traditional system (or even from the general internal vantage point of the culinary arts). Above all, the discussion regarding consumption of meat was on the table and the related issue of vegetarianism, which in the meantime – along with incalculable allergies and other no-gos – have strongly influenced the work of many restaurants. Added to that are the critical aspects of nutrition on the whole. These lie within the full bandwidth from ecology to the discussion of overeating versus malnutrition. The reactions to these "external" pressures have not been exhausted merely by the fact that virtually all restaurants now have vegetarian dishes or even entire menus – not by a long shot. It is precisely those chefs within the creative scene who have adopted the ecological aspect as a fixed component of their thinking and they often even have tight connections to similarly oriented groups outside their narrow "culinary scene". The changing views regarding regional resources in many creative kitchens, which have led to completely new evaluations of the usefulness of rare, never-before-used or as yet seen to be unsuitable products ('Nova Regio' cuisine), correspond remarkably well to the aims of the ecological movement, to many of the goals of vegetarianism and to a sort of food stuff that strives for all but the gluttonous bon-vivant characteristics of the traditional style.

In the process, many interesting details, connections and perspectives have arisen that many interested parties are not yet even aware of and that may stand for a significant change in the role of culinary arts in society. Via seemingly universal sounding criteria such as ease, wholesomeness, ecological correctness or the demand that all parts of the plants and animals be used, i.e., to abolish waste, so to speak, entirely new developments in the details of culinary arts are on the rise. Moreover, this is happening partly with a pronounced change in the entire aesthetic of cuisine itself. Suddenly, minimalistic compositions are being presented that also make a show of the least expensive vegetables including the parts that were once thrown away. For a little bit of extra time, a forest floor extract can be distilled for sauces or whole dishes created from "inedibles" like mosses and lichens. The words "top product" are hardly spoken in this context, and even the cult of cooking times only plays a minor role.

Is it nowadays the case that the culinary arts – at least in their creative forms – have fallen under the influence of societal movements and placed their old values at society's disposal too quickly? Not necessarily. Indeed, it is probably the case that at first the expansion of criteria within the culinary arts has played a role, which opened the possibility for work to be done in the creative scenes in turn, from molecular gastronomy to new Scandinavian cuisine. Only afterwards did many chefs discover the connections to ecological issues; meanwhile the ecologically interested parties are still not really united behind the contemporary cuisine based on ideas that stemmed from their own philosophies. Creative cuisine has always been a forge of sorts for all kinds of ideas – anything that has ever been presented as a novelty in gastronomy, right up to food services and the product ranges offered by the food industry. Banking on their current efforts, the creative cuisine could take on a role that it has rarely ever fulfilled before. It could assume a societally useful role of sorts, if not to say: a beneficial function. It could – inspired by societal currents but in no way indoctrinated by them – arrive at the forefront of a movement that has quite a bit to do with the future of nutrition on the whole. When it comes to preserving our resources to the greatest extent possible and finding uses for those that have hardly ever been used before, this cuisine could ensure that this is done in a way that would please everyone – even the classic gourmets. It is not enough to simply throw in some organic products. One must also arrive at ways of preparing food that convince the senses and give people pleasure.

The art of cooking could then be on its way to bringing people closer together on the whole; it could leave its luxury enclave and work for the greatest and most sensible purpose. The really big question is, however, whether it may not even have to do that at all to gain a societally relevant raison d'être in the future. It is in the process of opening up. But, can it do that without giving up its substance? Is it possible for this kind of expert system to become part of an open society in which every supposed truth will continuously be put to the test?

A while ago, I introduced the concept of "holistic gourmandise" for this field: a gourmandise that sees itself committed to comprehensive and social benefits, while taking into account all of the problematic issues – from the individual, like healthy nutrition, to the ecological. In such a context, would the "eternal values" of the culinary arts become rather like theories that hold until they are proven wrong but are essentially forever put to the test? Would everything then, also the formerly professional criteria, be placed under the discretionary power of societal movements? With very uncertain consequences?

WHAT IS UP FOR DISPOSITION?
CULINARY CRITERIA CREATION IN AN OPEN SOCIETY

Example 1: Product Quality

If one attempts to "play through" the usefulness of culinary criteria in a more or less holistic way, one very quickly runs up against how tremendously complex this field really is and how little we are accustomed to moving about within it. In the following, a few possible criteria are presented for discussion.

One of the most fiercely debated criteria is what a good quality product might be. This criterion already plays a central role in our society because it is universally used and abused and can be employed to serve all sorts of particular interests besides the obvious commercial ones. Determining what a good product is was for a long time essentially something for professionals, the chefs, the producers or the unions and organizations of professions relevant to the culinary industry – even if the latter groups are sometimes too generous in the positive evaluation of one another's products. With the rise of highly rated gourmet restaurants, an even more elite understanding of top quality began to grow among them. In the desire to reach absolute excellence, finding the rarest and most expensive products was not the central question anymore; rather, very quickly it was all about finding top products in all possible genres of product – from the best oysters to the best chickens to the best potatoes. Of course the quality of the preparation has a lot to do with the quality of dish presentation, but ultimately certain comparisons started to establish themselves, like a good turbot prepared by a bad chef is better than a bad turbot prepared by a good chef.

All the interests endeavoring towards cheaper food for the whole population of course stood in contrast to this – at first, however, a long way off from the "bourgeois" circles, whose culinary behavior still had a lot to do with solid home cooking and the associated skills right up to the final decades of the 20th century. Today, the situation looks very different. With concepts like a price-performance ratio, there is a move in the direction of relativization of product quality, which is actually even a sort of antithesis to the "cult" of top quality and considers spending huge amounts of money for excellent products to be fundamentally absurd. A good example of the problematic nature of this concept is that of the oft-cited wine lover: He goes to his friend overjoyed with the news that at discount store X you can buy a wine for ten euros that is a really good value for the money and it was also given 90 points in the *This-n-That* guide, which is supposedly really good quality. A couple of days later comes another friend that counters with his own wine find from discount store Y. This wine is almost as good but it only costs six euros – and so on and so on. The notion of a price-performance ratio is at the center of culinary life today. It is employed in almost all social circles and has even found its way into the gourmet guides, which never get tired of finding new addressees to offer "good cuisine for moderate prices" (the central criteria of *Michelin's Bib Gourmand*). In detail of course, the food quality in such establishments is considerably weaker than in the top restaurants with high ratings in almost every case. Even though one could easily guess what "good cuisine for moderate prices" might mean, there is nothing harder than taking impeccable products and preparing dishes with them that dispense with unnecessary (and expensive) extras. These dishes should actually create qualities that make culinary sense and lead to a pleasant experience for any and all – from the "normal eater" to the gourmet.

Take this real world example: In a town in the south of Germany, I once went to two restaurants that were widely praised, which served the typical bourgeois cuisine. These two breweries were listed as good addresses in every guidebook to the region. My project was to look very closely at the culinary performance of these places, concentrating thus on the relationship between textures, aromas and the proportions. The result was very disappointing and even alarming to some extent. All of the meat elements of my "brewery plate", from the sausage to the roast, were poor in quality with an unbalanced, lightly stale taste lurking in the background. These were laid on a huge mountain of sauerkraut that was, in contrast, extremely heavily spiced – or more truthfully, it had a high proportion of salt. The texture of the meat was the only thing to notice about it, while the already weak or imbalanced aroma was overpowered by the devastating spiciness of the sauerkraut. In the text I wrote about it for the 'Geschmackssache' food section of the FAZ (*Frankfurter Allgemeine Zeitung* newspaper), I mentioned that one could not really expect good quality meat for the price of this dish, in my opinion. The angry reactions I got from this article were varied and their objections ultimately boiled down to this: This cuisine cannot be reviewed like a gourmet temple. Above all, one has to think about the functional aspects – the hard working folks or the students, for example, who are just thankful that they can get such delicious food for such little money. Unfortunately, the day I dined the hard working folks and penniless students were few and far between. Instead, the lunch period was already full of large groups of seriously overweight and elderly gentlemen, thus exactly the kind that frequent such establishments. Can you use any "normal" criteria to review such cuisine? Or are the criteria of haute cuisine not "normal" at all? Within this context, one only has to think about the widespread product tests and various institutes and magazines that are all involved in the phenomenon of price-performance ratios to be confronted by the question of whether it makes any sense at all to have criteria that are exclusively expert-related and to place the best of each category at the top of a linear scale. Parallel to these questions, there would also be those who ask whether there can be a sort of medium quality, whose criteria is based on societal feedback and aspects of linear quality evaluation that are connected to such a functional quality assessment. A cut of lamb that has a "clean" taste with no unpleasant side notes would therefore perhaps amount to the "point zero" (as any central reference point should necessarily be referred to) from which poorer but also higher qualities would vary in the evaluation.

As reasonable as such a "solution" may sound to many, a whole gambit of questions and problems arise – ones that are typical for criteria creation in an open society. Where exactly does the point zero/reference point lie and what forces are involved in its definition? Does this reference point come into being in a balance between maximum and minimum? If so, how does it change if the content of the maximum and the minimum change? Who is responsible for the relative stability of the system? Will obligations or consequences for all of the participants arise from the constant struggle in relation to the reference point? Sticking to the example of product quality, must or will whatever exceptional product quality be transparent so that medium quality can even be defined, as derived from top quality?

One thing seems certain: The task of determining a medium quality can no longer be divorced from an open society. Simultaneously, however, the existence of a top quality that defines the latter is and remains indispensable so as to work against the downward slippage of the reference point. Thus, if a discount store offers wine that is of supposedly high quality, it is necessary that such allegations be clearly relativized. If industrially produced food exhibits the tendency to be considerably over seasoned and thereby leads to a manipulation of taste perception itself, it is very urgent that this be utterly transparent. If there are poor quality categories, these should also be subject to constant monitoring evaluation, as is the case for top quality. The criteria for good quality are therefore not divisible, but it depends on which function they flow into in the societal balance. And, the unwavering transparency of criteria is also so very important because the greatest enemy of a statistically unbalanced system forever in flux is that relativity becomes the absolute. No connaisseur of best quality would ever have something against a reputable medium quality. When the medium quality becomes absolute through various relativizations – as is often the case today ("reasonable cuisine for reasonable prices, whatever goes beyond that is decadent") – the system is susceptible to disruption – the consequence usually being a downward spiraling of quality. Hence, it seems to be the case for the product quality criterion that it is simply better if the classic linear quality scale is preserved and can withstand any quality pressure from society.

The questions of how to keep the balance and who could be responsible for doing so are, nevertheless, very complicated and beyond the scope of this text. Of course, one could discuss regulations for anything and everything, although the intervention of policymakers into certain culinary qualities seems very far off because they already seem to be overwhelmed by monitoring rather technical qualities (i.e., those that relate to health). What would be interesting is an institution that monitors the input into the societal system. The German Federal Cartel Office intervenes if an excessive concentration occurs in a particular area and the possibility of market manipulation arises. There should be an analog institution for product quality, one that ensures that the declared reference point for good product quality not only – as usually is the case – just swing back and forth, but rather moves into negative because the poorer quality products are increasing beyond measure. This is something one could at least imagine. The next question would be what measures could be made available to work against the negative developments. Ultimately, it can only amount to increases in the input from opposing opinions, for example, by demanding more media coverage and reports from dissenters. First of all, because one cannot really create an 'Institute for Societal Input' that would force TV stations to drop this or that popular cooking show based on impending unbalanced assessments of quality or secondly force discount stores not to sell certain products, and because – thirdly – the situation in schools is not really moving forward and the only thing left to do is to send out clear signals via policy. Due to the lack of any such signals and – quite to the contrary – the balance being negatively influenced by campaigns like "Currywurst is the Social Democratic Party" (the 2012 election North Rhine-Westphalia campaign), the current situation for guaranteeing, stabilizing and promoting good overall quality criteria is pretty bleak. Perhaps first off one should give some thought to the difference between a completely free market economy and a liberal market economy. In the former, things are left completely up to the interplay of forces, and the food industry's power would strengthen. The latter would be coupled to a liberal understanding of balanced interests and alignment to a picture of how positive societal development should look to everyone in the sense of holistic thinking.

Example 2: Throw Nothing Away!

The stipulation not to throw away as much food and use the food we have more efficiently has many sources, but for the publicly conscious part of society, it comes more or less from the societal middle. Wasting culinary resources can be seen as a typical flaw of a society that has forgotten to be aware of larger connections and has apparently subjected everything to the interests of the individual, rigorously and without regard for any consequences whatsoever. People who think and act that way prove that they have already become victims of industrial strategies with their behavior, and this fact has only recently come under discussion. Not throwing away food so readily is one thing. Using food in such a way that every bit is consumed is clearly different. It is also a waste – for lack of know-how – to only use the leaves one can pluck from a Savoy cabbage and tossing the excellent tasting rest (the trunk or the leaf spines) into the garbage. Another resource not adequately used is animal meat; tiny fillets play a role in top cuisine while the rest ends up in sausages, cat and dog food as well as glue. It is ultimately the respect for the animal that calls for a "high-quality" use for all of the animal parts for food. Within the same context one finds the old criticism of the long distances that products have to travel and everything being on offer all the time – even if it is simply not the season for certain vegetables at our latitude. There is criticism of the reduction of varietal diversity and the neglect of regional products associated with it, which all together builds into considerable pressure for change. Thus, the criticism is coming from multiple directions and is clearly aimed in this case against the advanced cuisine, which is otherwise considered – see above under product quality – to be a refuge for rigorous qualitative orientation. No, haute cuisine (better said: the more tradition-oriented haute cuisine) only seldom works with every part of the animal and picks out only – supposedly – the very best. It still has its products regularly flown in from all corners of the world regardless of the season and only rarely worries about ecological and regional contexts. In any case, the potentially new criteria for a responsible use of resources do not put this sort of cuisine in the best light.

And now of course, the question is who will actually bring about changes to align to this new vision. In this area – seen through the aspects of criteria creation – one finds himself indeed in an extraordinary situation: A few new aspects, like those mentioned above, are already leading to some sort of changed qualifications but are still a long way from being completely prevalent. To be precise, it is a phase of criteria creation – not so much a phase of criteria change or criticism of existing criteria. And it is a phase in which – probably for the first time in history – a sort of holistic consideration of nutrition is looming; alongside the ecological and ethnic considerations this also takes up aspects of health and civilization. Mind you, "holistic" as understood truly by the definition of holistic and not just being related to certain more or less ideological connections in alternative scenarios.

The current situation is first of all influenced by the fact that those who criticize how things are cannot offer many concrete alternatives. Not even the organic scene can do more than offer a few vegetarian dishes with conventionally prepared ingredients. Even the various books on the subject are pretty tame and of course confirm the suspicion of ideology right off with this lack of convincing alternatives, and generally the "ordinary" guy on the street is still clinging to that suspicion.

Let's stay with the Savoy cabbage for a moment, or even a leek whose roots have an excellent taste but end up in the trash anyway, or the tomato whose most aromatic part (the core of seeds) is still often taken out or products like the turnip whose use often does not even come into consideration. The solutions to their optimized and convincing use arrive for now, in part, from creative cuisine, which is rather less aligned to traditional high cuisine and goes its own way, hence from chefs like previously mentioned René Redzepi, Kobe Desramaults and Alexandre Gauthier, from chef duo André Köthe/Yves Ollech in 'Essigbrätlein' in Nuremberg, Jean-Luc Rabanel in Arles or Heinz Reitbauer Jr. from the 'Steirereck' in Vienna. The list is growing longer and longer. A new regional cuisine with a completely new evaluation of regional resources and heavily modified cooking techniques, thus a combination of regional cuisine and avant-garde, has clearly been the world's dominant trend in creative cuisine for several years now ('Nova Regio' cuisine). It is in these kitchens that things are being created that will give these new ideas the shine and appeal that they need to even have a chance at competing against people's ingrained eating habits. Good 'Nova Regio' cuisine is already pretty clear to the connaisseurs. Many observers, however, would still be hard pressed to follow the new developments as quickly as they arise.

So, there are ideas from the middle of society and paths to solutions from the progressive sectors of quality-oriented cuisine. Is that enough to develop clear criteria for a holistic gourmandise? Well, in principle, it is – if the forces working in the same direction are able to merge together. There are already indications that the tradition-oriented sector of advanced cuisine simply cannot continue on its path up to now; the image of the obese gourmand who does not want anything other than lobster, Pauillac lamb and truffles has no future. There are indications that a new type of chef is out there. One who suddenly no longer belongs solely to the culinary avant-garde but also to the social because he promotes socially desired developments and thereby gains a multifaceted role-model function. There are even indications that the I-based, completely unthinking culinary behavior of large population circles is succumbing to pressure – one day it may even go as far as it did with smoking.

Criteria creation in an open society proves itself to be a very complex topic as exemplified here because it does not – as is the case for product quality – revolve around a field in which one can clearly determine between a certain input and its effects and insofar develop straightforward strategies. When it comes to a holistic view of nutrition, it is not only about eating good instead of bad meat, or changing one's eating habits, but also about recognizing the goodness in interesting preparation methods and products that until now hardly ever played a role and in popular opinion simply do not taste as good as what we have been eating so far. Such changes in behavior are major. To aid in these changes, one effect may come into play that is already well known from the organic movement: Someone who generally has a holistic view of the world will be more capable of opening up to the culinary aspects. Getting used to new taste profiles, and this much is clear, does not take much else – I, myself, am an obvious example, having gone from fast-food eater to food critic. Like with product quality, developing the criteria for this example also, of course, involves adequate input from influential institutions. But even more important will be promoting concrete encounters between people and the "new" nutritional means and the changed cuisine. That happens above all via convincing culinary solutions and a concomitant aesthetic of the holistic – from schools out into public life, from private kitchens to restaurants throughout all of gastronomy. Development in this direction seems to be the inevitable path for the decades to come.

Bibliography

Adorno, T. W. (1997): *Aesthetic Theory*, tr. R. Hullot-Kantor, London/New York.

Adrià, A./Soler, J./Adrià, F. (2008): *A Day at elBulli. An insight into the ideas, methods and creativity of Ferran Adrià*, London/New York.

— (2014): *elBulli 2005-2011*, London.

Aduriz, A. L. (2012): *Mugaritz. A Natural Sciene of Cooking*, London/New York.

Aicher, O. (2005): *Die Küche zum Kochen. Werkstatt einer neuen Lebenskultur*, Staufen b. Freiburg.

Albers, I./Franke, A. (2012): *Animismus. Revisionen der Moderne*, Zürich.

Anderson, M. et al. (2009): *Agriculture at a crossroads: evaluación internacional del conocimiento, ciencia y tecnología en el desarrollo agrícola* (IAASTD), No. E14-199.

Anonymous (1925): Die Küche – die Fabrik des Hauses, in: *Wohnungswirtschaft* 3.

Atala, A. (2013): *D. O. M.. Die neue brasilianische Küche*, Hamburg.

Autsch, S. (2015): Essen als Material. Kulinarische Praktiken und künstlerische Produktion, in: Autsch, S./Hornäk, S. (eds.): *Materialität und künstlerisches Handeln* (in preparation).

BAG Bundesamt für Gesundheit Schweiz (ed.) (2010): *Wie essen und bewegen wir uns?*, Bern.

Baier, B./Müller, C./Werner, K. (2013): *Stadt der Commonisten. Neue urbane Räume des Do it yourself*, Bielefeld.

Barber, D. (2014): *The Third Plate. Field Notes on the Future of Food*, London.

Barlösius, E. (1999): *Soziologie des Essens. Eine sozial- und kulturwissenschaftliche Einführung in die Ernährungsforschung*, Weinheim/München.

Barthes, R. (1961): Pour une psycho-sociologie de l'alimentation contemporaine, in: *Annales. Economies, Sociétés, Civilisations.* 16e année, N. 5, pp. 977–986.

Beauvilliers, A. (1814): *L'art du cuisinier*, Paris.

Beil, R. (2002): *Künstlerküche*, Köln.

Belasco, W. (2013): *Food. The Key Concepts*, London/New York.

Bendiner, K. (2004): *Food in Painting. From the Renaissance to the Present*, London.

Berlant, L. (2010): Risky Bitness: On Obesity, Eating and the Ambiguity of „Health", in: Metzel, J./Kirkland, A. (eds.): *Against Health. How Health Became the New Morality*, New York, pp. 26–39.

Betsy, D. et al. (2010): Re-regionalizing the Food system?, in: *Cambridge Journal of Regions, Economy and Society* (vol. 3), pp. 171–175.

Bippus, E. (ed.) (2009): *Kunst des Forschens. Praxis eines ästhetischen Denkens*, Schriftenreihe des Instituts für Gegenwartskunst ZHdK, Zürich.

Birnbaum, D. (2015): Rirkrit Tiravanija: Meaning is use, in: Davidson, Cynthia (ed.): *Log*, New York.

Bittman, M. (2008): *How to Cook Everything*, Boston.

Blumenthal, H. (2002): Weird but wonderful. Life and style, in: *The Guardian*, May 4, available online at: https://www.theguardian.com/lifeand style/2002/may/04/foodanddrink.shopping

Boehm, G. (2003): Der Topos des Lebendigen. Bildgeschichte und Ästhetische Erfahrung, in: Menke, C. (ed.): *Dimensionen ästhetischer Erfahrung*, Frankfurt/M., pp. 94–112.

Boer, J./Herman, S. (2010): *Eten, Drinken en Slapen. Lees-kookboek met (on) mogelijke recepten voor thuis*, Zwolle.

Bourriaud, N. (2002): *Relational Aesthetics*, Dijon.

— (2009): *A Precarious Existence. Precarious Constructions: Answer to Jacques Rancière on Art and Politics*, online available at: http://online open.org/precarious-constructions

— (2015): Diet of the Authors, in: Celant, G. (ed.): *Arts and Foods*, Verona.

Brillat-Savarin, A. [1825] (1979): *Physiologie des Geschmacks oder Betrachtungen über das höhere Tafelvergnügen* [fr. 1825, dt. 1866], Frankfurt/M.

Brunner, K.-M. et al. (2007): *Ernährungsalltag im Wandel: Chancen und Nachhaltigkeit*, Wien.

Bruno, N./Martani, M. et al. (2013): The effect of the color red on consuming food does not depend on achromatic (Michelson) contrast and extends to rubbing cream on the skin, in: *Appetite* 71, pp. 33–37.

Buergel, R. (2009): One Artist, in: Hamilton, R./Todoli, V. (eds.): *Food for Thought*, New York.

Burckhardt, J. (1998): Long river – a single line, in: Migros Museum für Gegenwartskunst (ed.): *Supermarket*, Zürich.

Busch, K. (2009): Artistic Research and the Poetics of Knowledge, in: *Art & Research* 2/2, pp. 1–4.

Butler, J. (2002): Was ist Kritik? Ein Essay über Foucaults Tugend, tr. Jürgen Brenner, in: *Deutsche Zeitschrift für Philosophie* 50/2, pp. 249–265.

Butter, S. (2013): Why dinner Now Comes in a Bag, Bath and Flowerpot, in: *London Evening Standard*, 31 October.

Caduff, C. et al. (eds.) (2010): *Kunst und künstlerische Forschung*, Zürich.

Caraher M. et al. (1999): The state of cooking in England: the relationship of cooking skills to food choice, in: *British food journal* 101.8, pp. 590–609.

Carême, M.-A. (1815): *Le Pâtissier pittoresque*, Paris

— (1828): *Le Cuisinier parisien*, Paris.

Carrigan, M. A. et al. (2015): Hominids adapted to metabolize ethanol long before human-directed fermentation, in: *Proceedings of the National Academy of Sciences*, 112 (2), pp. 458–463.

Carta, A. C. A. (ed.) (2013): *Alla Carta. Dissertations Around a Table* (vol. 3), Milano.

Caviezel, F./Florenz, B./Franke, M./Wiesel, J. (2013): *Forschungsskizzen. Einblicke in Forschungspraktiken der Hochschule für Gestaltung und Kunst FHNW*, Zürich.

Caveziel, R./Vilgis, T. (2012): *Foodpairing – Harmonie und Kontrast*, Lenzburg.

Clausen, M. (2012): *Prinzessinnengärten. Anders gärtnern in der Stadt*, Köln.

Cockrail-King, J. (2012): *Food and the City. Urban Agriculture and the New Food Revolution*, New York.

Crutzen, P. (2002): The Geology of Mankind, in: *Nature* (vol. 415).

Därmann, I. (2005): *Fremde Monde der Vernunft*, Paderborn.

— (2009): *Figuren des Politischen*, Frankfurt/M.

Därmann, I./Lemke, H. (eds.) (2008): *Die Tischgesellschaft. Philosophische und kulturwissenschaftliche Annäherungen*, Bielefeld.

Dell'Agli, D. (2009): *Essen als ob nicht. Gastrosophische Modelle*, Frankfurt/M.

Denker, W. C. (2015): *Vom Geist des Bauches: Für eine Philosophie der Verdauung*, Bielefeld.

Derrida, J. (1997): *Aufzeichnung eines Blinden*, München.

Diaconu, M. (2013a): *Phänomenologie der Sinne*, Stuttgart.

— (2013b): *Tasten, riechen, schmecken. Eine Ästhetik der anästhesierten Sinne*, Würzburg.

Dollase, J. (2005): *Geschmacksschule*, Wiesbaden.

— (2006): *Kulinarische Intelligenz*, Wiesbaden.

— (2014): *Himmel und Erde. In der Küche eines Restaurantkritikers*, München/Aarau.

Douglas, M. (1979): Les structures du culinaire, in: *Daedalus* 101/2, pp. 61–81.

— (1988): *Reinheit und Gefährdung. Eine Studie zu Vorstellungen von Verunreinigung und Tabu*, Frankfurt/M.

Ekstedt, N. (2016): *Food from the Fire. The Scandinavian Flavours of Open-Fire Cooking*, London.

Elias, Norbert (1969): *The Civilizing Process (vol. 1), The History of Manners*, Oxford.

Eliasson, S. O. (ed.) (2013): *TYT (Take your Time), vol. 5: The Kitchen*, Berlin.

Emmison, M. (2003): Social Class and Cultural Mobility: Reconfiguring the Omnivore Thesis, in: *American Journal of Sociology* 39, pp. 211–30.

Endres, E.-M. (2002): *Genussrevolte: Von der Diät einer neuen Esskultur*, Wiesbaden.

Fan, J. E. (2013): Can ideas about food inspire real social change?, in: *Gastronomica. The Journal of Food and Culture* 13, pp. 29–40.

Fischer, D. (s. a.): *Essen und die Interkulturalität von Ernährung. Ein paradigmatisches Lernfeld der Bildung für nachhaltige Entwicklung*, avail-

able online at: http://www.umweltbildung.uni-osnabrueck.de/pub/up
loads/Baikal/fischer08esskulturen.pdf.

Fischer, M. (2011): *Die Kunst des Essens. Anleitung zum Genuss*, München/
Berlin.

Fischler, D. (1990): *L'hommivore*, Paris.

Flaig, B. B./Meyer, T./Ueltzhöffer, J. (1993): *Alltagsästhetik und politische
Kultur. Zur ästhetischen Dimension politischer Bildung und politischer
Kommunikation*, Bonn.

Flammer, D./Müller, S. (2013a): *Das kulinarische Erbe der Alpen. Das Kochbuch*, Aarau.

— (2013b): *Das kulinarische Erbe der Alpen. Die Ernährungsgeschichte des
Alpenraums*, Aarau.

Froelich, D. (2010): *Topografie der Gemengel und Gehäcksel. Kloß, Knödel,
Pudding, Klops, Wurst, Pastete, Terrine. Ein Kochbuch nebst weiteren
Betrachtungen über vermengte und gehackte Speisen*, Hannover.

— (2012): *supen. Getränk, Brühe, Sülze, Mus, Suppe, Eintopf. Eine Betrach-
tung der flüssigen Speisen*, Hannover.

Gibbons, A. (2007): Food for Thought, in: *Science*, vol. 316, iss. 5831,
pp. 1558–1560, available online at: http://science.sciencemag.org/con
tent/316/5831/1558.full.

Gilmore, P. (2012): *QUAY. Nature-based Cuisine*, Stuttgart.

Grassi, F./Tiravanija, R. (eds.) (2007): *Rirkrit Tiravanija. A Retrospective.
Tomorrow is another fine day*, Zürich.

Greeley, A. (2009): Finding Pad Thai, in: *Gastronomica*, vol. 9:1, available
online at: http://www.gastronomica.org/finding-pad-thai/.

Gremillion, K. (2011): *Ancestral Appetites: Food in Prehistory*, Cambridge/
MA.

Grober, U. (2013): *Die Entdeckung der Nachhaltigkeit. Kulturgeschichte eines
Begriffs*, München.

Hall, C. M./Gössling, S. (eds.) (2013): *Sustainable Culinary Systems. Local
foods, innovation, tourism and hospitality*, New York.

Halligan, M. (1990): *Eat my words*, London.

Harman, G. (2010): *Towards Speculative Realism*, Winchester/WA.

Harrar, V./Piqueras-Fiszman, B./Spence, C. (2011): There's more to taste in
a coloured bowl, in: *Perception* 40, pp. 880–882.

Hartmann, C./Dohle, S./Siegrist, M. (2013): Importance of cooking skills
for balanced food choices, *Appetite* 65, pp. 125–131.

Hauschild, J. (2014): Von Wurstsalat und Weltfrieden, in: *Die Zeit Wissen* 01,
available online at: http://www.zeit.de/zeit-wissen/2014/01/ernaehrung-
gemeinsame-mahlzeiten.

Hayn, D. et al. (2005): *Trends und Entwicklungen von Ernährung im Alltag.
Ergebnisse einer Literaturrecherche* (vol. 2), Institut für sozialökologische
Forschung (ISOE), Frankfurt/M.

Heindl, I. (1999): *Essen. Trinken und Ernähren zwischen Naturwissenschaf-
ten und Kulturphänomen*, Neuwied.

Herriman, K. (2015): A Restaurant where Art is on the Menu, in: *New York
Times Style Magazine* 11.

Hilbeck A./Hilbeck, H. (2015): Subsistence farming – the survival strategy, in: Scott J. (ed.): *Transdiscourse 2: Turbulent Societies*, Wien/New York.

Hilbeck A./Oehen, B. (2015): Post-industrial Agriculture – Competing Proposals for the Transformation of Agriculture, in: *Feeding the People. Agroecology for nourishing the world and transforming the agri-food system*, Brüssel, pp. 12–19.

Hirschfelder, G. et al. (2015): *Was der Mensch essen darf. Ökonomischer Zwang, ökologisches Gewissen und globale Konflikte*, Wiesbaden.

Hirschfelder, G./Ploeger, A. (eds.) (2009): *Purer Genuss? Wasser als Getränk, Ware und Kulturgut*, Frankfurt/M.

Hladik, C. M./Pasquet, P./Simmen, B. (2002): New perspectives on taste and primate evolution: the dichotomy in gustatory coding for perception of beneficent versus noxious substances as supported by correlations among human thresholds, in: *American Journal of Physical Anthropology*, 117 (4), pp. 342–348.

Hobsbawm, E. (2012): Introduction: Inventing Traditions, in: Hobsbawm, E./Ranger, T. (eds.): *The Invention of Tradition*, 20th print.

Hofstadt, C. et al. (eds.) (2009): *Gastrosophical Turn. Essen zwischen Medizin und Öffentlichkeit*, Bochum/Freiburg.

Home, R./Angelone, S./Hunziker, M./Bolliger, J. (2014): Public preferences for ecosystem enhancing elements in agricultural landscapes in the Swiss lowlands, in: *Journal of Integrative Environmental Sciences*, vol. 11, No. 2, pp. 93–108.

Huber, J. et al. (2007): *Ästhetik der Kritik. Verdeckte Ermittlung*, Zürich.

Ingendahl, W. (2001): Ästhetische Praxis, in: *Schulmagazin* 5-10/12, pp. 49–52.

Jaeggi, R./Wesche, T. (eds.) (2009): *Was ist Kritik?*, Frankfurt/M.

Jahic, A./Röthlisberger, C. (2015): *Artists' Recipes. Contemporary Artists and their Favourite Recipes*, Basel.

Janecke, C. (2011): *Maschen der Kunst*, Springe.

Johnston, J./Baumann, S. (2007): Democracy versus Distinction: A Study of Omnivorousness in Gourmet Food Writing, in: *American Journal of Sociology* (vol. 113:1), pp. 165–204.

Juul, J. (2015): *Was gibt's heute? Gemeinsam Essen macht Familie stark*, Weinheim.

Käsmayr, A. (ed.) (2012): *No ART Around. About the (Im)Possibility to Operate a Restaurant as Art*, Berlin.

Katz, S. E. (2012): *The Art of Fermentation. An in-depth exploration of essential concepts and processes from around the world*, Vermont.

Kaufmann, J.-C. (2006): *Kochende Leidenschaft. Soziologie vom Kochen und Essen*, Konstanz.

Kellein, T. (ed.) (2010): *Rirkrit Tiravanija Cookbook*, Bangkok/London.

Keller, T. (1999): *The French Laundry Cookbook*, New York.

Kimmich, D./Schahadat, S. (2012): *Essen, Zeitschrift für Kulturwissenschaft* (vol. 1), Bielefeld.

King, G. F./Williams, N. (eds.) (2014): *Kinfolk. Discovering new things to cook, make and do* (vol. 11), Portland.

Kirchhoff, T. (2007): *Systemauffassungen und biologische Theorien. Zur Herkunft von Individualitätskonzeptionen und ihrer Bedeutung für die Theorie ökologischer Einheiten*, Freising.

Kirchner, C. (1999): Ästhetisches Verhalten von Kindern im Dialog mit Bildender Kunst, in: Neuß, Norbert (eds.): *Ästhetik der Kinder. Interdisziplinäre Beiträge zur ästhetischen Erfahrung von Kindern*, Frankfurt/M.

Kleinspehn, T. (1987): *Warum sind wir so unersättlich?*, Frankfurt/M.

Klink, V. (2014): *Voll ins Gemüse mit Vincent Klink – 'wir schnallen den Gürtel weiter'*, Stuttgart.

Kneafsey, M. (2010): The region in food. Important or irrelevant?, in: *Cambridge Journal of Region, Economy and Society*, available online at: http://cjres.oxfordjournals.org/content/early/2010/05/10/cjres.rsq012.full.

Kogge, W./Krämer, S./Gruber, G. (eds.) (2007): *Spur. Spurenlesen als Orientierungstechnik und Wissenskunst*, Frankfurt/M.

Krause-Wahl, A. (2006): *Konstruktionen von Identität: Renée Green, Tracey Emin, Rirkrit Tiravanija*, München.

Krausse, J. (1992): Gedanken über das Feuer beim Wassertragen, in: Andritzky, M. (ed.): *Oikos. Von der Feuerstelle zur Mikrowelle*, Gießen.

Kunstforum International (2002): *Essen und Trinken. Die große Enzyklopädie* (vol. 159/160).

Kurihara, K. (2015): Umami the fifth basic taste: history of studies on receptor mechanisms and role as a food flavour, in: *BioMed research international*, Article ID 189402.

Küster, H. (2013): *Am Anfang war das Korn. Eine andere Geschichte der Menschheit*, München.

Lanier, J. (2014): *Wem gehört die Zukunft?*, Hamburg.

Leinfelder, R. (2012): Paul Joseph Crutzen, The 'Anthropocene', in: Leggewie, C. et al. (eds.): *Schlüsselwerke der Kulturwissenschaften, Edition Kulturwissenschaft* (vol. 7), Bielefeld, pp. 257–60.

Leinfelder, R. et al. (2016): *Die Anthropozän-Küche. Matooke, Bienenstich und eine Prise Phosphor – in zehn Speisen um die Welt*, Berlin/Heidelberg.

Leinfelder, R./Hamann, A./Kirstein, J. (2015): Wissenschaftliche Sachcomics: Multimodale Bildsprache, partizipative Wissensgenerierung und raumzeitliche Gestaltungsmöglichkeiten, in: Bredekamp, H./Schäffner, W. (eds.): *Haare hören, Strukturen wissen, Räume agieren. Berichte aus dem Interdisziplinären Labor Bild-Wissen-Gestaltung*, Bielefeld, pp. 45–59.

Lemke, H. (2007a): *Die Kunst des Essens: Eine Ästhetik des kulinarischen Geschmacks*, Bielefeld.

— (2007b): *Ethik des Essens. Eine Einführung in die Gastrosophie*, Berlin.

— (2012): *Politik des Essens. Wovon die Welt von morgen lebt*, Bielefeld.

Lévi-Strauss, C. [1964] (2000): *Mythologica I. Das Rohe und das Gekochte*, Frankfurt/M.

— [1964] (1976): *Mythologica III. Der Ursprung der Tischsitten*, Frankfurt/M.

Lévi-Strauss, C./Weightman, J. (1994): *The raw and the cooked: Introduction to a science of mythology*, New York.

Levitsky, D./Youn, T. (2004): The more food young adults are served, the more they overeat, in: *Journal of Nutrition* (vol. 134), pp. 2546–2549.

Lihotzky, M. (1927a): Die ‚Frankfurter Küche'. Typisierte Küche des Hochbauamtes Frankfurt/M., in: *Stein, Holz, Eisen*, vol. 8.

— (1927b): Streamlinedisierung im Haushalt, in: *Das Neue Frankfurt*, vol. 5.

Löwenstein, F. zu (2011): *Food Crash*, München.

Łuczak, A./Pinkpank, T./Schacht, A./Sommer, W./Vilgis, T. A. (2016): The valence of food in pictures and on the plate: impacts on brain and body, in: *International Journal of Gastronomy and Food Science* (vols. 5-6), pp. 33–40.

Lutz-Auras, L./Gottschlich, P. (eds.) (2013): *Aus dem politischen Küchenkabinett. Eine kurze Kulturgeschichte der Kulinaristik. Festschrift zum 65. Geburtstag von Professor Jakob Rösel*, Baden-Baden.

Mackay, R./Negarestani, R. (eds.) (2011): *Collapse VII: Culinary Materialism*, Falmouth.

Maggi, M. (2014): *Essbare Stadt. Wildwuchs auf dem Teller. Vegetarische Rezepte mit Pflanzen aus der Stadt*, Aarau/München.

Marchiori, D./Corneille, O./Klein, O. (2012): Container size influences snack food intake independently of portion size, in: *Appetite*, Jun 2012, 58(3), pp. 814–817.

Mather, G. (2006): *Foundations of sensation and perception*, Hove.

Matthiesen, U. (2005): Esskultur und Regionale Entwicklung – unter besonderer Berücksichtigung von "Mark und Metropole": Strukturskizzen zu einem Forschungsfeld, in: *Berlin Blätter. Ethnographische und Ethnologische Beiträge* 34, Berlin, pp. 111–145.

Mauss, M. [1923/24] (1990): *Die Gabe. Form und Funktion des Austauschs in archaischen Gesellschaften*, Frankfurt/M.

May, Ernst (1928): Grundlagen der Frankfurter Wohnungsbaupolitik, in: *Das Neue Frankfurt*, vols. 7-8.

Menke, C. (1996): *Tragödie im Sittlichen. Gerechtigkeit und Freiheit nach Hegel*, Frankfurt/M.

— (2013): *Die Kraft der Kunst*, Frankfurt/M.

Menke, C./Loick, D./Graw, I. (2010): *The Power of Judgment*, Berlin.

Mepham, B. (ed.) (1996): *Food Ethics. Professional Ethics*, London/New York.

Merleau-Ponty, M: (1968): *The Visible and the Invisible*, Evanston.

Meyer, E. (1926): *Der neue Haushalt. Ein Wegweiser zur wissenschaftlichen Haushaltsführung*, Stuttgart.

Michel, C. et al. (2015): Rotating plates: Online study demonstrates the importance of orientation in the plating of food, in: *Food Quality and Preference*, vol. 44, pp. 194–202.

Miller, J./Deutsch, J. (2009): *Food Studies. An Introduction to Research Methods*, London et al.

Möhring, M. (2012): *Fremdes Essen. Die Geschichte der ausländischen Gastronomie in der Bundesrepublik Deutschland*, München.

Muche, G. (1925): Das Versuchshaus des Bauhauses, in: Meyer, A.: *Ein Versuchshaus des Bauhauses in Weimar*, Bauhausbücher, vol. 3.

Müller, K. (2003): *Kleine Geschichte des Essens und Trinkens. Vom offenen Feuer zur Haute Cuisine*, München.

Muñoz, C. L./Wood, N. T. (2009): A recipe for success: understanding regional perceptions of authenticity in themed restaurants, in: *International Journal of Culture, Tourism and Hospitality Research*, vol. 3, iss. 3, pp. 269–280.

Murata, Y. (2006): *Kaiseki: The Exquisite Cuisine of Kyoto's Kikunoi Restaurant*, New York.

Murphy, S. et al. (2012): *Cereal secrets: the world's largest grain traders and global agriculture*, Oxfam Research Reports.

Neumann, G. (1993a): „Jede Nahrung ist ein Symbol". Umrisse einer Kulturwissenschaft des Essens, in: Wierlacher, A./Neumann, G./Teuteberg, H. J. (eds.): *Kulturthema Essen. Ansichten und Problemfelder*, Berlin, pp. 385–444.

— (1993b): Filmische Darstellungen des Essens, in: Wierlacher, A./Neumann, G./Teuteberg, H. J. (eds.): *Kulturthema Essen. Ansichten und Problemfelder*, Berlin, pp. 343–366.

Nilsson, M. (2012): *Fäviken*, London/New York.

Obrist, H. U. (2010): *Rirkrit Tiravanija – The Conversation Series*, Köln.

Ott, C. (2011): *Feinschmecker und Bücherfresser. Esskultur und literarische Einverleibung der Moderne*, München.

Park, M. Y. (2013): *A history of how food is plated, from medieval bread bowls to Noma*, available online at: http://www.bonappetit.com/trends/article/a-history-of-how-food-is-plated-from-medieval-bread-bowls-to-noma.

Parodi, O. et al. (eds.) (2010): *Wechselspiele: Kultur und Nachhaltigkeit. Annäherungen an ein Spannungsfeld*, Berlin.

Pellerin, A./Lane, D./Tweed, M. (eds.) (2013): *The Gourmand. A food and culture journal*, London.

Pence, G. E. (ed.) (2002): *The Ethics of Food. Reader for the 21st century*, Lanham/Oxford.

Pfeifer, K. (2000): *Medizin der Goethezeit: Christoph Wilhelm Hufeland und die Heilkunst des 18. Jahrhunderts*, Köln et al.

Pimbert, M. (2009): *Towards food sovereignty*. International Institute for Environment and Development, London.

Pingali, P. (2007): Westernization of Asian diets and the transformation of food systems: Implications for research and policy, in: *Food Policy* 32 (3), pp. 281–298.

Piqueras-Fiszman, B./Spence, C. (2012a): The weight of the container influences expected satiety, percieved density, and subsequent expected fullness, in: *Appetite* 58, pp. 559–562.

— (2012b): The influence of the feel of product packaging on the perception of the oral-somatosensory texture of food, in: *Food Quality and Preference* 26, pp. 67–73.

Piqueras-Fiszman, B./Harrar, V./Alcaide, J. et al. (2011): Is it the plate or is it the food? The influence of the color and shape of the plate on the perception of the food placed on it, in: *Food Quality and Preference* 24, pp. 205–208.

Pollan, M. (2013): *Cooked: A Natural History of Transformation,* New York.

Raby, F. (2001). *Design Noir: The Secret Life of Electronic Objects,* Basel.

Rebentisch, J. (2013): *Theorien der Gegenwartskunst,* Hamburg.

Redzepi, R. (2010): *Noma. Time and Place in Nordic Cuisine,* London/New York.

— (2011): René Redzepi au Thuriès magazine: Juste avant d'ouvrir le NOMA, j'avais fait un long voyage, in: *Thuriès Gastronomie du mois d'octobre.*

— (2013): *A Work in Progress,* 3 vols., London.

Rheinberger, H.-J. (2001): *Experimentalsysteme und epistemische Dinge. Eine Geschichte der Proteinsynthese im Reagenzglas,* Göttingen.

— (2005): *Iterationen,* Berlin.

Rockström J. et al. (2009): A safe operating space for humanity, in: *Nature* 461.7263, pp. 472–475.

Rogoff, I. (2006): *Smuggling – An Embodied Criticality,* available online at: http://eipcp.net/dlfiles/rogoff-smugglin.

Röttgers, K. (2009): *Kritik der kulinarischen Vernunft. Ein Menü der Sinne nach Kant,* Bielefeld.

Rückert-John, J. (2006): *Natürlich essen. Kantinen und Restaurants auf dem Weg zu nachhaltiger Ernährung,* Frankfurt/M.

— (2010): Semantik der Natürlichkeit als sichernder Sinnhorizont des Lebensmittelkonsums, in: Soeffner, H.-G. (ed.): *Unsichere Zeiten: Herausforderungen gesellschaftlicher Transformationen. Verhandlungen des 34. Kongresses der Deutschen Gesellschaft für Soziologie in Jena 2008,* Wiesbaden.

Rudolph, T./Bassett, M. (2014): *Food Consumption 2014. Ess- und Verzehrverhalten in der Schweiz,* St. Gallen.

Rumohr, C. F. [1822] (2010): *Geist der Kochkunst,* Frankfurt/M.

Schareika, H. (2008): *Die alten Römer bitten zu Tisch,* Stuttgart.

Schlegel-Matthies, K. (1995): *„Im Haus und am Herd“: Der Wandel des Hausfrauenbildes und der Hausarbeit 1880-1930,* Stuttgart.

Seel, M. (1993): Zur ästhetischen Praxis der Kunst, in: Welsch, W. (ed.): *Die Aktualität des Ästhetischen,* München, pp. 398–416.

Selby, T. (2012): *Edible Selby/Todd Selby,* New York.

Selfa, T./Qazi, J. (2005): Place, taste, or face-to-face? Understanding producer–consumer networks in „local“ food systems in Washington State, in: *Agriculture and Human Values* 22, pp. 451–464.

Serres, M. (1998): *Die fünf Sinne. Eine Philosophie der Gemenge und Gemische,* Frankfurt/M.

Shepard, G. (2011). *Neurogastronomy: How the Brain Creates Flavor and Why It Matters,* New York.

Simmel, G. (1957): Soziologie der Mahlzeit, in: Ibid.: *Brücke und Tür,* Stuttgart, pp. 243–250.

Smith, S. (2013): Introduction. Of Feasts, Hospitality, and Art, in: Ibid. (ed.): *Feast. Radical Hospitality in Contemporary Art,* Chicago.

Spang, R. (2001): *The Invention of the Restaurant: Paris and Modern Gastronomic Culture,* Cambridge/MA.

Spechtenhauser, K. (ed.) (2006): *Die Küche. Lebenswelt, Nutzung, Perspektiven*, Basel.

Spence, C./Piqueras-Fiszman, B. (2014a): *The Perfect Meal. The multisensory science of food and dining*, Hoboken.

— et al. (2014b): *The plating manifesto (I): From decoration to creation*, available online at: http://flavourjournal.biomedcentral.com.

— et al. (2014c): *The plating manifesto (II): From decoration to creation*, available online at: http://flavourjournal.biomedcentral.com.

Spence, C./Michel, C. et al. (2015): Studying the impact of plating on ratings of the food served in a naturalistic dining context, in: *Appetite* (vol. 90), pp. 45–50.

Spence, C. (2016): *The Art and Science of Plating* (in press).

Stahl, A. (2011): Künstler als Köche verderben den Brei. Frankreichs Kunststreit, in: *FAZ* 09.05.2011.

Steffen, W. et al. (2015): Planetary boundaries: Guiding human development on a changing planet, in: *Science*, vol. 347, iss. 6223.

Stewart, P. C./Goss, E. (2013): Plate shape and colour interact to influence taste and quality judgments, in: *Flavour* (vol. 2), p. 27.

Stierand, P. (2014): *Speiseräume: Die Ernährungswende beginnt in der Stadt*, München.

Stone, M. (2015): *Cooking for Artists*, London.

Taleb, N. T. (2014): *Antifragilität. Anleitung für eine Welt, die wir nicht verstehen*, München.

Tanner, J. (1996): Der Mensch ist, was er isst, in: *Hist. Anthropologie. Kultur Gesellschaft Alltag* (vol. 4), Köln et al., pp. 399–419.

Taut, B. (1924): *Die neue Wohnung. Die Frau als Schöpferin*, Leipzig.

Teasdale, P. (2012): Sculptures don't eat, in: D. Lane/M. Tweed (eds.): *The Gourmand. A food and culture journal*, London, pp. 20–27.

Teuteberg, H.-J. (1997): *Essen und kulturelle Identität. Europäische Perspektiven*, Berlin.

Texte zur Kunst (2014): *Spekulation, Speculation* (vol. 93).

Thimm, U./Wellmann, K.-H. (2004): *In aller Munde. Ernährung heute*, Frankfurt/M.

Trippi, L. (1998): Untitled Artists' Projects by Janine Antoni, Ben Kinmont, Rirkrit Tiravanija, in: Scapp, R./Seitz, B. (eds.): *Eating Culture*, New York.

Trubek, A. (2000): *Haute Cuisine: How the French Invented the Culinary Profession*, Philadelphia.

Tschofen, B. (2007): Vom Geschmack der Regionen. Kulinarische Praxis, europäische Politik und räumliche Kultur – eine Forschungsskizze, in: *Zeitschrift für Volkskunde* (vol. 103), pp. 169–195.

Tsuji, Kaichi (1972): *Kaiseki: Zen Tastes in Japanese Cooking*, New York.

UNCTAD (2013): Wake up before it's too late. Make agriculture truly sustainable now for food security and changing climate, in: *Trade and Environment Review*.

van der Meulen (2013): Ästhetische Praxis als eine Theorie der Praxis in Gestaltung und Kunst, in: Langkilde, K. (ed.): *Verortung: Das Wissen der Künste*, Basel, pp. 33–40.

van der Meulen, N./Wiesel, J. (2016): Ästhetische Praxis als Dialog, in: Kauppert, M./Eberl, H. (eds.): *Selbstentgrenzung der Künste oder Entkunstung der Kunst*, Wiesbaden, pp. 263–282.

van der Sande, B./Lauwaert, M./de Rooden, P./van Westrenen, F. (eds.) (2012): *Food for the City. A Future for the Metropolis*, Den Haag/Rotterdam.

Vilensky, D./Bibkov, A. (2008): *On Practice and Critique*, available online at: http://www.chtodelat.org.

Vilgis, T. A. (2007): Geschmackssache. Mitunter eine physikalische Angelegenheit, in: *Journal Culinaire* 5, pp. 19–32.

— (2008): Geschmackswahrnehmung. Physikalisch-chemische Ansichten, in: *Journal Culinaire. Kultur und Wissenschaft des Essens* 7, pp. 20–28.

— (2009): *Die Molekularküche*, Wiesbaden.

— (2010): Physik und Kulinaristik, in: Schütze, I. (ed.): *Über Geschmack lässt sich doch streiten. Zutaten aus Küche, Kunst und Wissenschaft*, Berlin.

— (2011): Genuss und Ernährung aus naturwissenschaftlicher Perspektive, in: Ploeger, A./Hirschfelder, G./Schönberger, G. (eds.): *Die Zukunft auf dem Tisch – Analysen, Trends und Perspektiven der Ernährung von morgen*, Wiesbaden.

— (2013a): Komplexität auf dem Teller – Ein naturwissenschaftlicher Blick auf das „kulinarische Dreieck" von Lévi-Strauss, in: *Journal Culinaire* 16, pp. 109–122.

— (2013b): Texture, taste and aroma: multi-scale materials and the gastrophysics of food, in: *Flavour*, 2(1), p. 12.

— (2014): *Kochen für Angeber – die besten Tricks der Spitzenköche*, Stiftung Warentest.

Vilgis, T. A./Lendner, I./Caviezel, R. (2014): *Ernährung bei Pflegebedürftigkeit und Demenz – Lebensfreude durch Genuss*, Wien.

Vilgis, T. A./Tzschirner, H. (2014): *Roh! Die neue Defintion von Rohkost*, Köln.

Vilgis, T. A./Vierich, T.-A. (2013): *Aroma: Die Kunst des Würzens*, Stiftung Warentest.

von Müller, A. von (2010): Carl Friedrich von Rumohr entdeckt die Kulturgeschichte und antizipiert die Klassiker, in: Bastek, A./von Müller, A. (eds.): *Kunst, Küche und Kalkül. Carl Friedrich von Rumohr (1785–1843) und die Entdeckung der Kulturgeschichte*, Petersberg, pp. 215–218.

von Vaerst, E. [1851] (1975): *Gastrosophie oder die Lehre von den Tafelfreuden* (2 vols.), München.

Waldenfels, B. (2008): *Fremdspeise. Zur Phänomenologie von Essen und Trinken*, Bielefeld.

— (2010): *Sinne und Künste im Wechselspiel*, Frankfurt/M.

Wansink, B./Cheney, M. M. (2005): Super bowls: Serving bowl size and food consumption, in: *Journal of the American Medical Association* 293, pp. 1727–1728.

Waters, A. (2010): *In the Green Kitchen. Techniques to Learn by Heart*, Luton.

Waters, C. et al. (2016): The Anthropocene is functionally and stratigraphically distinct from the Holocene, in: *Science* (vol. 351, no. 6269).

WBGU (2016): *Der Umzug der Menschheit: Die transformative Kraft der Städte. Zusammenfassung*, Berlin.

Wierlacher, A./Neumann, G./Teuteberg, H. J. (eds.) (1993): *Kulturthema Essen. Ansichten und Problemfelder*, Berlin

Wierlacher, A./Bendix, R. (eds.) (2008): *Kulinaristik. Forschung – Lehre – Praxis*, Münster.

Wiesner, S. (2011): *Wiesner. Avantgardistische Naturküche*, Aarau/München.

Wiesner, S./Räber, G. (2003): *Gold Holz Stein. Sinnliche Sensationen aus Wiesners alchemistischer Naturküche*, Aarau.

Wilk, N. (2010): *Esswelten. Über den Funktionswandel der täglichen Kost*, Frankfurt/M. et al.

Wilk, R. (2006): *Fast Food/Slow Food. The Cultural Economy of the Global Food System*, Lanham.

Wilke, S. (2005): *Die verspeiste Esskultur. Nahrung und Nahrungstabus*, Marburg.

Will, S. et al. (2015): Planetary boundaries: Guiding human development on a changing planet, in: *Science* 347.6223: 1259855.

Williams, N. (ed.) (2013): *The Kinfolk Table. Recipes for small gatherings*, New York.

Wrangham, R. (2009): *Catching Fire. How Cooking Made Us Human*, London.

Wrangham, R. et al. (1999): The Raw and the Stolen. Cooking and the Ecology of Human Origins, in: *Current Anthropology* (vol. 40, no. 5), pp. 567–94.

Yalouf, I. (2016): *Food and the City. New York's Professionals, Chefs, Restaurateurs, Line Cooks, Street Vendors, and Purveyors Talk About What They Do and Why They Do it*, New York.

Yang, J. (2011): *The Art of Food Representation*, available online at: www.cravemag.com/features/the-art-of-food-presentation.

Zeuch, U. (2000): *Umkehr der Sinneshierarchie. Herder und die Aufwertung des Tastsinns seit der frühen Neuzeit*, Tübingen.

List of Figures

Fig. 8, p. 49: Mobile kitchen trolley *Cucina minima*, Joe Colombo, 1964. Taken from: Anonymous: Boffi. La non cucina, in: *Ottagono*, vol. 107/1993, p. 119

Fig. 9, p. 49: English kitchen island *Masterplan*, John Heritage, 1963. Taken from: Snelling, J. (1963): "Masterplan-Küche" erfüllt die Träume der Hausfrau, in: *Die moderne Küche*, vol. 20/1963, p. 56

Fig. 10, p. 49: *Novellipsenküche*, by Novelectric, 1965. Taken from: Anonymous: dmk international. Luxus-Küchen aus der Schweiz, in: *Die moderne Küche* supplement, vol. 31/1965, S. D.

Fig. 11, p. 49: Model *Experiment 70* by the designer Luigi Colani, Poggenpohl, 1970. Taken from: Lübbert-Griese, K. (1970): Wird die Küche ein Gerät? Küchengestaltung in Bewegung, in: *Die moderne Küche*, vol. 2/1970, p. 13

Fig. 11a, p. 49: Model *Typ 1*, by Bulthaup. Taken from: Anonymous: Cologne Furniture Fair 1970, in: *Form*, vol. 50/1970, p. 5

Fig. 12, p. 49: Kitchen block by Haas und Sohn KG. Taken from: Schulz, G. (1972): Internationale Möbelmesse Köln 1972. Gemütlich – wohnlich – mobil. 1. Bericht, in: *MD*, vol. 3/1972, p. 43

Fig. 13, p. 47: Model *Mal-Zeit*, Coop Himmelb(l)au, 1987–1989. Taken from: Cecarelli L./Doveil, F./Goldschmiedt, M. (1991): La cucina – produzione e tendenze: Il luogo e la macchina, in: *Modo*, vol. 133/1991, p. 54

Fig. 14, p. 49: Model *Eroica*, Alberto Rizzi, Rossano Didaglio, 1990. Taken from: Ibid.: p. 58, 59

Fig. 15, p. 49: Kitchen model from 1989. Taken from: Advertisement, in: *Die moderne Küche*, vol. 5/1989, p. 67

Hanni Rützler/Wolfgang Reiter:
Fig. 1, p. 59: Cooking table, photo: Caspar Sessler © 2015, Studio Moritz Putzier
Fig. 2, p. 59: Cooking table, photo: Caspar Sessler © 2015, Studio Moritz Putzier
Fig. 3, p. 59: Cooking workbench © 2016, bulthaup
Fig. 4, p. 60: flow 2 © 2016, Studio Gorm
Fig. 5, p. 61: Farm 432 © 2016, Livin Farms
Fig. 6, p. 61: The Hive © 2016, Livin Farms
Fig. 7, p. 61: The Hive © 2016, Livin Farms

Lucky Peach:
Fig. 1, p. 63: La Brigade de Cuisine © Carolyn Bahar for Lucky Peach

Iliana Regan:
Fig. 1–2, p. 65: Iliana Regan, Photo © Jeffrey Marini

Kobe Desmaraults:
Fig. 1, p. 68: Kobe Desmaraults, Dish, Photo © Piet De Kersgieter
Fig. 2, p. 69: Kobe Desmaraults, Dish, Photo © Piet De Kersgieter

Holger Stromberg:
Fig. 1–2, p. 71: Holger Stromberg, Photo © Erwin Lanzensberger

Fig. 4, p. 156: © 2013, Thomas A. Vilgis
Fig. 5, p. 157: © 2017, Thomas A. Vilgis

Chus Martinez:
Fig. 1, p. 161: Eduardo Navarro, Metabolic drawing, 2016, eatable ink on rice paper, Courtesy of the artist

Felix Bröcker:
Fig. 1, p. 173: Rirkrit Tiravanija handing out food, *Do We Dream Under The Same Sky*, Art Basel 2015, Photo © Felix Bröcker
Fig. 2, p. 173: Standing in line to wash the dishes, *Do We Dream Under The Same Sky*, Art Basel 2015, Photo © Felix Bröcker

Paola Bonino:
Fig. 1, p. 194: Allen Ruppersberg, Al's Grand Hotel, 1971, Courtesy of the artist and Greene Naftali, New York
Fig. 2, p. 194: Allen Ruppersberg, Al's Grand Hotel, 1971, Courtesy of the artist and Greene Naftali, New York
Fig. 3, p. 195: Gordon Matta-Clark, Food, Courtesy of White Columns, New York
Fig. 4, p. 195: Gordon Matta-Clark, Food, Courtesy of White Columns, New York
Fig. 5, p. 195: Rirkrit Tiravanija, Untitled 1994 (angst essen Seele auf), with the kind permission of the Rirkrit Tiravanija Archive Berlin
Fig. 6, p. 199: Finissage dreijahre dining room project, 2010, photo: Jan Meier, Courtesy dilettantin produktionsbüro
Fig. 7, p. 199: Invitation to the Finissage, 2010, courtesy dilettantin produktionsbüro
Fig. 8, p. 201: Eating the Forest, 2015, DOCVA, Milan, photo: Angelo Becci. Courtesy of Estonian Contemporary Art Development Center (ECADC)
Fig. 9, p. 201: Eating the Forest, 2015, DOCVA, Milan, photo: Angelo Becci. Courtesy of Estonian Contemporary Art Development Center (ECADC)
Fig. 10, p. 203: The Secret Club in the Basement of dreijahre, 2008, courtesy dilettantin produktionsbüro
Fig. 11, p. 204: Carsten Höller, The Double Club, photo: Attilio Maranzano, Courtesy Fondazione Prada

Sandra Knecht:
Fig. 1, p. 211: Lukmanier © 2015, Sandra Knecht

Nicolaj van der Meulen:
Fig. 1, p. 238: © Thomas A. Vilgis
Fig. 2, p. 239: © Museum Frankenthal, Germany
Fig. 3, p. 241: © Dominic Davies
Fig. 4, p. 241: © Sarah_Ackerman/Flickr
Fig. 5–7, p. 244: Photo © Nicolaj van der Meulen
Fig. 8, p. 246: © Nicolaj van der Meulen
Fig. 9, p. 247: © Nicolaj van der Meulen

International Gastronautical Society:

Anton Studer:

Jürgen Dollase:

Contributors

Sonja Alhäuser is an artist; she draws the stages of recipes, produces margarine and chocolate sculptures, and her exhibition openings feature such elements as lavish banquets with fountains of red wine and people stepping into baths of chocolate. She loves working with unusual materials and quantities of foods, using them to highlight the boundaries between decadent profligacy and unbridled self-indulgence in orgiastic proportions. She exhibits her work in numerous solo and group shows in the national and international context. Alhäuser lives and works in Berlin.

Born in Basel in 1961, **Béla Bartha** developed an enthusiasm for crop plants and their diversity back in his days as a Biology student. After spending several years teaching scientific subjects at major national exhibitions (Pfahlbauland, Heureka) and working as a teacher in a high school, where it was his job to pass on his passion for nature to his students, he found his vocation in 1995 at ProSpecieRara. He has been CEO of the organization for the past twelve years, managing its affairs together with his dedicated team.

Paola Bonino graduated in Italian Literature (Bologna University, Italy) and Visual Arts (IUAV University, Venice, Italy; Hochschule für Künste, Bremen, Germany) and took part in the post-Master's international curatorial program at École du Magasin (Grenoble, France), where she co-curated the exhibition LIAM GILLICK: FROM 199C TO 199D. She currently runs the contemporary art gallery Placentia Arte (Piacenza, Italy), with its focus on artistic research and young artists. She also contributes to Juliet, an Italian contemporary art magazine.

After training as a chef, **Felix Bröcker** gained extensive gastronomic experience in Switzerland, Portugal and Australia. He then obtained a diploma in Hotel Management from Heidelberg's School of Hotel Management, before enrolling for Film Studies and Philosophy in Mainz. As well as working in the family business on Lake Constance, he contributes to projects involving art and cuisine, most recently for Arpad Dobriban at the exhibition *Food* (Triennale der Kleinplastik, Fellbach), for Rirkrit Tiravanija at Art Basel, for Peter Kubelka for his lecture at the Städelschule and with Frankfurt's Freitagsküche at the Ruhrtriennale and the Kunst-festspiele Herrenhausen in Hanover. He is currently working on a doctorate on visual staging strategies in Haute cuisine at HfG Offenbach.

Rebecca Clopath is an organic chef and, until recently, worked as head chef for Stefan Wiesner. Her cooking philosophy does not start in the kitchen, but with how her ingredients are grown and kept. She grew up on an organic farm in Lohn, Switzerland, and her culinary creations rely on local, organic, fair-trade products. Her focus is always on simple, healthy, unpretentious food. She is currently training as a farmer in order to broaden her knowledge and enrich her personal style of cooking. At the same time, Clopath organizes various events in which she combines her understanding of culture, history, agriculture, crop growing and cuisine.

Born in Oberhausen in the Ruhr region of Germany in 1948, **Jürgen Dollase** studied Art, Music and Philosophy at Kunstakademie Düsseldorf and the universities of Cologne and Düsseldorf. A professional Rock musician from 1970 through 1983, he established, led and wrote songs for the Rock band "Wallenstein" and recorded with BASF, RCA and EMI, after which he continued to work as an author and producer. He went back to painting in 1988 and started taking an increasing interest in cooking as of around 1983. After corresponding with publicist Johannes Gross the latter invited him to start writing a cookery column. He started working for the newspaper F.A.Z. in 1999, then later for the F.A.S., for Feinschmecker, Port Culinaire and Fine – European Wine Magazine. He started writing books on fine dining in 2005. Dollase is considered "Germany's most important gourmet" (Südkurier), its "most influential one" (taz) and "the best German food critic" (SZ-Magazin, 9/2016).

Daniel de La Falaise trained as a chef at Harry's Bar in London, later opening the George Club in London's Mayfair. Today, he works as an itinerant chef for eclectic international clients, catering bespoke events for brands and private individuals. He approaches cooking as a sensual task, involving as little interference as possible from the cook. His focus is on the inherent synergies that occur between the realms of vegetables, fruit and herbs. The result is a celebration of the vitality of natural ingredients. The descendent of a long line of gardeners and cooks, La Falaise focuses on sourcing ingredients from independent producers, thus honoring sustainable agriculture and farming traditions. His first cookbook, "Nature's Larder: Cooking with the Senses", was published in 2015 by Rizzoli. He has been profiled in T, The New York Times Style Magazine, The Wall Street Journal, and Vogue. He lives with his wife and son on their farm in southwest France.

Since 2003, the artists' collective **dilettantin produktionsbüro** (dilettante production bureau) has been producing conceptual work that is at once art and everyday life, using gustatory elements as a means of communication.

With its installations and performances *dilettantin produktionsbüro* creates sensual, temporary spaces in the everyday world, illustrates or stages them. The group's work often targets the kind of everyday audience that has not come to consume art. At the same time, one of its perennial topics is the question of art per se. Can something be art if it does not look like art? Can art manage without a "product"? What role does culinary taste play in perception so as to "proceed [from] tasting to thinking and speaking"? *dilettantin produktionsbüro* sees itself as an open, discourse-oriented collective. Its recent work has included a series of performative dinners *(Eating the Forest)*, a food trailer and fashion project *(SLOE)*, a temporary art club/ Kunstverein *(Thisisnotashop)*, a record shop *(sex®shop)*, a restaurant *(drei-jahre dining room project)*, and a hotel business *(HOTEL)*. Since 2014, the collective has been staging a series of works by the name of *"Tu dir Gutes – Do Thee Good"* – site-specific productions and interventions on the basis of recent findings on nutritional science, quantum physics and psychology. www.dilettantin.com

For 30 years now **Dominik Flammer** has been investigating the history of nutrition. His books are among the standard works of Central European literature on cookery and nutrition. Flammer is currently in charge of establishing a competence center on regional Alpine cuisine at Kloster Stans in the Swiss canton of Nidwalden.

Born in 1959, **Dieter Froelich** studied Sculpture under Michael Croissant at the Städelschule in Frankfurt/Main in the 1980s, also attending Peter Kubelka's cookery seminars there. In 2003, he established "Restauration a.a.O." One facet of this mobile eatery is organizing lectures, seminars and banquets. As an exponent of purist culinary practices he developed his own model for "archetypes of fare". His "Topografie der Gemengsel und Gehäcksel" was published in 2010 and his treatise on liquid food "supen – Getränk, Brühe, Suppe, Brei und Eintopf" in 2012. www.restauration-a-a-o.de

Sonja Frühsammer was born near Adelaide, Australia in 1969. She trained as a chef with Siemens in Berlin before being hired by starred chef Karl Wannemacher for his restaurant Alt-Luxemburg. She established SerVino, a catering business, together with starred chef Peter Frühsammer in 1998. She then established Frühsammer's restaurant in 2007 and was put in charge of running the kitchen there. She was named Achiever of the Year by Berlin-Partner in 2008. Her cuisine is aromatic and strong on taste and she consciously avoids theatricality. In 2014 she was named Achiever of the Year by the newspaper F.A.Z., received her first *Michelin* star and was awarded 17 *Gault Millau* points.

Samuel Herzog is an art historian and, until 2016, was arts editor for the newspaper Neue Zürcher Zeitung. He now writes mainly on food and continues to develop his fictitious island Santa Lemusa, in existence since 2001 and located in the middle of the Atlantic Ocean.

Robert Home holds a Ph. D. in the natural sciences, and is a social scientist who works in the field of agrarian knowledge systems at the Research Institute for Organic Agriculture (FiBL)'s department of socio-economics. He researches the relationship between man and nature. He is an Australian and has been living in Switzerland with his two children since 2004. He currently resides in Bangerten, a small village with some 60 residents, surrounded by the forest in the canton of Berne.

The **International Gastronautical Society** (Internationale Gastronautische Gesellschaft) is a critical research unit and design offensive that is all about eating and food. It organizes tangible experiments, produces works of art and initiates innovative undertakings. Alongside its three main protagonists the society boasts a team of more than 20 staffers.

Anneli Käsmayr has, since 2003, been part of *dilettantin produktionsbüro* (dilettante production bureau), an artist collective which realizes projects at the interface of culinary taste and staging. From 2007–2010 the group operated a restaurant *(dreijahre dining room project)* which explored the question of the extent to which a hospitality location based on economic considerations can be art. Since 2004 she has been a member of *SEX*, an artist-cum-musician collective, and of *sexsoundsystem*, a DJ collective. Käsmayr is interested in the question of the relationship between being affected emotionally by and enjoying something through taste, and intuition, as well as in both the kind of atmospheric parameters that determine a hospitality space and in transdisciplinary work at the interface of artistic practices. She works in food consulting and conducts workshops. She is currently working on her doctorate in the context of the research project, "Cooking and Eating as Aesthetic Practice". www.dilettantin.com and www.thisissex.de

Marius Keller has been involved in the artist collective *dilettantin produktionsbüro* since 2007 and completed his training as a chef with it in 2009 as part of its "dreijahre dining room project" in Bremen. He has been operating the restaurant Canova at Kunsthalle Bremen since 2011 and is committed to regional production and enjoyment in Bremen and Lower Saxony. His cuisine is based on a careful approach to good products, with a predilection for old species and varieties.

Sandra Knecht, born in 1968, artist. Sandra Knecht graduated with a Master of Fine Arts from Zurich's Hochschule der Künste. She works in different media, although in recent years food has emerged as her key expressive means and research instrument. Sandra Knecht lives in the village of Buus in the Canton of Basel-Landschaft. She uses artistic means to explore the topics of "home" and "identity". In 2015, she transferred a barn that was about 80 years old from the village of Boncourt in the Jura to the Basel inland port and re-erected it as the "Chnächt". The life-span of the "Chnächt" has not been fixed, whereas the conceptual format used there has: Once a month, Knecht cooks at the "Chnächt" for 30 persons – the event is called "Immer wieder Sonntags"/"It's Sunday again". www.sandraknecht.ch

Joachim Krausse, Emeritus Professor of Design Theory, is currently teaching at Bauhaus Dessau on the degree program COOP DESIGN Research. Associate investigator in the excellence cluster "Bild Wissen Gestaltung" at the Humboldt-Universität, Berlin, he is a contributor to ARCH+, an architecture periodical. He has published on architecture and design, amongst other things, on the Frankfurt Kitchen and the small apartment (DVD Das Neue Frankfurt, absolut Medien, 2015), and on the work of R. Buckminster Fuller ("Your Private Sky", new edition Zurich, Lars Müller, 2017), including "Operating Manual for Spaceship Earth". A selection of writings is in preparation (Gebaute Weltbilder [Built World Views], Spector Books, Leipzig, 2017).

Reinhold Leinfelder, a university professor of Geology and Paleontology, heads a working party on geo-biology and research into the Anthropocene at Freie Universität Berlin. He is a member of the International Anthropocene Working Group and Principal Investigator in the excellence cluster "Bild Wissen Gestaltung" at Humboldt-Universität. He works in the fields of the evolution and ecology of coral reefs, fluctuations in sea levels, systemic research into the Anthropocene, museology and new methods of Science communication. Amongst other things, he is coeditor of an intercultural educational comic produced within the excellence cluster entitled "Die Anthropozän-Küche. Matooke, Bienenstich und eine Prise Phosphor – in zehn Speisen um die Welt" ([Anthropocene Kitchen. Matooke, Bienenstich and a Pinch of Phosphorous – around the world in ten dishes] Heidelberg, Berlin: Springer, 2016).

Born in Spain, **Chus Martínez** has a background in philosophy and art history. Currently Martínez is Director of the Institute of Art at the Hochschule für Gestaltung und Kunst FHNW in Basel, Switzerland. She was previously chief curator at El Museo Del Barrio, New York and was head of department and a member of the Core Agent Group for dOCUMENTA (13). Other previous roles include chief curator at MACBA, Barcelona (2008–2011), director of Frankfurter Kunstverein (2005–08) and artistic director of Sala Rekalde, Bilbao (2002–2005). Martínez curated the National Pavilion of Catalonia for the 56th Biennale di Venezia (2015) and the Cyprus National Pavilion for the 51st Biennale (2005). In 2014–2015, she served as part of a curatorial "alliance" for the Istanbul Biennial (2015); in 2008 she served as a curatorial advisor for the Carnegie International and in 2010 for the 29th Bienal de São Paulo. Martínez lectures and writes regularly for publications including numerous catalog texts and critical essays, and is a regular contributor to Artforum, among other international journals. Among her recent projects are the exhibitions *The Metabolic Age* at Malba in Buenos Aires (2015–2016) and *Undisturbed Solitude* at Künstlerhaus Hamburg (2016). She is currently preparing a project for the Sculpture Park in Cologne, opening in June 2017.

Bernadette Oehen is a biologist and economist and works as a senior researcher at Research Institute for Organic Agriculture (FiBL). Her research interests are farmers' decision-making processes and types of cooperation along supply chains. She has managed several EU projects on the coexistence of agricultural production systems with and without transgenic plants. Currently she is responsible for agroecology at FiBL and involved in the EU projects Diversifood and Healthy Minor Cereals.

Iliana Regan is a self-taught chef who began washing dishes at age 15 and hasn't left the restaurant industry since. Her cuisine highlights her Midwestern roots as a small farmer's daughter and emphasizes the pure flavor of the ingredients from her upbringing. It was tradition in her family to farm, forage, and homestead. Her dishes highlight these practices, sometimes sung and sometimes whispered, within her seasonally focused menus. She orchestrates tasting menus aimed at pleasing the senses and extracting the essence of terroir, telling the story of her Midwestern heritage. www.elizabeth-restaurant.com, www.kitsunerestaurant.com, www.bunny bakeryandworkshop.com

Hanni Rützler is a nutritionist and founder of futurefoodstudios in Vienna. A food expert and trend researcher, she has been investigating changes in our gastronomic culture for many years now. Together with cultural scientist **Wolfgang Reiter**, she produces studies and books on the future of eating and the challenges facing the food industry. Her "Food Report", published annually since 2013, has become established as an important identifier of trends in the food and beverage industry.

Holger Stromberg grew up in Waltrop in a family in the hospitality business boasting more than 180 years of hospitality experience. He was awarded his first *Michelin* star at the age of 23, the youngest chef to do so in Germany, and after training in renowned award-winning restaurants, became chef de cuisine at Mark's Restaurant in the Hotel Mandarin Oriental, Munich in 2002. As a founding member and president of Junge Wilde e. V., Stromberg and other up-and-coming chefs revolutionized the young avant-garde cuisine and hospitality scene in Germany. In 2003, Stromberg started up on his own as the founder and managing partner of f. e. b. GmbH in Munich. He and his team offer a wide range of services from catering & events-related services to consulting, nutritional advice, cookery courses, school catering and advice on systems & hospitality. Stromberg also runs various hospitality and event formats. As chef for Germany's national soccer squad, he has been on the team of advisers for the German Football Association since 2007. www.holgerstromberg.de

Anton Studer has been a perfumer for the past 40 years. In the 1990s, because of the growing demand for gourmand notes, he trained as an aromatics specialist. His field of expertise is herbs and spices and how to combine them to effect. His experience in distillation and extraction techniques and in investigating chemical processes led to a fruitful collaboration with organic cook Stefan Wiesner, resulting in a large number of creative "food pairings".

Antonia Surmann is a freelance art historian and teacher in Berlin. She works in fields such as welfare organizations of the 19th and 20th centuries, public housing and 20th-century design history.

Professionally, in the media and in private, **Thomas A. Vilgis** investigates the subject of science in the kitchen and likes to enjoy simple things with a glass of wine or beer. For him, cooking starts at the market, which is why he takes any opportunity that presents itself to visit the markets in unfamiliar cities and surroundings and, when time allows, to visit regional restaurants. At Mainz's Max Planck Institute for Polymer Research he conducts research into such subjects as the theory of soft material and food chemistry. Vilgis is coeditor of the magazine Journal Culinaire – Kultur und Wissenschaft des Essens and the author of numerous books and specialist articles on the science of cooking and on the physics and chemistry of foods.

Bernhard Waldenfels is Emeritus Professor of Philosophy at Ruhr-Universität Bochum. He has been awarded an honorary doctorate by the universities of Rostock and Freiburg. He has been visiting professor in such places as Hong Kong, New York, Prague, Rome and Vienna. His work focuses on the responsive phenomenology of the foreign, the body and the senses as well as on French philosophy.

Together with Jörg Wiesel, (Prof.) **Nicolaj van der Meulen** has since 2013 headed the Institute of Aesthetic Practice and Theory at Hochschule für Gestaltung und Kunst FHNW in Basel. He studied History of Art and Philosophy in Berlin and Basel. He qualified as a university professor in 2014 in the field of fine arts at Universität Hildesheim with a thesis on images, space and performance in the late-Baroque Benedictine Abbey of Zwiefalten. Van der Meulen's work focuses on the theories of pictorial practices and art from the late 18th century to the present day. Publications: *Der parergonale Raum. Zum Verhältnis von Bild, Raum und Performanz in der spätbarocken Benediktinerabtei Zwiefalten*, Wien/Köln/Weimar, 2016; van der Meulen/Wiesel: Ästhetische Praxis als Dialog, in: Kaupert, M./Eberl, H. (2016): *Ästhetische Praxis*, Wiesbaden, pp. 263–282; Ästhetische Praxis als eine Theorie der Praxis in Gestaltung und Kunst, in: Langkilde, K. (ed.) (2013): *Verortung: Das Wissen der Künste*, Basel, pp. 33–40.

Julia von Mende, a graduate engineer, investigates spatial constellations and the structures of human nutrition in the context of cuisine, house-keeping and the urban sphere. Her last position was as research assistant in the base project "Anthropocene Kitchen" for the excellence cluster "Bild Wissen Gestaltung" at Humboldt-Universität in Berlin.

Together with Nicolaj van der Meulen, (Prof.) **Jörg Wiesel** has headed the Institute of Aesthetic Practice and Theory at Hochschule für Gestaltung und Kunst FHNW in Basel since 2013. He graduated in Theater Studies and German in Munich. In 2007, he qualified as a university professor in Theater Studies at FU Berlin with a thesis on the cultural history of piracy. The focus of Wiesel's work is on fashion and performance as well as on the theory and history of the theater. In their joint work, Wiesel and van der Meulen look into the theoretical differentiation of aesthetic practices as criticism. The topics in which they are currently interested are images, fashion, performativity and cookery. Publications: van der Meulen & Wiesel: Ästhetische Praxis als Dialog, in: Kaupert, H. M./Eberl, H. (2016): *Ästhetische Praxis*, Wiesbaden, pp. 263–282; Reenactment. Zur Dramaturgie kulturhistorischen Wissens bei Rimini Protokoll und Friedrich Dürrenmatt, in: Caviezel, F./Florenz, B./Franke, M./Wiesel, J. (eds.) (2013): *Forschungsskizzen. Einblicke in Forschungspraktiken an der Hochschule für Gestaltung und Kunst FHNW*, Zürich, pp. 107–113; Tierähnlichkeit – kulturelle Verortung des Animalischen, in: Langkilde, K. M. (ed.) (2013): *Verortung. Aufzeichnungen der Hochschule für Gestaltung und Kunst FHNW*, Basel, pp. 155–166.

Stefan Wiesner is a renowned chef and author of books. Together with his wife Monica he has, since 1984, been managing Gasthof Rössli in Eschholzmatt, Lucerne, an establishment which boasts 17 *Gault Millau* points and a *Michelin* star. Wiesner made his name as the "alchemist" and "wizard" of Entlebuch; his is an "avant-garde organic cuisine" based on the use of organic regional products and elements and on the experimental techniques used to process them. His gourmet menus combine culinary/gustatory experiences with reflections on ethics, ecology, music, aesthetics and art.

Kulturwissenschaft

Eva Horn, Peter Schnyder (Hg.)
Romantische Klimatologie
Zeitschrift für Kulturwissenschaften, Heft 1/2016

Mai 2016, 152 S., kart., 14,99 € (DE),
ISBN 978-3-8376-3434-1
E-Book: 14,99 € (DE), ISBN 978-3-8394-3434-5

Fatima El-Tayeb
Undeutsch
Die Konstruktion des Anderen
in der postmigrantischen Gesellschaft

September 2016, 256 S., kart., 19,99 € (DE),
ISBN 978-3-8376-3074-9
E-Book: 17,99 € (DE), ISBN 978-3-8394-3074-3

Arianna Ferrari, Klaus Petrus (Hg.)
Lexikon der Mensch-Tier-Beziehungen

2015, 482 S., kart., 29,99 € (DE),
ISBN 978-3-8376-2232-4
E-Book: 26,99 € (DE), ISBN 978-3-8394-2232-8

Kulturwissenschaft

Andreas Langenohl, Ralph Poole,
Manfred Weinberg (Hg.)
Transkulturalität
Klassische Texte

2015, 328 S., kart., 24,99 € (DE),
ISBN 978-3-8376-1709-2
E-Book: € (DE), ISBN

María do Mar Castro Varela, Nikita Dhawan
Postkoloniale Theorie
Eine kritische Einführung

2015, 376 S., kart., 24,99 € (DE),
ISBN 978-3-8376-1148-9
E-Book: 21,99 € (DE), ISBN 978-3-8394-1148-3
EPUB: 21,99 € (DE), ISBN 978-3-8394-1148-3

Thomas Hecken, Moritz Baßler, Robin Curtis,
Heinz Drügh, Nadja Geer, Mascha Jacobs,
Nicolas Pethes, Katja Sabisch (Hg.)
POP
Kultur & Kritik (Jg. 5, 2/2016)

September 2016, 176 S., kart., zahlr. Abb., 16,80 € (DE),
ISBN 978-3-8376-3566-9
E-Book: 16,80 € (DE), ISBN 978-3-8394-3566-3

Leseproben, weitere Informationen und Bestellmöglichkeiten
finden Sie unter www.transcript-verlag.de